Lucy Tappan

Topical Notes on American Authors

Lucy Tappan

Topical Notes on American Authors

ISBN/EAN: 9783337279295

Printed in Europe, USA, Canada, Australia, Japan

Cover: Foto ©Thomas Meinert / pixelio.de

More available books at **www.hansebooks.com**

ON

AMERICAN AUTHORS

BY

LUCY TAPPAN

Teacher of English Literature in the Gloucester (Mass.) High School

SILVER, BURDETT, AND COMPANY

New York   BOSTON   Chicago

1896

C. J. PETERS & SON, TYPOGRAPHERS.

BERWICK & SMITH, PRINTERS.

PREFACE.

THE following notes were gathered for the use of classes in the Gloucester High School, and are the outgrowth of several years' teaching in the department of literature.

The aim in their preparation was to create an interest in the personality of the authors as revealed in characteristic utterances and in their lives, in order to heighten the enjoyment of individual writings.

The general plan of treatment is as follows: (1) Short selections from works, (2) list of reference books and magazines, (3) topical outline of life, (4) appellations, (5) notes on writings, (6) miscellaneous notes. In the case of Irving and of Thoreau, the notes on the life and those on the writings have been combined.

The brief extracts from the verse and prose of Whittier, Longfellow, Lowell, Holmes, Emerson, Hawthorne, and Thoreau are used by permission of and by arrangement with Messrs. Houghton, Mifflin, & Co., the authorized publishers of their works; the selections from Irving, through the courtesy of Messrs. G. P. Putnam's Sons; and those from Bryant, through the courtesy of Messrs. D. Appleton & Co.

LUCY TAPPAN.

GLOUCESTER, MASS.
March, 1896.

CONTENTS.

SUGGESTIONS.

In connection with TOPICAL NOTES, the pupil should be encouraged to do as much of the reading referred to in them as time and material will allow, and to keep a list of such reading for his own satisfaction, and for the aid of the teacher. This list should include both what has been read from the author himself, and the books and magazines consulted with regard to him or his works.

The periodical literature alluded to may be found, to a greater or less extent, at the nearest public library, in the homes of various members of the class, or upon application to the publishers. The school itself can secure for its own possession many of the books named, if interested to do so. The Gloucester High School, by annual courses of public lectures and entertainments, has been able to purchase, within a few years, most of the text-books and miscellaneous works indicated in the general reference list, one biography of each writer, and such voluminous publications as Wilson and Fiske's *Cyclopædia of American Biography*, the Stedman-Hutchinson *Library of American Literature*, Allibone's *Dictionary of Authors*, and *The Encyclopædia Britannica*.

Information gained from the various sources upon any one topic may frequently be wrought into composition form, either by impromptu ten-minute writing in the recitation hour, or by essays formally prepared outside of the class-room.

7

Pupils will find pleasure in making scrap albums of clippings and views pertaining to the lives and writings of the authors. For these albums, unmounted photographs, old magazines, portrait catalogues, and current literature will furnish abundant material. The search for this material will give new interest to the periodical literature of the day, and a keener appreciation of it.

A visit to any literary Mecca that may be accessible to one or to all members of a class serves as stimulus to the regular work, and often makes an impression that will give pleasurable vividness to subsequent reading.

The study of Hawthorne, of Cooper, and of Holmes, would be quite incomplete without the reading in its entirety of a novel by each. It is desirable, also, that the student should read a biography of at least one writer among those included in the course; he may by this means win a lifelong personal friend (for is not a loved writer to be classed with our truest and most helpful friends ?), and create a taste for biographical literature in general.

The memorizing of choice thoughts from the writings of an author is one of the most valuable phases of literary study, and is worthy of emphatic attention. Some such thoughts may be pointed out by the teacher, while the pupil may be expected to cull others for himself.

Inexpensive copies of selected works from most of the authors treated can readily be obtained for class-room use. (See list of general reference books.)

Topical Notes will prove helpful only as made subordinate and supplementary to the study of the literature itself.

GENERAL REFERENCE BOOKS.

MAINLY BIOGRAPHICAL.

WILSON AND FISKE'S *Cyclopædia of American Biography.* (Illustrated.)

LIPPINCOTT'S *Dictionary of Biography.*

APPLETONS' *American Encyclopædia.*

The *Encyclopædia Britannica.* (With Supplement.)

ARTHUR GILMAN'S *Poets' Homes.* (Illustrated.)

RICHARD H. STODDARD'S *Poets' Homes.* (This and its predecessor are supplementary. Illustrated.)

G. W. CURTIS'S *Homes of American Authors.* (1853. Illustrated.)

HATTIE T. GRISWOLD'S *Home Life of Great Authors.*

SARAH K. BOLTON'S *Famous American Authors.*

MAINLY CRITICAL.

CHARLES F. RICHARDSON'S *American Literature.*

EDMUND C. STEDMAN'S *Poets of America.*

ALLIBONE'S *Dictionary of Authors.* (With two supplementary volumes.)

EDGAR ALLAN POE'S *Literati.* (Bryant. Cooper. Hawthorne. Longfellow. Lowell.)

T. W. HIGGINSON'S *Short Studies of American Authors.* (Hawthorne. Poe. Thoreau.)

MOSES COIT TYLER'S *History of American Literature.*

BIOGRAPHICAL AND CRITICAL.

American Men of Letters Series. —

WILLIAM CULLEN BRYANT.   By John Bigelow.

JAMES FENIMORE COOPER.   By T. R. Lounsbury.

RALPH WALDO EMERSON.   By Oliver Wendell Holmes.

WASHINGTON IRVING.   By Charles Dudley Warner.

JAMES RUSSELL LOWELL.   By George E. Woodberry.
   (In preparation.)

EDGAR ALLAN POE.   By George E. Woodberry.

HENRY D. THOREAU.   By Frank B. Sanborn.

JOHN G. WHITTIER.   By G. R. Carpenter.
   (In preparation.)

9

English Men of Letters Series. —

    HAWTHORNE.　　　　　　By Henry James.

Great Writers Series. —

LIFE OF EMERSON.	By Richard Garnett, LL.D.
LIFE OF HAWTHORNE.	By Moncure D. Conway.
LIFE OF LONGFELLOW.	By E. S. Robertson.
LIFE OF WHITTIER.	By W. J. Linton.

Text-Books and Cyclopædias. —

    HENRY A. BEERS's *Initial Studies in American Literature.*

    HAWTHORNE AND LEMMON's *American Literature.* (Illustrated.)

    CHARLES F. RICHARDSON's *Primer of American Literature.*

    CHARLES D. CLEVELAND's *Compendium of American Literature.*

    FRANCIS H. UNDERWOOD's *Hand-Book of American Authors.*

    FRANCIS H. UNDERWOOD's *Builders of American Literature.*

    N. K. ROYSE's *Manual of American Literature.*

    HORACE H. MORGAN's *English and American Literature.*

    MILDRED C. WATKINS's *Primer of American Literature.*

    DUYCKINCK's *Cyclopædia of American Literature.*

    RUFUS GRISWOLD's *Prose Writers of America.*

    RUFUS GRISWOLD's *Poets and Poetry of America.*

    F. L. PATTEE's *History of American Literature.*

    JENNIE E. KEYSOR's *Sketches of American Writers.* (Illustrated.)

    HENRIETTA C. WRIGHT's *Children's Stories in American Literature.*

MISCELLANEOUS.

ALFRED H. WELSH's *Digest of English and American Literature.*

G. J. SMITH's *Synopsis of English and American Literature.*

SELDEN L. WHITCOMB's *Chronological Outlines of American Literature.*

GREENOUGH WHITE's *Philosophy of American Literature.*

LOUISE M. HODGKINS's *Guide to the Study of Nineteenth Century Authors.*

OSCAR FAY ADAMS's *Hand-Book of American Authors.*

H. R. HAWEIS's *American Humorists.*

J. R. LOWELL's *A Fable for Critics.*

WILLIAM SHEPARD's *Pen Pictures of Modern Authors.*

ALFRED S. ROE's *American Authors and Their Birthdays.*

J. C. DERBY's *Fifty Years Among American Authors, Books, and Publishers.*

ALONZO CHAPPEL's *National Portrait Gallery of Eminent Americans.* (1864. Illustrated.)

ALFRED H. WELSH's *English Masterpiece Course.* (Critical References.)

R. E. THOMPSON's *Syllabus of University Extension Lectures on the History of American Literature.*

J. H. PENNIMAN's *Syllabus of University Extension Lectures on American Authors.* (Franklin. Irving. Poe. Lowell.)

POOLE's *Index to Periodical Literature.* (With two supplements, bringing the work down to January, 1892.)

Portrait Catalogues.

BOOKS CONTAINING EXTRACTS FROM AUTHORS SELECTED.

The STEDMAN-HUTCHINSON *Library of American Literature.*

UNDERWOOD's *American Authors.*

CLEVELAND's *American Literature.*

Masterpieces of American Literature.

American Poems. (Edited by Horace E. Scudder.)

American Prose. (Edited by Horace E. Scudder.)

BEERS's *Initial Studies.* Appendix.

BEERS's *Century of American Literature.*

WILLIAM SWINTON's *Studies in English Literature.* (Annotated Selections from Bryant, Emerson, Hawthorne, Holmes, Longfellow, and Whittier.)

GRISWOLD's *Prose Writers of America.*

CHARLES MORRIS's *Half Hours with American Authors.*

CHARLES MORRIS's *Half Hours with Humorous Authors.*

CHAMBERS's *Cyclopædia of English Literature.*

Leaflets. — (For class-room use. Annotated, and with biographical sketches.)

The Riverside Literature Series. (Bryant. Emerson. Hawthorne. Holmes. Irving. Longfellow. Lowell. Thoreau. Whittier.) Portraits and Biographical Sketches of Twenty American Authors.

MAYNARD's *English Classic Series.* (Irving. Emerson. Longfellow. Whittier.)

WASHINGTON IRVING.

WASHINGTON IRVING.

Essayist, Romancer, Historian, Biographer, Traveller.

EXTRACTS.

A man as he grows old must take care not to grow musty, or fusty, or rusty — an old bachelor especially.

LETTER.

The Almighty Dollar, that great object of universal devotion throughout our land, seems to have no genuine devotees in these peculiar villages.

The Creole Village.

He [Governor Van Twiller] was exactly five feet six inches in height, and six feet five inches in circumference. His head was a perfect sphere, and of such stupendous dimensions, that Dame Nature, with all her sex's ingenuity, would have been puzzled to construct a neck capable of supporting it; wherefore she wisely declined the attempt, and settled it firmly on the top of his backbone, just between the shoulders. His body was oblong, and particularly capacious at bottom; which was wisely ordained by Providence, seeing that he was a man of sedentary habits, and very averse to the idle labor of walking. His legs were short, but sturdy in proportion to the weight they had to sustain; so that, when erect, he had not a little the appearance of a beer-barrel on

15

skids. His face, that infallible index of the mind, presented a vast expanse, unfurrowed by any of those lines and angles which disfigure the human countenance with what is called expression. Two small gray eyes twinkled feebly in the midst, like two stars of lesser magnitude in a hazy firmament, and his full-fed cheeks, which seemed to have taken toll of everything that went into his mouth, were curiously mottled and streaked with dusky red, like a Spitzenburg apple.

HISTORY OF NEW YORK.

Her mighty lakes, like oceans of liquid silver; her mountains, with their bright aerial tints; her valleys, teeming with wild fertility; her tremendous cataracts, thundering in their solitudes; her boundless plains, waving with spontaneous verdure; her broad, deep rivers, rolling in solemn silence to the ocean; her trackless forests, where vegetation puts forth all its magnificence; her skies, kindling with the magic of summer clouds and glorious sunshine,—no, never need an American look beyond his own country for the sublime and beautiful of natural scenery.

PREFACE TO THE SKETCH-BOOK.

THE WIDOW AND HER SON.

Pittie olde age, within whose silver haires
Honor and reverence evermore have raign'd.
MARLOWE'S *Tamburlaine.*

During my residence in the country, I used frequently to attend at the old village church. Its shadowy aisles, its mouldering monuments, its dark oaken panelling, all reverend with the gloom of departed years, seemed to fit it for the haunt of solemn meditation. A Sunday, too, in the country, is so holy in its repose—such a pensive quiet reigns over the face of nature, that every restless passion is charmed down, and we feel all the natural religion of the soul gently springing up within us.

"Sweet day, so pure, so calm, so bright,
The bridal of the earth and sky!"

I cannot lay claim to the merit of being a devout man; but there are feelings that visit me in a country church, amid the beautiful serenity of nature, which I experience nowhere else; and, if not a more religious, I think that I am a better, man on Sunday, than on any other day of the seven.

But in this church I felt myself continually thrown back upon the world by the frigidity and pomp of the poor worms around me. The only being that seemed thoroughly to feel the humble and prostrate piety of a true Christian was a poor, decrepit old woman, bending under the weight of years and infirmities. She bore the traces of something better than abject poverty. The lingerings of decent pride were visible in her appearance. Her dress, though humble in the extreme, was scrupulously clean. Some trivial respect, too, had been awarded her, for she did not take her seat among the village poor, but sat alone on the steps of the altar. She seemed to have survived all love, all friendship, all society; and to have nothing left her but the hopes of heaven. When I saw her feebly rising and bending her aged form in prayer; habitually conning her prayer-book, which her palsied hand and failing eyes would not permit her to read, but which she evidently knew by heart; I felt persuaded that the faltering voice of that poor woman arose to heaven far before the responses of the clerk, the swell of the organ, or the chanting of the choir.

I am fond of loitering about country churches; and
this was so delightfully situated that it frequently attracted me. It stood on a knoll, round which a small
stream made a beautiful bend, and then wound its way
through a long reach of soft meadow scenery. The church
was surrounded by yew-trees, which seemed almost coeval
with itself. Its tall Gothic spire shot up lightly from
among them, with rooks and crows generally wheeling
about it. I was seated there one still sunny morning,
watching two laborers who were digging a grave. They
had chosen one of the most remote and neglected corners
of the churchyard, where, by the number of nameless
graves around, it would appear that the indigent and
friendless were huddled into the earth. I was told that
the new-made grave was for the only son of a poor widow.
While I was meditating on the distinctions of worldly
rank, which extend thus down to the very dust, the toll
of the bell announced the approach of the funeral. They
were the obsequies of poverty, with which pride had nothing to do. A coffin of the plainest materials, without pall
or other covering, was borne by some of the villagers. The
sexton walked before with an air of cold indifference.
There were no mock mourners in the trappings of affected
woe, but there was one real mourner who feebly tottered
after the corpse. It was the aged mother of the deceased
— the poor old woman whom I had seen seated on the
steps of the altar. She was supported by an humble friend,
who was endeavoring to comfort her. A few of the
neighboring poor had joined the train, and some children
of the village were running hand in hand, now shouting
with unthinking mirth, and now pausing to gaze, with
childish curiosity, on the grief of the mourner.

As the funeral train approached the grave, the parson issued from the church porch, arrayed in the surplice, with prayer-book in hand, attended by the clerk. The service, however, was a mere act of charity. The deceased had been destitute, and the survivor was penniless. It was shuffled through, therefore, in form, but coldly and unfeelingly. The well-fed priest moved but a few steps from the church door; his voice could scarcely be heard at the grave; and never did I hear the funeral service, that sublime and touching ceremony, turned into such a frigid mummery of words.

I approached the grave. The coffin was placed on the ground. On it were inscribed the name and age of the deceased — "George Somers, aged 26 years." The poor mother had been assisted to kneel down at the head of it. Her withered hands were clasped, as if in prayer; but I could perceive, by a feeble rocking of the body, and a convulsive motion of the lips, that she was gazing on the last relics of her son with the yearnings of a mother's heart.

Preparations were made to deposit the body in the earth. There was that bustling stir, which breaks so harshly on the feelings of grief and affection; directions given in the cold tones of business; the striking of spades into the sand and gravel, which, at the grave of those we love, is of all sounds the most withering. The bustle around seemed to waken the mother from a wretched reverie. She raised her glazed eyes, and looked about with a faint wildness. As the men approached with cords to lower the coffin into the grave, she wrung her hands, and broke into an agony of grief. The poor woman who attended her took her by the arm, endeavoring to raise her from the earth, and to whisper something like consolation — " Nay, now — nay, now — don't take it so sorely to heart." She could only shake her head, and wring her hands, as one not to be comforted.

As they lowered the body into the earth, the creaking of the cords seemed to agonize her; but when, on some accidental obstruction, there was a jostling of the coffin, all the tenderness of the mother burst forth; as if any harm could come to him who was far beyond the reach of worldly suffering.

I could see no more — my heart swelled into my throat — my eyes filled with tears — I felt as if I were acting a barbarous part in standing by and gazing idly on this scene of maternal anguish. I wandered to another part of the churchyard, where I remained until the funeral train had dispersed.

THE SKETCH-BOOK.

I MUST not omit to mention that this village is the paradise of cows as well as men. . . . The same scrupulous cleanliness which pervades everything else, is manifest in the treatment of this venerated animal. She is not permitted to perambulate the place; but in winter, when she forsakes the rich pasture, a well-built house is provided for her, well painted, and maintained in the most perfect order. Her stall is of ample dimensions, the floor is scrubbed and polished; her hide is daily curried and brushed and sponged to her heart's content, and her tail is daintily tucked up to the ceiling, and decorated with a ribbon.

BROEK ; OR, THE DUTCH PARADISE.

THE trumpets were about sounding for the encounter, when the herald announced the arrival of a strange knight; and Ahmed rode into the field.

A steel helmet studded with gems rose above his turban; his cuirass was embossed with gold; his cimeter and dagger were of the workmanship of Fez, and flamed with precious stones.

A round shield was at his shoulder, and in his hand he bore the lance of charmed virtue. The caparison of his Arabian steed was richly embroidered and swept the ground, and the proud animal pranced and snuffed the air, and neighed with joy at once more beholding the array of arms.

The lofty and graceful demeanor of the prince struck every eye, and when his appellation was announced, "The Pilgrim of Love," a universal flutter and agitation prevailed among the fair dames in the galleries.

The Alhambra : Legend of Prince Ahmed Al Kamel.

SIR WALTER SCOTT AND HIS DOGS.

After my return from Melrose Abbey, Scott proposed a ramble to show me something of the surrounding country. As we sallied forth, every dog in the establishment turned out to attend us. There was an old stag-hound, Maida, that I have already mentioned, a noble animal, and a great favorite of Scott's; and Hamlet, the black greyhound, a wild, thoughtless youngster, not yet arrived to the years of discretion; and Finette, a beautiful setter, with soft silken hair, long pendent ears, and a mild eye, the parlor favorite. When in front of the house we were joined by a superannuated greyhound, who came from the kitchen wagging his tail, and was cheered by Scott as an old friend and comrade.

In our walks, Scott would frequently pause in conversation to notice his dogs and speak to them, as if rational

companions; and, indeed, there appears to be a vast deal
of rationality in these faithful attendants on man, derived
from their close intimacy with him.   Maida deported himself with a gravity becoming his age and size, and seemed
to consider himself called upon to preserve a great degree
of dignity and decorum in our society.   As he jogged
along a little distance ahead of us, the young dogs would
gambol about him, leap on his neck, worry at his ears, and
endeavor to tease him into a frolic.   The old dog would
keep on for a long time with imperturbable solemnity, now
and then seeming to rebuke the wantonness of his young
companions.   At length he would make a sudden turn,
seize one of them, and tumble him in the dust; then
giving a glance at us, as much as to say, "You see, gentlemen, I can't help giving away to this nonsense," would
resume his gravity and jog on as before.

Scott amused himself with these peculiarities.   "I
make no doubt," said he, "when Maida is alone with
these young dogs, he throws gravity aside, and plays the
boy as much as any of them; but he is ashamed to do
so in our company, and seems to say, 'Ha' done with
your nonsense, youngsters; what will the laird and the
other gentleman think of me if I give away to such
foolery?'" . . .

Scott amused himself with the peculiarities of another
of his dogs, a little shamefaced terrier with large glassy
eyes, one of the most sensitive little bodies to insult and
indignity in the world.   If he ever whipped him, he said,
the little fellow would sneak off and hide himself from
the light of day in a lumber-garret, whence there was
no drawing him forth but by the sound of the chopping-
knife, as if chopping up his victuals, when he would steal

forth with humbled and downcast look, but would skulk
away again if any one regarded him.

While we were discussing the humors and peculiarities
of our canine companions, some object provoked their
spleen, and produced a sharp and petulant barking from
the smaller fry, but it was some time before Maida was
sufficiently aroused to ramp forward two or three bounds,
and join in the chorus with a deep-mouthed bow-wow!

It was but a transient outbreak, and he returned in-
stantly, wagging his tail, and looking dubiously in his
master's face; uncertain whether he would censure or
applaud.

"Aye, aye, old boy!" cried Scott, "you have done wonders. You have shaken the Eildon hills with your roaring; you may now lay by your artillery for the rest of
the day. Maida is like the great gun at Constantinople,"
he continued; "it takes so long to get it ready that the
small guns can fire off a dozen times first, but when it
does go off it plays the very d——l." . . .

At dinner, Scott had laid by his half-rustic dress, and
appeared clad in black. The girls, too, in completing
their toilet, had twisted in their hair the sprigs of purple
heather which they had gathered on the hillside, and
looked all fresh and blooming from their breezy walk.

There was no guest to dinner but myself. Around the
table were two or three dogs in attendance. Maida, the
old stag-hound, took his seat at Scott's elbow, looking
up wistfully in his master's eye, while Finette, the pet
spaniel, placed herself near Mrs. Scott, by whom, I soon
perceived, she was completely spoiled.

The conversation happening to turn on the merits of
his dogs, Scott spoke with great feeling and affection

of his favorite, Camp, who is depicted by his side in the earlier engravings of him. He talked of him as a real friend whom he had lost; and Sophia Scott, looking up archly into his face, observed that papa shed a few tears when poor Camp died. I may here mention another testimonial of Scott's fondness for his dogs, and his humorous mode of showing it, which I subsequently met with. Rambling with him one morning about the grounds adjacent to the house, I observed a small antique monument, on which was inscribed, in Gothic characters, —

> " Cy git le preux Percy."
> (Here lies the brave Percy.)

I paused, supposing it to be the tomb of some stark warrior of the olden time, but Scott drew me on. "Pooh!" he cried, "it's nothing but one of the monuments of my nonsense, of which you'll find enough hereabouts." I learnt afterwards that it was the grave of a favorite greyhound.

THE CRAYON MISCELLANY: *Abbotsford.*

REFERENCES.

Biographies by Charles Dudley Warner, Pierre Irving, R. H. Stoddard, and David J. Hill.

James Grant Wilson's *Bryant and His Friends* (Chapter on Irving).

H. R. Haweis's *American Humorists.*

H. T. Griswold's *Home Life of Great Authors.*

Irvingiana; a Memorial of Washington Irving.

Stedman-Hutchinson's *Library of American Literature.* Vol. V.

Richardson's *American Literature.* Vol. I. chap. vii.

Lowell's *Fable for Critics.*

Chambers's Cyclopædia of English Literature.

Duyckinck's *Cyclopædia of American Literature.* Vol. I.

R. W. Griswold's *Prose Writers of America.*

Allibone's *Dictionary of Authors.*

Appletons' Cyclopædia of American Biography.

Lippincott's Biographical Dictionary.

Text-books on American Literature. (Beers; Hawthorne and Lemmon; Morgan; Underwood; Tuckerman; Cleveland.)

Report of the Commemoration of Irving's Hundredth Birthday. (By the Washington Irving Association, Tarrytown.)

Harper's Magazine. March, 1860 (Article by Thackeray). February, 1862. April, 1876 (Illustrated). April, 1883 (Portrait by Stuart Newton). September, 1883.

The Century Magazine. May, 1887 ("Irving at Home," by Clarence Cook).

The Atlantic Monthly. November, 1860. June, 1864 (Article by Donald G. Mitchell).

The Critic. Irving Number. March 31, 1883.

Bryant's Address on Irving before the New York Historical Society.

Longfellow's Address on Irving before the Massachusetts Historical Society.

Chappel's *Portrait Gallery of Eminent Americans.* Vol. II.

LIFE AND WORKS.

NOTE. — The two are intimately connected.

April 3, 1783.
Nov. 28, 1859.

Father.

Scotch, from the Orkneys. Descended from the armor-bearer of Robert Bruce. Officer on a British packet. Strict disciplinarian. Blue Presbyterian. Thoroughly patriotic through the American Revolution.

Mother.

English. William Irving met her when in port. Gentle, cheerful, sympathetic. All the children adopted their mother's religion, Episcopacy. Washington was confirmed without his father's knowledge.

The family were friends with both the Dutch and the English residents of New York City.

Born the year in which the treaty between Great Britain and the United States was signed. (Irving's diplomatic and literary careers cemented the union between the countries.)

On William Street, New York, midway between Fulton and Joy Streets. No trace of birthplace left.

New York then a city of but twenty-three thousand inhabitants.

Youngest of eleven children.

Name and Blessing of George Washington.

"That blessing has attended me through life."

Youth.

Puritan home-training. "I was led to believe that everything that was pleasant was wicked." His mischievous propensities caused his father much anxiety.

Education.

Desultory. A little Latin and music.

" In school he feasted on travels and tales, but hated arithmetic.
He wrote compositions for boys who, in return, worked his
sums for him."

Not sent to Columbia College, as his brothers were, because of
his delicate health and dislike of study.

Early Books.

*Sindbad the Sailor, Gulliver's Travels, Robinson Crusoe, Pil-
grim's Progress.*

Studies Law (like Bryant, Lowell, and Holmes).

In Judge Hoffmann's office, New York. " A heedless student."
Little work. Much reading. Becomes enamored of Miss Hoffmann.

Contributes to The Morning Chronicle, his brother's paper.

Letters on the drama and the customs of New York.

Delicate Health.

Pulmonary weakness. An obstacle to him through most of his
life.

Voyage up the Hudson.

(Irving first wrote of the beauties of this river.)

Trip to Europe, 1804, at his brothers' expense.

Two years of absence.

The captain remarked, " That chap will go overboard before we
get across."

Boat boarded by a privateer.

Saw Nelson's fleet in the Mediterranean, off Messina, ready for
Trafalgar.

Rome. Met Washington Allston, and was almost persuaded to
become an artist. (He had a strong love of color.)

Gay Paris. He excused his neglect of home correspondence by
saying, " I am a young man and in Paris."

London. Enjoyed intensely Mrs. Siddons and John Kemble.

Resumes Law Studies in New York, although feeling " a fatal pro-
pensity to *belles-lettres.*"

Brilliant social life. " A champion at the tea-parties."

Death of Miss Hoffmann, at eighteen. 1809.

> Irving never recovered from the effects. (Her Bible and prayer-book were always with him. Her picture and a lock of her hair were found at his death among his private papers.)
>
> Miss Hoffmann's friend, Rebecca Gratz, a Jewess, who cared solicitously for Miss Hoffmann in her illness, is the original of Scott's heroine Rebecca. Irving's enthusiasm prompted her creation.
>
> (Later love, Emily Foster, known when in Dresden.)

Writes for Salmagundi.

> Fortnightly magazine. Twenty numbers.
>
> Edited by Irving's brother William, and J. K. Paulding, William's brother-in-law.
>
> Local allusions. Personal hits. Continuous humor.
>
> "A complete triumph of local genius."
>
> "The American Spectator." (The last example of this type of literature.)
>
> "Whim-Whams and Opinions of Launcelot Langstaff."

Publishes Diedrich Knickerbocker's History of New York. 1809.

> America's earliest literary flower from native soil.
>
> Begun as a burlesque of a hand-book just issued, — S. L. Mitchill's "A Picture of New York."
>
> Considered a veritable history by some Germans.
>
> Gave offence to some New Yorkers, but was read and praised by all other Americans and Englishmen.
>
> Great success. Income of $3,000 from it. Scott's appreciation. Advertisement in New York *Evening Post* before its appearance (as Carlyle "advertised" before publishing *Sartor Resartus*) for "a small elderly gentleman in black coat and cocked hat, who had left a MS. behind him at the Columbian Hotel, Mulberry St."
>
> "A most excellently jocose history." — WALTER SCOTT.
>
> "One of the few masterpieces of humor."

Trial of Aaron Burr.

> Irving held a semi-official connection with it. His sympathies were called out on Burr's behalf.

Silent Partner in his brother's business.

Second European Trip. 1815.

    Significant time historically.

    Bright prospects followed by depressing experiences.

Outings.

    Enjoys his sister's home near Birmingham. Becomes acquainted with Kean, Campbell, Moore, Rogers, Disraeli, Jeffrey, Murray. Meets Longfellow in Spain.

    Friendship with Scott and visit to him.

        Consult Lockhart's *Life of Scott*, and Irving's pleasing essay on Abbotsford.

    Welcomed everywhere for his Knickerbocker fame and for his social charms.

    He imbibes the spirit of the Romanticists.

Financial Reverses of 1818, following several years of gloom.

    Through the days of investigation of affairs by the commissioners, Irving sought relief in studying day and night the German language.

Declines, in favor of a literary profession, the mayoralty of New York, a seat in Congress, and the secretaryship of the navy ($2,500) under Van Buren.

The Sketch-Book.

    1819. By "Geoffrey Crayon."

    Written in England, and published serially in America.

    Anonymous at first, and attributed to Scott.

    Murray, the publisher and thereafter the lifelong friend of Irving, brings out through Scott's influence a London edition of the book, paying $2,400 to Irving for it.

    Warm reception on both sides of the ocean.

    "His Crayon — I know it by heart." — Lord Byron.

    Its Motto. — "I have no wife nor children, good nor bad, to provide for — a mere spectator of other men's fortunes." (Quoted.)

    Its Immortal Creations.

        Rip Van Winkle. (Joe Jefferson, the most famous stage exponent of the character.) Compare this story with the German legend of Frederick Barbarossa.

        Ichabod Crane.

Consult *Harper's Magazine*, September, 1883, for the " Genesis of the Rip Van Winkle Legend."

Bracebridge Hall.

The English Sketch-Book. 1822.

Written in Paris. Murray paid a thousand guineas for it without seeing the manuscript.

"The coronation of English country life." — HAWEIS.

The original, Ashton Hall, is in the vicinity of Birmingham.

Irving loved England and the English.

Tales of a Traveller.

Criticised severely, but contains some of Irving's best writing.

Secretary of Legation at Madrid. 1826-1829.

Under Alexander Everett, who commissioned him to translate Navarrete's *Voyages of Columbus*, then just published This led Irving to undertake later his *Life of Columbus.*

His most productive literary period.

He rooms in the summer of 1829 in Lindaraja's apartments in the Alhambra. (The room is shown to visitors to the palace.)

The Life of Columbus. Three thousand guineas.

Medal (fifty guineas) from George IV. for historical composition. Its companion medal was bestowed at the same time on the historian Hallam.

Clear, judicious, accurate. It still holds its own, despite the wealth of Columbian literature issued in 1893.

The Conquest of Granada and the Alhambra.

The Spanish Sketch-Book.

Secretary of Legation at London. 1829-1832.

Degree of D.C.L. from Oxford to Irving in person.

Last interview with Walter Scott, in London.

Edits Bryant's poems, and thus secures for them an English public.

Returns to New York. 1832.

Great ovation. Unsuccessful attempt to make a speech at a New York banquet.

Purchase of " Sunnyside." *Wolfert's Roost.*

X A Dutch stone cottage on the banks of the Hudson, at Tarrytown (now Irvington), once the home of the Van Tassels.
Cosey and picturesque. Mantled with ivy brought as a
slip from Melrose Abbey by Mrs. Jane Renwick (famous in
literature as " The Blue-Eyed Lassie " of Burns), and given
to Irving.

Its hospitality, generous.

The household consisted of the family of Irving's brother, with
a number of nieces, two of whom still occupy the home
(1894). Here Irving was visited by Napoleon III. and by
Daniel Webster.

Its gable-ends hold aloft a venerable weathercock that once
surmounted the Stadt-House of New Amsterdam.

See illustrated article on Sunnyside in *Harper's Magazine* for
December, 1856, and Irving's *Wolfert's Roost.*

Travels West, to become acquainted with his own country, after
his seventeen years of life in Europe.

Resultant Works.

*A Tour on the Prairies. Astoria. The Adventures of Captain
Bonneville.*

Surrenders, at considerable sacrifice, his plan to write a history of
Mexico, when he learns that Prescott is at work on the
same theme.

Appointment as Minister to Spain. 1842. Wholly unsought.

Name proposed by Daniel Webster, then Secretary of State.
Reluctance to leave his home. " It is hard, very, but I must
try to bear it," he humorously remarked.
Troublesome times in Spain. (Queen Isabella II. and her
regents.)
Little literary activity. Resigns in 1846.

Life of Washington. Five volumes. 1855-1859.

The outcome of thirty years of thought.
A standard authority.

Other Biographies.

Oliver Goldsmith. His most spontaneous and fascinating one. "One of the best biographies in the whole range of English literature."

Mahomet. Not a success.

Columbus. (See preceding note.)

Last Years at Tarrytown. Thirteen.

Putnam, of New York, now becomes his publisher and friend.

A happy, kindly, cheerful old age.

Death, from Heart Disease, the same year with Prescott and Macaulay.

Buried at Sleepy Hollow, Tarrytown.

(As Emerson and Thoreau, in Concord's "Sleepy Hollow.")

Lies by the side of his mother.

Second tombstone much mutilated; the first was wholly destroyed by relic-seekers.

Read Longfellow's sonnet, "In the Churchyard at Tarrytown."

See article on Sleepy Hollow in *Munsey's Magazine* for June, 1892.

First Biographer.

Pierre Irving, his nephew.

"One million copies have been sold in America, and as many more elsewhere."

Character.

"His character is perfectly transparent."

"Genial, sunny, modest, humorous, sensitive." ("One condemning whisper sounded louder in his ears than a thousand plaudits.") Fond of society, amiable, and of gentle manners. A charming talker. Popular, but not a speechmaker. Very ready to acknowledge merit in others. "He had a boundless capacity for good-fellowship." His company was sought by kings and queens.

"He was thoroughly a gentleman, not merely in external manners and look, but to the innermost fibres and core of his heart." — EMILY FOSTER.

See his account of himself in the Preface to the *Sketch-Book*, and Lowell's verses on him in the *Fable*.

Appearance and Voice.

Medium height. Somewhat stout. Dark gray eyes with delicate eyebrows; handsome straight nose; shapely head. Wore a dark brown wig. Winning smile.

"He seemed to have stepped out of his own books." — G. W. CURTIS.

Well-modulated voice.

APPELLATIONS.

A Spontaneous Optimist.
The Best Beloved among American Authors.
The Father of American Letters.
The Earliest Classic Writer of America.
The Morning Star of American Literature.
Society's Darling.
The Dutch Herodotus.
The American Goldsmith.
The Addison of American Literature.
The First Ambassador sent by the New World of Letters
     to the Old. — *Thackeray.*
The Gentle Humorist.
The Second American to make Literature a Profession.
     (Charles Brockden Brown was the first.)
A Mediator between England and America.
Our First Picturesque Tourist.
The Genial Conservative in Literature and Life.
The First of the American Humorists.
The George Washington of American Literature.

PSEUDONYMS.

Jonathan Oldstyle,	*The New York Morning Chronicle.*
Launcelot Langstaff,	*Salmagundi.*
Diedrich Knickerbocker,	*Historian of New York.*
Fray Antonia Agapida,	*Chronicler of Granada.*
Geoffrey Crayon,	*The Sketch-Book.*

MISCELLANEOUS NOTES.

Tributes to Irving.

Scott said to one of his friends, "When you see Tom Campbell, tell him that I have to thank him for making me known to Mr. Washington Irving, who is one of the best and pleasantest acquaintances I have made this many a day."

" His writings are my delight." — BYRON.

" For fifty years, Irving charmed and instructed the American people, and held the foremost place in their affections."—WARNER.

" Nothing bitter, morbid, or sensational ever came from him." — HAWTHORNE and LEMMON.

"The mild and beautiful genius of Mr. Irving was the morning star that led up the march of our heavenly host." — ALEXANDER EVERETT.

" Irving's genius was what in the old English phrase would have been called sauntering. It cast the glamor of idlesse over our sharp, positive, and busy American life. . . . While one lurid letter spells Puritan, and the keen laughter of Hosea Biglow nails fast the counterfeit American, still Rip Van Winkle lounges idly by, and the vagabond of the Hudson is an unwasting figure of the imagination, the earliest, constant, gentlest satirist of American life." — GEORGE W. CURTIS.

Lowell's verses on Irving in his *Fable for Critics.*

Longfellow's sonnet *In the Churchyard at Tarrytown.*

Consult *Irvingiana: a Memorial to Washington Irving.*

His Literary Style.

Fluent, graceful, picturesque.

" His language was full of grace; his sympathies were true; his humor, genuine and abiding."

Sale of Works.

Six hundred thousand volumes were sold in his lifetime. From 1859 to 1887 the average annual sale was thirty thousand.

His literary income was more than $36,000.

Illustrated Editions.

The Darro Edition of *The Alhambra.* 1891. G. P. Putman. ($6.00.) Illuminated cover and page borders. Thirty photogravures.

Rip Van Winkle. 1893. Macmillan. ($2.00.) George H. Boughton, artist.

Legend of Sleepy Hollow. G. P. Putman.

Memorials.

Busts in Central Park, N.Y., and Prospect Park, Brooklyn.

Irving Memorial Church at Tarrytown.

Edition of his Life and Works.

Formation of the Irving Society at Tarrytown, 1883.

First American author thus honored.

Memorial volume published by the society.

Donald G. Mitchell, the orator of the Centennial Celebration of his birth.

His Admiration for Women.

"I am superstitious in my admiration for them, and like to walk in a perpetual delusion, decking them out as divinities. I thank no one to undeceive me, and to prove that they are mere mortals."

Irving's Worldly Wisdom.

"When I cannot get a dinner to suit my taste, I get a taste to suit my dinner."

Anecdotes of interest concerning Irving.

See Griswold's *Home Life of Great Authors*, Warner's *Life of Irving*, Lockhart's *Life of Scott*.

Selected Readings.

The Sketch-Book. Rip Van Winkle. ("One of those strokes of genius that re-create the world and clothe it with the unfading hues of romance.") The Spectre Bridegroom, Rural Funerals, Westminster Abbey, The Legend of Sleepy Hollow, Stratford-on-Avon, Little Britain, The Pride of the Village.

The Alhambra. The Court of Lions, Legends of The Three Beautiful Princesses, The Rose of the Alhambra, The Moor's Legacy, The Two Discreet Statues, The Arabian Astrologer, Governor Manco and the Soldiers.

Knickerbocker's History of New York. Governor Van Twiller (Bk. III., ch. i.); How the Streets were made, (Bk. III., ch. iii.); Military Reception (Bk. VI., ch. ii.).

The Crayon Miscellany. Newstead Abbey, Abbotsford.

Bracebridge Hall. The Stout Gentleman. (Greatly admired by Dickens.)

Columbus. Landing of Columbus in the New World (Vol. I, Bk. IV.).

Life of Washington. Washington's Farewell Address (Vol. V., chap. xxx.).

" For nearly half a century, Niagara Falls and Washington Irving were the two American subjects most interesting to Englishmen."

" Irving attributed the success of his books in England to the astonishment of Englishmen that an American could write good English."

" Irving's imagination, like that of Spenser and Scott, was fascinated by the past and its associations."

" His pen was the first to give to literature the Dutch legends of the New World and the romances of the Moors in Spain."

" Irving regarded life purely from the literary point of view."

" There was never any one who so carried the whole of himself in each of his writings." — HAWEIS.

" Irving's first literary work was a play, written for an entertainment at the house of a friend."

" Before Irving there was no laughter in the land."

" The influence of his writings is sweet and wholesome."

" His writings are the literature of leisure and retrospection ; and already Irving's gentle elaboration, the refined and slightly artificial beauty of his style, and his persistently genial and sympathetic attitude, have begun to pall upon readers who demand a more nervous and accentuated kind of writing." — BEERS.

JAMES FENIMORE COOPER.

JAMES FENIMORE COOPER.

NOVELIST AND CONTROVERSIALIST.

EXTRACTS.

SCENE BETWEEN MAJOR DUNWOODIE AND HARVEY BIRCH.

"If I am to be murdered, fire! I will never become your prisoner."

"No, Major Dunwoodie," said Birch, lowering his musket; "it is neither my intention to capture nor to slay."

"What then would you have, mysterious being?" said Dunwoodie, hardly able to persuade himself that the form he saw was not a creature of the imagination.

"Your good opinion," answered the pedler with emotion; "I would wish all good men to judge me with lenity."

"To you it must be indifferent what may be the judgment of men; for you seem to be beyond the reach of their sentence."

"God spares the lives of his servants to his own time," said the pedler solemnly; "a few hours ago I was your prisoner, and threatened with the gallows; now you are mine; but, Major Dunwoodie, you are free. There are men abroad that would treat you less kindly. Of what

41

service would that sword be to you against my weapon and a steady hand? Take the advice of one who has never harmed you, and who never will. Do not trust yourself in the skirt of any wood, unless in company and mounted."

"And have you comrades, who have assisted you to escape, and who are less generous than yourself?"

"No — no; I am alone truly; none know me but my God and *him.*"

"And who?" asked the major, with an interest he could not control.

"None," continued the pedler, recovering his composure. "But such is not your case, Major Dunwoodie; you are young and happy; there are those who are dear to you, and such are not far away; danger is near them you love most — danger within and without. Double your watchfulness, strengthen your patrols, and be silent. With your opinion of me, should I tell you more, you would never suspect an ambush. But remember and guard them you love best."

The pedler discharged the musket in the air, and threw it at the feet of the astonished auditor. When surprise and smoke allowed Dunwoodie to look again on the rock where he had stood, the spot was vacant.

THE SPY.

SCENE BETWEEN MOHEGAN AND MISS TEMPLE.

"DAUGHTER, the Great Spirit made your father with a white skin, and he made mine with a red; but he colored both their hearts with blood. When young, it is swift and warm; but when old, it is still and cold. Is there difference below the skin? No. Once John

had a woman. She was the mother of so many sons," —
he raised his hand with three fingers elevated, — "and
she had daughters that would have made the young
Delawares happy. She was kind, daughter, and what I
said she did. (You have different fashions; but do you
think John did not love the wife of his youth — the
mother of his children ? ")

" And what has become of your family, John, — your
wife and your children ?" asked Elizabeth, touched by
the Indian's manner.

" Where is the ice that covered the great spring ? It
is all melted, and gone with the waters. John has lived
till all his people have left him for the land of spirits;
his time has come, and he is ready."

Mohegan dropped his head in his blanket and sat in
silence. Miss Temple knew not what to say. - She wished
to draw the thoughts of the old warrior from his gloomy
recollections; but there was a dignity in his sorrow and
in his fortitude that repressed her efforts to speak. After
a long pause, however, she renewed the discourse by
asking, —

" Where is Leatherstocking, John ? I have brought
this canister of powder at his request; but he is nowhere
to be seen. Will you take charge of it and see it
delivered ? "

The Indian raised his head slowly, and looked earnestly
at the gift, which she put into his hand.

" This is the great enemy of my nation. Without this
when could the white men drive the Delawares ?
Daughter, the Great Spirit gave your fathers to know
how to make guns and powder, that they might sweep
the Indians from the land. There will soon be no red-

skin in the country. When John is gone, the last will leave these hills, and his family will be dead." The aged warrior stretched his body forward, leaning an elbow on his knee, and appeared to be taking a parting look at the objects of the vale, which were still visible through the misty atmosphere; though the air seemed to thicken at each moment around Miss Temple, who became conscious of an increased difficulty of respiration.

The eye of Mohegan changed gradually from its sorrowful expression to a look of wildness that might be supposed to border on the inspiration of a prophet, as he continued, " But he will go to the country where his fathers have met. The game shall be plenty as the fish in the lakes. No woman shall cry for meat; no Mingo can ever come. The chase shall be for children; and all just red-men shall live together as brothers."

THE PIONEERS.

" WHEN the tide falls," Dillon said, in a voice that betrayed the agony of fear, though his words expressed the renewal of hope, "we shall be able to walk to land."

" There was One, and only One, to whose feet the waters were the same as a dry deck," returned the cockswain; "and none but such as have His power will ever be able to walk from these rocks to the sands." The old seaman paused, and turning his eyes, which exhibited a mingled expression of disgust and compassion, on his companion, he added, with reverence : " Had you thought more of Him in fair weather, your case would be less to be pitied in this tempest."

THE PILOT.

REFERENCES.

Thomas R. Lounsbury's *James Fenimore Cooper*.

J. G. Wilson's *Bryant and His Friends* (Chapter on Cooper).

Richardson's *American Literature*. Vol. II. chap. ix.

Stedman-Hutchinson's *Library of American Literature*. Vol. V.

Allibone's *Dictionary of Authors*.

Chambers's *Cyclopædia of English Literature*.

Griswold's *Prose Writers of America*.

Poe's *Literati*.

Bryant's Memorial Address on Cooper (see Bryant's Prose Works).

Brander Matthews's *Americanisms and Briticisms*.

Duyckinck's *Cyclopædia of American Literature*. Vol. I.

Chappel's *Portrait Gallery of Eminent Americans*. Vol. II.

Lowell's *Fable for Critics*.

Appletons' Cyclopædia of American Biography.

Text-books on American Literature.

The Atlantic Monthly. February, 1887 ("A Glance Backward," by Susan Fenimore Cooper).

The North American Review. July, 1895.

Poole's *Index to Periodical Literature*, with Supplements.

T. S. Livermore's *History of Cooperstown*.

OUTLINE OF HIS LIFE.

September 15, 1789.
September 14, 1851.

Descent.

From James Cooper, of Stratford-on-Avon (Shakespeare's birth-place).   Quaker family.

Father.

English. A judge.   Cultured, wealthy, energetic.   Several times a Representative in Congress, and a leading Federalist.

Mother.

Of Swedish blood.   A Fenimore, whose ancestors had lived for a century in Burlington, N. J.

Birth.

In Burlington, N. J.   (The youngest but one of twelve children, many of whom died in infancy.)

Removal.

When a year old, to the western frontier of New York State.
The founding by his father, William Cooper, of Cooperstown, on Otsego Lake.   (See notes under "Cooperstown.")
A family of fifteen live six years in a log house.
Building of the "Hall," the manor-house of the town.
Life in contact with Indians, primeval forests, rivers, and lakes.

As a Youth.

"Brave, blithe-hearted, impetuous, most generous and upright."

Education.

"The wilderness was his earliest and most potent teacher."
Fitted for college in Albany with the rector of St. Peter's Church, a man thoroughly English in his training and ideas.

Three Years at Yale College.

> (Entered at thirteen years of age.)
>
> Youngest student, save the poet Hillhouse, in his class.
>
> His class, he said, was Yale's first Freshman class able to scan Latin.
>
> Dismissed for pranks. His father defended his course.

Midshipman and Lieutenant. Several years.

> Gained material, to be worked later into his sea novels.

Marriage.

> In 1811, to Miss De Lancey, sister to the Bishop of Western New York. The De Lanceys were Tories. Leaves the navy, and loses the opportunity of taking an active part in the War of 1812.
>
> Settles for a time in Westchester County, N. Y., the home of the De Lanceys.
>
> A serene family life, although his literary career was a stormy one.

A "Gentleman Farmer" for Ten Years.

Accidentally Takes Up Literature as a Profession.

> When reading an English novel aloud to his wife, he exclaimed, "I believe I could do better myself."
>
> Result. *Precaution*, an English society novel.
>
> Not a success.
>
> Reviewed somewhat favorably in England, however, and not suspected to be of American origin.

Publication of The Spy; A Tale of the Neutral Ground. 1821.

> Brought out at his own expense, since no publisher was willing to risk an American novel on an American theme.
>
> Cooper, unlike Scott, had to create his own public.
>
> Made its author famous in both Europe and America.
>
> Determined Cooper's career.
>
> Translated into many languages, including Arabic, Russian, Norwegian, and even Persian.

Rapid Succession of Other Works.

> Eleven books published between 1821 and 1830.

"Cooper's prodigal pen was a mark of the English fiction of the period. . . .   Labor was hardly more than recreation to him."

Seven Years' Residence Abroad.   1826–1833.

Paris, Berne, Florence, Naples, Rome.

Friendly with Sir Walter Scott and the Marquis Lafayette.

Consul for two years at Lyons.

In Paris at the breaking out of the Revolution of 1830.

His company was sought, wherever he lived, by distinguished people, although he rarely made use of letters of introduction.

Loved Italy for its skies and scenery.

Wrote several novels, the scenes of which are laid in his native land: *The Prairie, The Red Rover*, and others.

Return to the United States.   Period of Controversy.

Twenty lawsuits at one time.

Made himself personally unpopular.   Misunderstood by his countrymen and his townspeople.

Took up his abode again at Otsego Hall.   Unpleasant legal disputes with local authorities.

Death and Burial at Cooperstown.

Died on the eve of his sixty-second birthday.

Death-bed Injunction.   The family should furnish no material for a biography.

Lies in the grounds of Christ Church, by the side of his wife, who died a few months later than he.

Monument at Cooperstown.

In Lakeside Cemetery.

A column surmounted by a figure of Leatherstocking.

Character.

Decided, original, frank, independent, generous, critical, somewhat reserved; not over-refined either by nature or by culture; intensely patriotic, manly, sincere, of lofty principles.

He made bitter enemies and warm friends.   Lacked humor. Possessed a combative disposition.   Was opposed to New England Puritans and Puritanism.

"An aristocrat in feeling and a democrat in conviction."
(Contrast his character with that of Washington Irving.)

Appearance.

Fine, massive build. Face strongly intellectual and manly.
Impressive port and vivacious presence.

Manner.

Self-assertive, somewhat arrogant, earnest, and at times
brusque. It repelled at first sight, rather than attracted.
Bryant spoke of his "emphatic frankness."

Family.

Susan Fenimore Cooper, the authoress. Lived at Cooperstown.
Paul Cooper, an Albany lawyer (who died in 1895, leaving a
son and three daughters)

Memorial Meeting.

Held in New York six months after his death.
Daniel Webster the presiding officer. Irving present.
William Cullen Bryant orator.

Autobiographic Glimpses.

Home as Found. His characters of John and Edward Elling-
ham show Cooper himself.
Sketches of Switzerland. Gleanings in Europe.

APPELLATIONS.

A NATIONAL NOVELIST OF INTERNATIONAL FAME.

A LARGE LITERARY CREATOR IN A FIELD OF HIS OWN DIS-
COVERY.

THE FIRST NOVELIST WEST OF THE ATLANTIC.

THE SEA-NOVELIST OF THE ENGLISH LANGUAGE.

THE AMERICAN SCOTT.

AMERICA'S NOVELIST OF ACTION.

THE STORY-TELLER OF AMERICAN WOODS AND WATERS.

A PANORAMIC NOVELIST.

A PHILISTINE OF ABOUNDING VITALITY.

THE MOST PROLIFIC OF AMERICAN AUTHORS.

THE ORIGINATOR OF THE RED MAN AS A CHARACTER IN LIT-
ERATURE.

A DEFENDER OF REPUBLICAN INSTITUTIONS.

THE PUGNACIOUS AMERICAN.

A MASTER IN DESCRIPTION.

THE DISCOVERER OF A NEW REGION OF ROMANCE.

ONE OF AMERICA'S LITERARY PIONEERS.

A STRIKING FIGURE IN AMERICA'S LITERARY ANNALS.

NOTES ON HIS WRITINGS.

Cooper's present fame rests wholly on his novels.

His Literary Domain.
" The borderland between barbarism and civilization."

His Themes.
The Sea. The Forest. The Sailor. The Hunter. The Pioneer.
The Indian.

Literary Merits.
Stirring action. Vigorous description.

Literary Faults.
Prolixity. Haste. Crudity. Inability to delineate women and
children.

Original Fields.
The novel of the sea and the novel of the Indian.

Three Literary Creations.
Leatherstocking. Long Tom Coffin. Harvey Birch.

His Novels.
Thirty-two in number. (Walter Scott wrote twenty-seven.)
Welcomed eagerly on both sides of the Atlantic.
" His works are published as soon as he produces them, in thirty-
four places in Europe." — S. F. B. MORSE.
Of the romantic type.
Read most by young people.
Stories of action. Not like modern novels, largely analytical.
The Prefaces to his books were written " not to conciliate the reader,
but to hurl scorn at the reviewer."

CLASSIFICATION.

Novels of the American Revolution.
The Spy ; or, A Tale of the Neutral Ground.
SCENE. Laid in Westchester Co., N.Y. (Cooper's home at time
of writing). Along the shores of the Hudson.

HERO. Harvey Birch, a Revolutionary patriot. Suggested by a story which the author heard from Chief Justice Jay, of Revolutionary fame.

The reading of this novel led a French patriot to assume the name of Harvey Birch, and pay the same service to his government in the reign of Louis Philippe.

It called forth a complimentary letter from Maria Edgeworth, the Irish novelist.

The best known English novel in Mexico and South America.

Appeared the same year with Irving's *Sketch-Book* and Dana's *Idle Man.*

Lionel Lincoln; or, The Leaguer of Boston.

Intended as one of a series of novels of the Revolution, to illustrate the history of each of its thirteen States.

Bancroft calls Cooper's description in this tale of the Battle of Bunker Hill the best written account of that engagement.

The Red Rover. The Revolutionary struggle on the water.

Written when Cooper was near Paris.

Scene opens in the harbor of Newport, R.I.

Sea Novels.

Here Cooper reigns an unchallenged master. (Frederick Marryat, the English marine novelist, ranks second.)

The Pilot. 1823. Instantaneous success.

Prompted by a conversation with a New York man, in which Scott's knowledge of sea-life as shown in *The Pirate*, just published, was called in question.

Founded on the exploits of John Paul Jones.

The first sea novel of the English language.

Translated early into German, French, and Italian.

Dramatized by Fitzball.

HERO. Long Tom Coffin.

"The finest thing since Parson Adams."—MARY RUSSELL MITFORD.

The Red Rover (see note above). *The Water Witch,* and others.

Political Novels.

Satanstoe. The Chain-bearer. The Red-skins. The Bravo. The Headsman of Berne. The Heidenmauer

The Leatherstocking Series.

A famous literary quintette.

"A drama in five acts."

The "perpetual delight" of the elder Dumas, the French novelist.

LOGICAL ORDER.

   The Deerslayer. 1811. The latest in date of publication.
      On the war-path.

   The Last of the Mohicans. "Hawkeye." (Daniel Boone?) 1826.
      Scene laid in the neighborhood of Lake George.
      The writing of the story was suggested to Cooper by Lord
        Derby.
      Career of activity and love.
      Leatherstocking appears here at his best.

   The Pathfinder. 1840.
   The Pioneers. "Natty Bumpo." 1823.
      The least interesting of the series.
      Written "to please himself."
      Thirty-five hundred copies sold the morning of its issue.
   The Prairie. "The Trapper." 1827.
      Old age and death.

HERO. Leatherstocking, or Natty Bumpo.
   "One of the greatest prize-men of fiction." — THACKERAY.
   "A philosopher of the wilderness."
   "A half-christian and a half-savage chevalier of American
      wild life."
   Brave, cool, slow of word and act, slightly suspicious, honest,
      manly.
   One of the noblest characters in fiction.

   "One wild flower he's plucked that is wet with the dew
      Of this fresh Western world; and, the thing not to mince,
      He has done naught but copy it ill ever since."
                   LOWELL'S *Fable.*

   Cooper introduced the Indian into literature; Mrs. Stowe, the
      Negro.

NOTE. — Cooper intended to write a sixth Leatherstocking novel, the
scene to be laid at Niagara at the time of the Revolution, but he was dis-
suaded from doing so by his publisher.

Other Works by Cooper.

   Naval History of the United States.
   Lives of Distinguished Naval Officers.
   Gleanings of Europe and *Sketches of Switzerland.*
   Homeward Bound and *Home as Found.*
      Harsh criticism on America and its people.
   Ways of the Hour.
      Criticism of trial by jury.

MISCELLANEOUS NOTES.

Tributes.

"Have you read the American novels? In my mind they are as good as anything Sir Walter ever wrote. . . . I envy the Americans their Mr. Cooper." — MARY RUSSELL MITFORD.

"Fenimore Cooper saved me from despair after my second return to Italy, and has, up to this moment, been a father to me in kindness." — Letter of GREENOUGH, the sculptor. 1833.

In 1833 Victor Hugo remarked to James Grant Wilson that, excepting the authors of France, Cooper was the greatest novelist of the century.

"To plunge into one of his great books brings a refreshment only to be likened to that of the sea and forest which they describe." — HAWTHORNE and LEMMON.

"His writings are instinct with the spirit of nationality. In his productions every American must take an honest pride." — WILLIAM H. PRESCOTT.

"While the love of country continues to prevail, his memory will exist in the hearts of the people." — DANIEL WEBSTER.

Cooperstown.

"The home of the 'Last of the Mohicans.'"

"Placed in a gateway of mountains," sixty miles west of Albany.

Inhabitants, about twenty-five hundred. A popular summer resort.

Judge Cooper was the founder of the village, the father and magistrate of the community, and its representative in Congress.

On Otsego Lake, the scene of several of the Leatherstocking tales.

Lake Steamer, "Natty Bumpo," and tug, "Pioneer."

Otsego Rock. The traditional meeting-place of Indians for hundreds of miles.

Leatherstocking Falls. On the west side of the lake.

Leatherstocking's Cave, in a cliff a mile and a half from the village.

Otsego Hall. "Templeton," prominent in *The Pioneers*.

Destroyed by fire soon after Cooper's death.

Here Judge Cooper entertained Washington, Talleyrand, and many other notable personages, including a number of political exiles of the French Revolution.

See R. B. Coffin's *The Home of Cooper;* also views in Duyckinck, Vol. I., and *Appleton's American Biography.*

Influence of Cooper's Early Environment.

"He learned wood-lore as the young Indian learned it, face to face with the divinities of the forest. He knew the calls of the wild animals far across the gloomy wilderness. He could follow the deer and bear to their secluded haunts. He could retrace the path of the retreating wolf by the broken cobwebs glistening in the early sunlight; and the cry of the panther, high overhead in the pines and hemlocks, was a speech as familiar as his own tongue. When he was thirsty he made a hunter's cup of leaves, and drank in the Indian fashion. When fatigued he lay down to rest with that sense of security that comes only to the forest-bred. When thoughtful he could learn, from the lap of the waves against the shore, the murmur of leaves, and the rustle of wings, those lessons which nature teaches in her quiet moods." — HENRIETTA C. WRIGHT.

Cooper's Continental Fame "could be said to hold its own with that of Walter Scott."

His Preferences among his own books.

The Pathfinder and *The Deerslayer.*

(These two novels are considered his most artistic ones.)

Unfitness of His Novels for Dramatization.

See William Winter's "Thought on Cooper" in *Old Shrines and Ivy.*

Cooper. Depicter of the external and active side of the Indian character.

Longfellow. Depicter of the inward and imaginative side of his character.

Cooper. The romancer of adventure and external incident.

Hawthorne. The romancer of the passions and experiences of the human heart.

Irving. The first American prose writer.

Cooper.   The first American novelist.

Bryant.   The first American poet.

Cooper.   "Colonel of the American literary regiment."

Irving.   "Lieutenant-colonel."

Bryant.   "Major."

Lowell, Whittier, Hawthorne, Dana, Halleck.   "Captains." — HALLECK.

Comments on Cooper by Charles F. Richardson.

"Let no one go to Cooper, as to Hawthorne, for instruction in the arts of style. . . . Instead of recognizing his defects, and trying either to correct them or modify his choice of themes and his methods of treatment, he fell into an inveterate habit of replying to, or suing at law, those who had criticised him."

"When free he could be as destructive as Victor Hugo's loose cannon on shipboard [see Hugo's novel, *Ninety-Three*]; when self-contained in his own proper field, no American could dispute, as none could equal, his solid success."

"Like a trained hound, his powers and beauty were visible in motion rather than at rest; in conflict, not in home life."

"We go to Cooper with the demand, 'Tell us a story;' not with the plea, 'Help us in solving the riddle of existence.' "

"After all, a novel must entertain, and a cloud of witnesses attest Cooper's entertainingness."

William Winter's Characterization of Cooper.

"Often, when Cooper is imaginative, his mind revels over vast spaces, alike in the trackless wilderness and on the trackless ocean — forests that darken half a continent, and tremendous icebergs that crash and crumble upon unknown seas. More often he is descriptive and meditative, moralizing, like Wordsworth, on rock and river and the tokens of a divine soul in the wonders of creation. His highest mood of feeling is that of calm-eyed philosophy. His highest ideal of virtue is self-sacrifice."

WILLIAM CULLEN BRYANT.

WILLIAM CULLEN BRYANT.

Poet, Journalist, and Commemorative Orator.

EXTRACTS.

He who, from zone to zone,
Guides through the boundless sky thy certain flight,
In the long way that I must tread alone,
    Will lead my steps aright.
To a Waterfowl.

To him who in the love of nature holds
Communion with her visible forms, she speaks
A various language.
Thanatopsis.

Old ocean's gray and melancholy waste.
Ibid.

All that tread
The globe are but a handful to the tribes
That slumber in its bosom.
Ibid.

So live, that when thy summons comes to join
The innumerable caravan, which moves
To that mysterious realm where each shall take
His chamber in the silent halls of death,
Thou go not, like the quarry-slave at night,

Scourged to his dungeon; but, sustained and soothed
By an unfaltering trust, approach thy grave
Like one who wraps the drapery of his couch
About him, and lies down to pleasant dreams.

THANATOPSIS.

MAN foretells afar
The courses of the stars; the very hour
He knows when they shall darken or grow bright;
Yet doth the eclipse of Sorrow and of Death
Come unforewarned.

AN EVENING REVERY.

ROBERT of Lincoln's Quaker wife,
    Pretty and quaint, with plain brown wings,
Passing at home a patient life,
    Broods in the grass while her husband sings:
        Bob-o'-link, bob-o'-link,
        Spink, spank, spink;
Brood, kind creature; you need not fear
Thieves and robbers while I am here.
        Chee, chee, chee.

ROBERT OF LINCOLN.

MAIDEN's hearts are always soft:
    Would that men's were truer!

SONG.

TRUTH crushed to earth shall rise again;
    The eternal years of God are hers;
But Error, wounded, writhes in pain,
    And dies among his worshipers.

THE BATTLE-FIELD.

The water, as the wind passed o'er,
    Shot upward many a glancing beam,
Dimpled and quivered more and more,
    And tripped along, a livelier stream,
The flattered stream, the simpering stream,
The fond, delighted, silly stream.

THE WIND AND STREAM.

GLIDE on in your beauty, ye youthful spheres,
To weave the dance that measures the years;
Glide on, in the glory and gladness sent
To the farthest wall of the firmament —
The boundless visible smile of Him
To the veil of whose brow your lamps are dim.

THE SONG OF THE STARS.

THE groves were God's first temples.

A FOREST HYMN.

THE melancholy days are come, the saddest of the year,
Of wailing winds, and naked woods, and meadows brown
    and sear.

THE DEATH OF THE FLOWERS.

THERE are notes of joy from the hang-bird and wren,
    And the gossip of swallows through all the sky;
The ground-squirrel gayly chirps by his den,
    And the wilding bee hums merrily by.

THE GLADNESS OF NATURE.

WHAT heroes from the woodland sprung,
    When, through the fresh awakened land,
The thrilling cry of freedom rung,
And to the work of warfare strung
    The yeoman's iron hand!

Hills flung the cry to hills around,
　And ocean-mart replied to mart,
And streams, whose springs were yet unfound,
Pealed far away the startling sound
　　Into the forest's heart.

SEVENTY-SIX.

THE barley-harvest was nodding white,
When my children died on the rocky height,
And the reapers were singing on hill and plain,
When I came to my task of sorrow and pain.
But now the season of rain is nigh,
The sun is dim in the thickening sky,
And the clouds in the sullen darkness rest
Where he hides his light at the doors of the west.
I hear the howl of the wind that brings
The long drear storm on its heavy wings;
But the howling wind, and the driving rain
Will beat on my houseless head in vain:
I shall stay, from my murdered sons to scare
The beasts of the desert and fowls of air.

RIZPAH.

THERE is a day of sunny rest
　For every dark and troubled night;
And grief may bide, an evening guest,
　But joy shall come with early light.

"BLESSED ARE THEY THAT MOURN."

ERE russet fields their green resume,
　Sweet flower, I love, in forest bare,
To meet thee, when thy faint perfume
　Alone is in the virgin air.

THE YELLOW VIOLET.

"OH FAIREST OF THE RURAL MAIDS."

Oh fairest of the rural maids!
Thy birth was in the forest shades;
Green boughs, and glimpses of the sky,
Were all that met thy infant eye.

Thy sports, thy wanderings, when a child,
Were ever in the sylvan wild;
And all the beauty of the place
Is in thy heart and on thy face.

The twilight of the trees and rocks
Is in the light shade of thy locks;
Thy step is as the wind, that weaves
Its playful way among the leaves.

Thy eyes are springs, in whose serene
And silent waters heaven is seen;
Their lashes are the herbs that look
On their young figures in the brook.

The forests' depths, by foot unpressed,
Are not more sinless than thy breast;
And holy peace that fills the air
Of those calm solitudes, is there.

REFERENCES.

Biographies by Parke Godwin, John Bigelow, A. J. Symington, D. J. Hill.

James Grant Wilson's *Bryant and His Friends.*

Richardson's *American Literature.* Vol. II. pp. 36-49.

Griswold's *Poets of America.*

Stedman's *Poets of America.*

Lowell's *Fable for Critics.*

Stedman-Hutchinson's *Library of American Literature.* Vol. V.

Gilman's *Poets' Homes.*

George William Curtis's *Homes of American Authors.*

Mrs. Kirkland's *Homes of American Authors.*

Griswold's *Home Life of Great Authors.*

Shepard's *Pen Pictures of Modern Authors.*

Morris's *Half Hours with the Best American Authors.*

Chappel's *Portrait Gallery of Eminent Americans.* Vol. II.

Whipple's *Literature and Life.*

Poe's *Literati.* (Acrimonious.)

Bayard Taylor's *Critical Essays.*

Duyckinck's *Cyclopædia of American Literature.* Vol. I.

Appletons' Cyclopædia of American Biography.

Lippincott's Biographical Dictionary.

Preface to Complete Edition of Bryant's Poems.

Histories and text-books of American Literature.

Memorial Addresses —
  George William Curtis, before the New York Historical Society.
  Robert C. Winthrop, before the Massachusetts Historical Society.
  John Bigelow, before the Century Club.

Harper's Magazine. April, 1851. March, 1862.

Atlantic Monthly. February, 1864.

Scribner's Magazine. August, 1878 (G. W. Curtis's Address. Illustrated.
  Wyatt Eaton's portrait of Bryant).

Century Magazine. March, 1882 (Bryant and Longfellow).

Lippincott's Magazine. July, 1882.

New England Magazine. September, 1893 ("Literary Associations of Berkshire." Illustrated). March, 1892 ("Bryant's New England Home." Illustrated). October, 1894 ("Bryant, the Poet of Nature." The frontispiece, a portrait of Bryant).

The Review of Reviews. October, 1894 (Frontispiece, the latest portrait taken of Bryant. Articles on his place in American Literature, and the Bryant Centennial).

St. Nicholas. December, 1876. (Bryant's "Boys of My Boyhood.")

Alden's *Studies in Bryant.*

OUTLINE OF HIS LIFE.

November 3, 1794.
June 12, 1878.

It began in Washington's administration, and extended into
that of Hayes.

An Ancestor, Peter Bryant, settled in Plymouth, Mass., in 1632.

Father.

> A physician.   Cultured and travelled for his time.
> Trained his children well.   Fostered William's taste for poetry.
> See allusions to him in Bryant's poems, " Hymn to Death," and
> " To the Past."

Mother.

> Like Longfellow's, a descendant of John Alden.
> Thrifty, economical, intelligent; interested in neighborhood and
> public affairs.
> Kept a diary fifty-three years without missing a day.   Entry
> for Nov. 3, 1794: "Storming, wind N.E.; churned; seven
> in the evening, son born."
> " Bryant's mother was his reliance; his father was sunshine."

Birthplace.

> Cummington, Hampshire County, Massachusetts, in a pictur-
> esque mountain region.
> Bryant's poetry belongs to New England, although his life was
> lived mainly in New York City.
> Read his birthday poem, The Third of November, 1861.
> A whipping-post stood within a mile of his home, — a vestige of
> colonial times.   The poet once witnessed the scourging of a .
> thief.

Named for William Cullen, a physician friend of his father's.

Atmosphere of the Home.

Somewhat Puritanical. Severe discipline.

"The home of virtue, not of emotion." (Contrast with Tennyson's home.)

Frail Child, with an abnormally large head. To reduce the size of this, the infant was plunged daily in a spring.

His Youth.

Passed largely out of doors in the enjoyment of nature. "He ground his colors in the open air."

He often prayed fervently that he might receive the gift of poetic genius.

His mental diet was at first Watts's Hymns, his father's medical works, and Pope's *Iliad*; later, Thomson, Cowper, Burns, Wordsworth, Southey, and Henry Kirke White.

Precocity.

(Compare with that of Byron, Pope, and the Goodale sisters.)

He knew his letters when a year and a half old.

At four years of age read well, and was an almost faultless speller.

Repeated Watts's Hymns at five years.

Wrote verses at twelve, and recited them in public at the close of the school term.

In two months of study, he "knew the Greek Testament as if it had been English."

When fourteen he wrote "The Embargo," a political satire on Jefferson's administration. (He afterwards championed ably that president's democratic ideas.)

"Thanatopsis," his best known poem, was written in his eighteenth year.

Education.

Two terms at Williams College, entering as a Sophomore. (View of college seen in Duyckinck's *Cyclopædia*, Vol I.) Not satisfactory. (In later life, made an alumnus.)

Distinguished for linguistic and literary ability.

Planned to continue his studies at Yale, but his father's limited means did not permit this.

Studied law in private offices.

Practised Law nine years in Western Massachusetts, attaining high rank in local and State courts.

    Read the last stanza of his poem, Green River.

Manuscript of " Thanatopsis " discovered by the father, with other verses, in the son's desk during the latter's absence from home.

    " American poetry may be said to have begun with the September number of the *North American Review*, 1817, when this poem and the ' Inscription for the Entrance to a Wood ' appeared in it."

    Incident of R. H. Dana's visit to the Boston State House to see the supposed author.

A Copy of Wordsworth's Ballads "changed the face of nature to him."

Delivered " The Ages " before Harvard's Phi Beta Kappa Society. 1821.

    Honor secured through Dana's influence.

    A didactic poem on the history of the race. Stately, grave, philosophic. Written in the Spenserian Stanza. (See Analysis of Versification.)

    Perhaps the best poem of its kind ever recited before a college fraternity, American or English.

    Bryant's only occasional poem.

    (Macaulay's " Evening " was delivered the same year before the students of Trinity College, Cambridge.)

Removal to New York in 1825, where Bryant spent most of the remainder of his long life.

    Abandonment of law for journalism. (As in the cases of Lowell, Longfellow, and others.)

Marriage to Frances Fairchild.

    " Their union was a poem of the tenderest rhythm."

    His prayer at the time. — " May God Almighty mercifully take care of our happiness here and hereafter. May we ever continue constant to each other, and mindful of our mutual promises of attachment and truth. . . . Together may we lead a long, happy, and innocent life, without any diminution of affection till we die. . . . And that we may be less unworthy of so great a blessing, may we be assisted to cultivate all the benign and charitable affections, and offices not only toward each other, but toward our neighbors, the human race, and all the creatures of God."

Poems written to his Wife.

During her lifetime.

"O Fairest of the Rural Maids."

The Future Life.

The Life that Is. (After her dangerous illness in 1858.)

At her death.

October, 1866.

Seven years afterward.

A Memory. (Unfinished.)

"I never wrote a poem that I did not repeat to her, and take her judgment upon it."

Connection with The New York Evening Post. 1826–1878.

Bryant, as editor, protested vigorously against slavery, advocated free trade, and made the paper strongly Democratic.

Maintained in it an exceptionally high moral and intellectual tone.

Six Tours to Europe, one extended to Egypt and Syria.

Letters from a Traveller.

Letters from the East.

Letters from Spain and other countries.

Publication of Poems, second collection, complete. 1832.

Washington Irving (not then acquainted with Bryant) brought out an English edition of them, writing a complimentary preface. Professor Wilson reviewed the verses patronizingly in *Blackwood's Magazine.*

Received well by the English public.

Extensive Travel in the United States at different times ; in Mexico and Cuba.

Thirty Years of uneventful life.   Mellow old age.

" Beside a massive gateway built up in years gone by,
  Upon whose top the clouds in eternal shadow lie,
  While streams the evening sunshine on quiet wood and lea,
  I stand and calmly wait till the hinges turn for me."

WAITING BY THE GATE.

Memorial Discourses on Thomas Cole, the artist, James Fenimore
   Cooper, Goethe, Shakespeare, Scott, Irving, Mazzini.
   Bryant had a peculiar fitness for this sort of oration, — " He
   was an accomplished, graceful, and impressive speaker."

Translation of Homer.   A work requiring six years.   1866–1872.
   Undertaken when the poet was more than seventy years old,
      as a solace after the loss of his wife.   (As Longfellow
      turned to Dante under the same bereavement.)
   Done in Blank Verse.   Use of Roman names of gods and god-
      desses.
   In many respects the best English translation.   Homeric spirit.
      Saxon English.
   Some earlier translators: George Chapman, Alexander Pope,
      William Cowper, I. Charles Wright.
   A later translator, William Morris.
   (Read the fifth book of *The Odyssey.*)

Honors **Paid Him Living.**

   Celebration of his Seventieth Birthday by the Century Club,
      New York.   (Bryant had been one of its founders.)
      Congratulatory Address by George Bancroft, then Presi-
         dent.
      Poems by Lowell, Holmes, Bayard Taylor, Tuckerman,
         Julia Ward Howe, Whittier, Stoddard, and others.
      Letters from Longfellow, N. P. Willis, Dana, Edward
         Everett.
      Presentation of Folio of forty studies by the various art
         members of the club, including Huntington, Church,
         Durand, Bierstadt, and Eastman Johnson.
   Reception by the New York Legislature when he was visiting
      Governor Tilden.

Commemorative Vase, on his eightieth birthday, presented by
the citizens of New York.

> Designed by J. H. Whitehouse, — Greek in form, and
> adorned with symbols of Bryant's life and poems.

> Kept in New York's Metropolitan Museum. (This mu-
> seum possesses also a bronze bust of the poet.)

> See *Harper's Magazine*, July, 1876; and Gilman's *Poets'
> Homes.*

> (Another eightieth birthday gift was a cactus plant, brought
> from Vergil's tomb at Naples.)

Admitted to the Russian Academy. 1873.

Death, in the Month of June, after a fall and a short illness consequent upon it.

His desire to die in this month. See poem, "June."

His daughter, Mrs. Parke Godwin, also passed away in the same
season of the year (June, 1893).

Buried at Roslyn, L.I. His poem, "June," recited at the funeral.

His First Biographer.

Parke Godwin, his son-in-law.

Character.

> Unimpassioned, reserved, and lofty in nature; "clear in mind,
> sober in judgment, refined in taste;" considerate of the
> feelings of others; always controlled in temper; free from
> all vices and time-wasting habits. Intensely fond of nature
> and freedom. ("I like air and elbow-room, as one finds
> them about the Pyramids, as at Thebes and Baalbec.")
> Popular as a man when unpopular as a journalist. "He
> wrote a note to his butcher as faultlessly as an article for
> the press."

> Deeply religious. In doctrine he was of the Unitarian faith.
> Bryant received private baptism at the age of sixty-four,
> when in Naples, and during the all but fatal illness of his
> wife.

Appearance and Manner.

> Majestic, kingly, reverence-inspiring. ("He was a favorite
> with photographers and artists in crayon.") Tall and

slender. Well-shaped head, high forehead, overhanging eyebrows, deep-set and keen eyes, aquiline nose.

"He resembled a Greek philosopher more than Longfellow or Walt Whitman." "His face, like his voice, had the innate charm of tranquillity."

In manner he was modest, courteous, dignified, and kindly.

For views of Launt Thompson's bust of Bryant, see *Harper's Magazine*, September, 1894.

Habits.

Usually rose at five o'clock and retired at ten.

Took daily morning gymnastic exercises and a cold bath throughout his long life.

Walked much, two miles to his business every day. A pleasurable sight to New Yorkers for fifty years.

"The good gray head, which all men knew," is as applicable to Bryant as to the Duke of Wellington.

Never indulged in a stimulant (even coffee), a narcotic, or condiments.

"He treated his body as God's temple."

His perfect health was notable ; although when young he was threatened with pulmonary weakness, he threw off the trouble, and was never known to have a sickness in his more than fourscore years of active life.

Memory.

Marvellous.

He said that with a moment's reflection he could recall every poem he had ever written ; while his resources as to the poetry of English authors were inexhaustible.

"He was fastidious about his reading, believing that there was no worse thief than a bad book."

Linguistic Accomplishments.

Bryant spoke all the living European languages save Greek, and was familiar with the literatures of many of them.

APPELLATIONS.

The Nestor of our Poets.

The Father of our Song.

Our Meditative Poet of Nature.

The Poet of New England Wild Flowers.

The Great American.

Nature's Celebrant.

The Foremost Citizen.

A Typical Republican.

The American Wordsworth.

Our Puritan Greek.

A Prophet in the Wilderness.

The Poet of Painters.

A High Priest at the Altar of Nature.

The Literary and Civic Nestor of New York Society.

Our Early Landscape Poet.

Calm Priest of Nature.

Bard of the Elements.

NOTES ON HIS WRITINGS.

General Comments.

Style. Simple, clear, natural, stately. (Bryant protested against
the obscurity of Browning's style.)

Nature. His poetry is imbued with an austere, solemn, reverential
spirit.

Length of poems. Like Poe, Bryant did not sanction long poems;
he considered seventy-five lines a good limit.

No epic or drama is found among his writings.

Most of his poems have been translated into the Russian language.

There was no original writing in America when Bryant began his
literary career.

"In the whole range of his writings, there is no line or word that
appeals to an unworthy feeling."

"The writing of poetry was little more than an avocation to Bryant.
He once said, "I should have starved if I had been obliged to
depend on my poetry for a living.""

CLASSIFICATION.

Autobiographical Poems.

Inscription for the Entrance to a Wood. To a Waterfowl (written
in the poet's twenty-first year, after a journey on foot to Plain-
field in search of an opening for law practice). Hymn to Death
(evoked by the death of his father; read the tributary lines).
Death of the Flowers (in memory of a sister who died young
in consumption). Four poems to his wife. A Lifetime.

Two Humorous Poems.

To a Mosquito. Rhode Island Coal.

Nature Poems, that sing of

Trees.

A Forest Hymn. Tree-Burial. Autumn Woods. Among the
Trees. Inscription for the Entrance to a Wood. The Planting of the Apple-Tree.

Water.

The Rivulet (it ran by the Cummington home). Green River. The Fountain. To the River Arve. A Hymn of the Sea. A Rain-Dream. A Scene on the Banks of the Hudson. Catterskill Falls. The Tides. The Night Journey of a River. The Twenty-Second of February (the second half of the poem very poetically compares Washington's course to that of the "mighty Hudson").

(Symbolical: The Stream of Life. The Flood of Years.)

Winds.

The Evening Wind. The Hurricane. The Summer Wind. The West Wind. March. The Winds. The Wind and the Stream.

Flowers.

The Yellow Violet. To the Fringed Gentian. The Death of the Flowers. The Child's Funeral. Innocent Child and Snow-white Flower.

Other Nature Poems. (More than a hundred in number.)

The Gladness of Nature. To a Cloud. June. After a Tempest. The Song of the Sower. The Return of the Birds. Robert of Lincoln.

> "His heart throbbed rhythmic to the heart divine,
> That bird, flower, forest, stream, and mountain sway."

Poems on the Indian.

Monument Mountain (the scene of the narrative is laid near Stockbridge, Mass). An Indian Story. The Disinterred Warrior. The Indian Girl's Lament. An Indian at the Burial-Place of his Fathers. A Legend of the Delawares.

Patriotic Poems.

The Twenty-Second of December. [Two Poems.] Seventy-Six. O Mother of a Mighty Race. Our Country's Call. Not Yet. The Twenty-Second of February. The Death of Lincoln. The Antiquity of Freedom. Song of Marion's Men (Bryant's best lyric; the third and fourth lines were modified for Irving's English edition of the poems). Centennial Hymn.

Poems on Slavery.

The Death of Slavery. The African Chief.

Hebraic Poems.

Rizpah. The Song of the Stars.

Hellenic Poems.

> The Massacre at Scio. The Song of the Greek Amazon. The Greek Partisan. The Greek Boy.

Translations from the Spanish, Portuguese, French, Provençal, Italian, Latin, and Greek.

Two Exquisite Fairy Tales.

> Sella ("Shadow"). Little People of the Snow (has been illustrated).
>
> Written in the winter of 1862-1863 as recreation from the depression resulting from the war and the burden of editorial duties.
>
> For an article, "Sella, Illustrated," see *Art Journal*, 1876.

His Best Known Poem, "Thanatopsis." ("View of Death.")

> Not the writer's own favorite; he preferred "The Past."
>
> "Original in conception and execution. . . . The microcosm of the author's mind and powers. . . . A piece of verse of which any language or age may be proud. . . . Its morality and its trust are ethnic rather than Christian." — CHARLES F. RICHARDSON.
>
> Although this poem voices no belief in personal immortality, unmistakable expressions of such a belief are found in The Future Life, Hymn to Death, The Return of Youth, and other poems.
>
> Wordsworth committed the poem to memory.
>
> "Bryant rose in this poem from the lyrical expression of nature to an epic interpretation of her solemn majesty." — R. H. STODDARD.
>
> See *Harper's Magazine*, September, 1894 ("The Origin of a Great Poem"). This magazine shows a view of the Cummington home in which the verses were written.

The Song of the Sower.

> Read with Jean François Millet's picture, The Sower, at hand. (See "Selected Proofs," Century Co., No. 20.)

The Flood of Years.

> Written in Bryant's eighty-second year. "A fitting crown for an existence so beneficent and exalted."

His Poetic Measures.

> Bryant's poetry furnishes excellent material for the study of versification.
>
> (Consult Analysis of Versification.)

Favorite Metres. Blank Verse and the Iambic Quatrain.

Blank Verse. (Heroic Metre.) Used in most of his long poems.

Translation of Homer. Thanatopsis. Inscription for the Entrance to a Wood. An Evening Revery. Sella. The Little People of the Snow. Tree-Burial. Forest Hymn. The Antiquity of Freedom. A Hymn to the Sea. The Flood of Years.

Iambic Quatrain. (Long Metre Stanza).

To the Fringed Gentian. The Lapse of Time. The Massacre at Scio. The West Wind. Blessed are They that Mourn: O Fairest of the Rural Maids, and others.

Anapestic Verse.

The Song of the Stars. I Cannot Forget with what Fervid Devotion. The Land of Dreams. The Gladness of Nature. The Snow-Shower. Green River. Catterskill Falls.

Trochaic Verse. (Not often employed by poets.)

The Cloud on the Way. The Third of November.

Varieties of Stanza. (Analyze.)

The Ages. To a Mosquito. Song for New Year's Eve. To A Waterfowl (stanza suggested by Southey's Ebb Tide). The Past. An Indian Story. A Presentiment. The Voice of Autumn. O Mother of a Mighty Race. The Planting of an Apple-Tree. Robert of Lincoln. The Tides. Italy. Waiting by the Gate. The Death of Slavery. May Evening. Christmas in 1875. A Northern Legend. The New Moon. The Greek Boy. Seventy-Six. Hymn to the North Star (last line, an Alexandrine).

Sonnets.

William Tell. November. October. Consumption. Mutation. Bryant's sonnets are not, in general, constructed on the Italian model; they are fourteen-lined poems, rather than sonnets. Consult Deshler's *Afternoons with the Poets.*

NOTE. — Bryant's Poems Complete have been published by D. Appleton & Co.

Groups of Allied Works.

Bryant's The Yellow Violet and To the Fringed Gentian.

Lowell's To the Dandelion.

Emerson's The Rhodora.

Whittier's Arbutus and The Mayflowers.

Wordsworth's To the Small Celandine.
Burns's To a Mountain Daisy.

Bryant's June.
Lowell's Rhapsody on June in The Vision of Sir Launfal, and his
poem, Under the Willows.

Bryant's Thanatopsis.
Wordsworth's Ode to Immortality.

Bryant's Oh Fairest of the Rural Maids!
Wordsworth's Three Years She grew in Sun and Shower.

Bryant's Sella.
Hawthorne's The Marble Faun.
Shelley's The Witch of Atlas.
Milton's Comus.   (Sabrina).
Fouqué's Undine.

Bryant's Little People of the Snow.
Hawthorne's The Snow Image.
Hans Christian Andersen's The Ice Maiden.

MISCELLANEOUS NOTES.

Tributes.

> " He spoke and lived
> ' As ever in his great Taskmaster's eye.' "
>
> HAWTHORNE.

> " How shall we thank him that in evil days,
> He faltered never, — nor for blame nor praise,
> Nor hire, nor party, shamed his earlier lays ?
>
> But as his boyhood was of manliest hue,
> So to his youth, his manly years were true,
> All dyed in royal purple through and through."
>
> HOLMES.

> " His life is now his noblest strain,
> His manhood better than his verse."
>
> WHITTIER.

> " Not in vague tones or tricks of verbal art
> The plaint and pæan rung;
> Thine the clear utterance of an earnest heart,
> The limpid Saxon tongue."

Abraham Lincoln once said of him, " It was worth the journey to the East to see such a man."

When Dickens landed in America his first question is said to have been, " Where is Bryant ? "

" Wherever English poetry is read and loved, his poems are known by heart."

" As long as a wild duck shall cross the crimson sky of evening in his flight, so long shall Bryant's memory float heavenward with it." — C. E. NORTON.

Centennial Celebration of His Birth.

Observed at Cummington, Aug. 16, 1894.

Original poems read by John Howard Bryant, aged brother of William Cullen, and Mrs. Julia Ward Howe.

Notable literary personages present. Charles Eliot Norton. Charles
Dudley Warner. Mrs. Julia Ward Howe. Parke Godwin.
John Bigelow.

Illustrated booklet, issued by the Committee of Celebration.

New York Memorials to Bryant.

Bronze bust and vase in Metropolitan Museum.

Bryant Park, Forty-second Street, named for him.

Works Edited by Bryant.

The Talisman. A decorated annual. Three issues.

From this grew the Sketch Club, which became later the
Century Club, an association of artists and literary men.

Picturesque America. (Appleton & Co.)

Popular History of America.

A Library of Poetry and Song.

Its introduction is an admirable essay on English poets and
poetry.

Twenty thousand copies sold in six months.

Two Prose Tales.

Medfield. The Skeleton's Cave.

An Illustrated Edition of thirty "Nature Poems." Published by the
Appletons, 1894. Paul de Longpré, artist.

Critical Attitude Toward His own Writing.

He destroyed more poetry than he had published.

His Economy.

Bryant did his editorial writing largely on the backs of letters.

1820-1821. A significant year in Bryant's life.

Publication of his first volume of verse. Marriage. Death of his
father. Phi Beta Kappa oration.

His Friends.

They comprised all the prominent literary men and artists in the
country.

Acquaintance with British Poets.

In 1844 Bryant met in England, Wordsworth, Samuel Rogers, and
Thomas Moore.

Bryant and Lincoln.

When Lincoln was nominated for the presidency, Bryant wrote him
a friendly letter of counsel, which elicited a grateful letter in
response. (Bryant was presidential elector at the time.)

Bryant's Homes.

Cummington, Mass., a mountain village in the Berkshires; also the birthplace of Massachusetts' ex-Senator Henry L. Dawes.

Estate purchased in 1865 by Bryant, and a new house built, in which he was wont to pass the autumn months.

View of house and of monument. *The Critic*, Aug. 25, 1894, p. 123.

Great Barrington. Seven years of life as barrister.

View. *New England Magazine*, September, 1893.

New York City. 24 West Sixteenth Street, for many years.

" *Cedarmere,*" *Roslyn, L.I.* Summer residence.

Old house, built in 1787. A poet's home.

Grounds adorned with trees and plants brought from various quarters of the globe.

Hospitality extended to distinguished foreigners and to school children of the neighborhood.

Bryant never carried editorial work to Roslyn.

Views. *Art Journal*, 1876. Gilman's *Poets' Homes.* Duyckinck's *Cyclopædia*, II. p. 186.

Secretary of the Copyright League.

This League issued a circular of appeal in 1873, looking toward the passage of an International Copyright Law in America and England, which was signed by Bryant, Longfellow, Emerson, Whittier, Garrison, Beecher, Holmes, Mrs. Stowe, Miss Alcott, Howells, and Aldrich.

America's first organized work in this direction. (Note Lowell's connection later with the movement.)

NATHANIEL HAWTHORNE.

NATHANIEL HAWTHORNE.

PROSE ROMANCER.

EXTRACTS.

A FOREST WALK.

"MOTHER," said little Pearl, "the sunshine does not love you. It runs away and hides itself, because it is afraid of something on your bosom. Now, see! There it is, playing, a good way off. Stand you here, and let me run and catch it. I am but a child. It will not flee from me, for I wear nothing on my bosom yet."

"Nor ever will, my child, I hope," said Hester.

"And why not, mother?" asked Pearl, stopping short, just at the beginning of her race. "Will it not come of its own accord, when I am a grown woman?"

"Run away, child," answered her mother, "and catch the sunshine! It will soon be gone."

Pearl set forth, at a great pace, and, as Hester smiled to perceive, did actually catch the sunshine, and stood laughing in the midst of it, all brightened by its splendor, and scintillating with the vivacity excited by rapid motion. The light lingered about the lonely child, as if glad of such a playmate, until her mother had drawn almost nigh enough to step into the magic circle too.

"It will go now," said Pearl, shaking her head.

85

"See!" answered Hester, smiling, "now I can stretch out my hand, and grasp some of it."

As she attempted to do so, the sunshine vanished; or, to judge from the bright expression that was dancing on Pearl's features, her mother could have fancied that the child had absorbed it into herself, and would give it forth again, with a gleam about her path, as they should plunge into the gloomier shade. There was no other attribute that so much impressed her with a sense of new and untransmitted vigor in Pearl's nature, as this never-failing vivacity of spirits; she had not the disease of sadness, which almost all children, in these latter days, inherit, with the scrofula, from the troubles of their ancestors.

Perhaps this too was a disease, and but the reflex of the wild energy with which Hester had fought against her sorrows before Pearl's birth. It was certainly a doubtful charm, imparting a hard, metallic lustre to the child's character. She wanted — what some people want throughout life — a grief that should deeply touch her, and thus humanize and make her capable of sympathy. But there was time enough yet for little Pearl.

"Come, my child!" said Hester, looking about her from the spot where Pearl had stood still in the sunshine. "We will sit down a little way within the wood, and rest ourselves."

"I am not aweary, mother," replied the little girl. "But you may sit down, if you will tell me a story meanwhile."

"A story, child!" said Hester. "And what about?"

"O, a story about the Black Man," answered Pearl, taking hold of her mother's gown, and looking up, half earnestly, half mischievously, into her face. "How he haunts this forest, and carries a book with him, — a big, heavy book, with iron clasps; and how this ugly Black Man offers his book and iron pen to everybody that meets him here among the trees; and they are to write their names in their own blood. And then he sets his mark on their bosom! Didst thou ever meet the Black Man, mother?"

"And who told you this story, Pearl?" asked her mother, recognizing a common superstition of the period.

"It was the old dame in the chimney-corner at the house where you watched last night," said the child. "But she fancied me asleep while she was talking of it. She said that a thousand and a thousand people had met him here, and had written in his book, and have his mark on them. And that ugly-tempered lady, old Mistress Hibbins, was one. And, mother, the old dame said that this scarlet letter was the Black Man's mark on thee, and that it glows like a red flame when thou meetest him at midnight, here in the dark wood. Is it true, mother? And dost thou go to meet him in the night-time?"

"Didst thou ever awake, and find thy mother gone?" asked Hester.

"Not that I remember," said the child. "If thou fearest to leave me in the cottage, thou mightest take me along with thee. I would very gladly go! But, mother, tell me now! Is there such a Black Man? And didst thou ever meet him? And is this his mark?"

"Wilt thou let me be at peace, if I once tell thee?" asked her mother.

"Yes, if thou tellest me all," answered Pearl.

"Once in my life, I met the Black Man!" said her mother. "This scarlet letter is his mark."

THE SCARLET LETTER.

THE ARCHED WINDOW.

CLIFFORD sat at the window, with Hepzibah, watching the neighbors as they stepped into the street. All of them, however unspiritual on other days, were transfigured by the Sabbath influence; so that their very garments — whether it were an old man's decent coat, well brushed for the thousandth time, or a little boy's first sack and trousers, finished yesterday by his mother's needle — had somewhat of the quality of ascension-robes. Forth, likewise, from the portal of the old house, stepped Phœbe, putting up her small green sunshade, and throwing upward a glance and smile of parting kindness to the faces at the arched window. In her aspect there was a familiar gladness, and a holiness that you could play with, and yet reverence it as much as ever. She was like a prayer, offered up in the homeliest beauty of the mother-tongue. Fresh was Phœbe, moreover, and airy and sweet in her apparel; as if nothing that she wore — neither her gown, nor her small straw bonnet, nor her little kerchief, any more than her snowy stockings — had ever been put on before; or, if worn, were all the fresher for it, and with a fragrance as if they had lain among the rose-buds.

The girl waved her hand to Hepzibah and Clifford, and went up the street; a religion in herself, warm, simple, true, with a substance that could walk on earth, and a spirit that was capable of heaven.

"Hepzibah," asked Clifford, after watching Phœbe to the corner, "do you never go to church?"

"No, Clifford!" she replied, "not these many, many years!"

"Were I to be there," he rejoined, "it seems to me that

I could pray once more, when so many human souls were praying all around me!"

She looked into Clifford's face, and beheld there a soft natural effusion; for his heart gushed out, as it were, and ran over at his eyes, in delightful reverence for God, and kindly affection for his human brethren. The emotion communicated itself to Hepzibah. She yearned to take him by the hand, and go and kneel down, they two together, — both so long separate from the world, and, as she now recognized, scarcely friends with Him above, — to kneel down among the people, and be reconciled to God and man at once.

"Dear brother," said she earnestly, "let us go! We belong nowhere. We have not a foot of space in any church to kneel upon; but let us go to some place of worship, even if we stand in the broad aisle. Poor and forsaken as we are, some pew-door will be open to us!"

So Hepzibah and her brother made themselves ready, — as ready as they could, in the best of their old-fashioned garments, which had hung on pegs, or been laid away in trunks, so long that the dampness and mouldy smell of the past was on them, — made themselves ready, in their faded bettermost, to go to church. They descended the staircase together, — gaunt, sallow Hepzibah, and pale, emaciated, age-stricken Clifford! They pulled open the front door, and stepped across the threshold, and felt, both of them, as if they were standing in the presence of the whole world, and with mankind's great and terrible eye on them alone. The eye of their Father seemed to be withdrawn, and gave them no encouragement. The warm sunny air of the street made them shiver. Their hearts quaked within them at the idea of taking one step further.

"It cannot be, Hepzibah! — it is too late," said Clifford, with deep sadness. "We are ghosts! We have no right among human beings, — no right anywhere, but in this old house, which has a curse on it, and which therefore we are doomed to haunt! And, besides," he continued, with a fastidious sensibility, inalienably characteristic of the man, "it would not be fit nor beautiful to go! It is an ugly thought, that I should be frightful to my fellow-beings, and that children should cling to their mothers' gowns, at sight of me."

They shrank back into the dusky passage-way, and closed the door. But, going up the staircase again, they found the whole interior of the house tenfold more dismal, and the air closer and heavier, for the glimpse and breath of freedom which they had just snatched. They could not flee; their jailer had but left their door ajar, in mockery, and stood behind it, to watch them stealing out. At the threshold, they felt his pitiless gripe upon them. For what other dungeon is so dark as one's own heart! What jailer so inexorable as one's self!

THE HOUSE OF THE SEVEN GABLES.

It is a marvel whence this perfect flower [the white pond-lily] derives its loveliness and perfume, springing as it does from the black mud over which the river sleeps, and where lurk the slimy eel and speckled frog and the mud turtle, whom continual washing cannot cleanse. It is the very same black mud out of which the yellow lily sucks its obscene life and noisome odor. Thus we see, too, in the world that some persons assimilate only what is ugly and evil from the same moral circumstances which supply good and beautiful results — the fragrance of celestial flowers — to the daily life of others.   MOSSES FROM AN OLD MANSE.

REFERENCES.

George Parsons Lathrop's *Study of Hawthorne.*

Henry James's *Hawthorne.*

Julian Hawthorne's *Nathaniel Hawthorne and His Wife.*

Moncure Conway's *Hawthorne.*

James T. Fields's *Yesterdays with Authors.*

Horatio Bridge's *Personal Recollections of Hawthorne* (Eight Illustrations).

Mary Russell Mitford's *Recollections of a Literary Life.*

Higginson's *Short Studies of American Authors.*

Richardson's *American Literature.* Vol. II., chap. x.

Holmes's "Reminiscences of Hawthorne," in *Soundings from the Atlantic.*

H. T. Griswold's *Home Life of Great Authors.*

Conway's *Emerson at Home and Abroad* (Chapter on Nathaniel and Sophia Hawthorne).

Samuel Smiles's *Brief Biographies.*

Article by R. H. Stoddard in the *Encyclopædia Britannica.*

Leslie Stephen's *Hours in a Library.*

Shepard's *Pen Pictures of Modern Authors.*

Griswold's *Prose Writers of America.*

Whipple's *Character and Characteristic Men.*

H. T. Tuckerman's *Mental Portraits.*

Poe's *Literati.*

O'Connor's *The Hawthorne Index.*

Lowell's *Fable for Critics.*

Welsh's *Development of English Literature and Language.* Vol. II.

Stedman-Hutchinson's *Library of American Literature.* Vol. VI.

Appletons' American Biography.

Allibone's *Dictionary of Authors.*

G. W. Curtis's *Literary and Social Essays.*

R. H. Hutton's *Essays in Literary Criticism.*

Cyclopædias of English and American Literature.

Text-books and Histories of American Literature.

G. W. Curtis's *Homes of American Authors.*

G. B. Loring's *History of Essex County, Massachusetts.*

Margaret Sidney's *Old Concord : Her Highways and Byways.*

Bartlett's *Concord Guide.*

Theodore Wolfe's *Literary Shrines.*

The New England Magazine. November, 1893 ("Homes and Haunts of Hawthorne." Illustrated).

Harper's Magazine. October, 1872 (An illustrated biographical sketch by R. H. Stoddard). July, 1881. July, 1886. (Portrait of Hawthorne.) August, 1894 (Howells's "My First Visit to New England ").

The Atlantic Monthly. May, 1860. July, 1862. July, 1864. January, 1868.

The North American Review. October, 1864 (Article by G. W. Curtis).

The Century Magazine. January, 1888. May, 1884. May, 1886.

The Ladies' Home Journal. March, 1894 (Illustrated article by Rose Hawthorne Lathrop on her father's literary methods).

St. Nicholas. March, 1895.

OUTLINE OF HIS LIFE.

July 4, 1804.
May 19, 1864.

Birth in Salem, Mass., on Independence Day.

Contrast this fact with Hawthorne's temperament and life.

27 Union Street. House still standing, and the birth-room shown to interested visitors. (South-west corner of third story.)

Ancestors. "Hawthorne's literary offspring."

Strict Puritans. Persecutors of Quakers and witches.

"The best compensation for their lives was when they were turned into gloomily picturesque figures by the art of their descendant, and the blood shed by their thorns tinted the blossoms of Hawthorne." — CONWAY.

William Hathorne (Nathaniel inserted the *w* in the name) came to Dorchester, Mass., in 1630. His son John was chief judge in the witch trials at Salem.

Father.

A sea-captain, like his forefathers.

Fond of books and of children. Serious, reticent.

Died of yellow fever at Surinam, when Nathaniel was four years old; the boy's consequent life with the mother's family, the Mannings, on Herbert Street.

Mother.

Elizabeth Clark Manning, of Salem.

For a woodcut of her face, consult *The Ladies' Home Journal,* March, 1894.

A beautiful, sensitive, singularly pure woman, of fine gifts.

Shut herself in the house for thirty years after her husband's death.

Read Hawthorne's story, "The Wives of the Dead." (*The Snow Image and other Twice-Told Tales.*)

The only Son in a family of three children.

> "Beautiful and bright boy, indulged not only by his mother, but by all his uncles and aunts."

> Hawthorne considered that his elder sister had more genius than himself. Like her mother, she lived a life of seclusion; on her brother's death she could not be persuaded to attend the funeral.

Solitary Childhood and Youth.

> Due to his mother's retirement, his own melancholy temperament, the quietness of his native city, and his frequent absences at Raymond, Me.

Early Reading.

> Bunyan's *Pilgrim's Progress*, Thomson, Milton, Shakespeare, Pope, Johnson's *Idler*.

> First book bought with his own money, Spenser's *Faerie Queene*.

> Before fourteen years of age, he had read all of the Waverley novels.

> He liked to invent strange, wild stories, ending them always with the words, "And I'm never coming back again." (Effect of his father's death far from home?)

> His favorite declamatory line, before he could talk plainly, was (from *Richard III.*) —
>
> > "Stand back, my Lord, and let the coffin pass."

> For an illustrated article on Hawthorne's boyhood, see *The Wide Awake* for November, 1891.

Housed by an accident (lameness resulting from an injury received when playing base-ball), and for two years taught privately by the lexicographer, Joseph Worcester.

Removal of Family to Raymond, Me., in 1818, to live with Mrs. Hawthorne's brother.

> A wild, woody country. Out-door life for one year.

> Home near Sebago Lake, on the borders of which Hawthorne spent many hours, falling into his "cursed habit of solitude."

> On the death of Mr. Manning, the home was converted into a "free meeting-house."

Return to the Herbert Street home (Number 10), Salem.

Issue of a **Weekly Paper**, *The Spectator.* A few numbers.

Bowdoin College, Brunswick, Me. 1821–1825. (See *Scribner's Magazine*, May, 1876, illustrated article.)

Hawthorne went to Brunswick *via* stage-coach from Salem, and Franklin Pierce was a fellow-passenger.

Expenses largely defrayed by his uncle, Robert Manning.

Intimate Friend. Franklin Pierce, in the class above him.

Ranked number eighteen in a class of thirty-eight.

Excelled in English and Latin composition.

Enjoyed the languages, and gave considerable time to general reading.

Disliked mathematics and physics, and refused to submit to any exercises in declamation. (This refusal deprived him of a commencement part.)

Wrote one poem, Moonlight, and a few other verses.

See Bridge's *Recollections of Hawthorne*, pp. 35, 37; and Lathrop, p. 122.

Paradise Spring, now called Hawthorne Brook, a favorite resort.

NOTE. — The year Hawthorne entered Bowdoin, Bryant published his first volume of poems, and Cooper his novel, *The Spy.*

Some Classmates.

Henry W. Longfellow and his brother Stephen.

"Longfellow used to talk in poetry when his early days at Bowdoin with Hawthorne were the theme."

J. S. C. Abbott, a clergyman and a writer.

George B. Cheever, an early Abolitionist and worker in the cause of temperance.

Edward Preble, son of Commodore Preble.

Horatio Bridge, Paymaster-General of the U. S. Navy for twenty years, including those of the Civil War.

For a description of Hawthorne's college life, consult Bridge's *Recollections.*

Literary Product of life at Bowdoin. *Fanshawe.*

"A pleasant, old-fashioned little romance, of an idealized Bowdoin."

Published anonymously in 1828, and soon suppressed by the writer. It was not reissued until 1876.

For sketch of the story, consult Lathrop, pp. 127-132.

Renewal of Life in Salem.

A recluse for twelve years. Calls himself "the obscurest man of letters in America."

Said to have read at this time all the books in the Salem Athenæum Library.

Early Publications Unsuccessful.

Contributes to Periodicals sketches, collected later as *Twice-Told Tales.*

Stories, partly true and partly fictitious, of Colonial New England.

Their power recognized by his neighbors, the three Peabody sisters.

As book, brought out by Samuel G. Goodrich, known to the literary public by the pseudonym Peter Parley.

Longfellow reviews the book appreciatively in *The North American Review.* (July, 1837.)

Weigher and Gauger at the Boston Custom House. 1839.

Appointed by George Bancroft, the historian, then collector of the port. Salary, $1,200.

Filled the position ably, although it was not to his taste.

Deposed by Harrison. (Whig party.)

Experiences described in his *Note Books.*

Life at Brook Farm, West Roxbury, Mass. 1841. A second "Golden Age."

(See notes on Transcendentalism, under Emerson.)

Invests a thousand dollars in the experiment.

Health delicate. Overworks physically.

Not in sympathy with the other Socialists.

Has an antipathy for Margaret Fuller.

Records his life here in his novel, *The Blithedale Romance.*

"I went to live in Arcady, and found myself up to the chin in a barnyard."

Marriage to Sophia Peabody, of Salem, 1842. An ideal union.

"If you want a new feeling in this weary life, get married. It renews the world from the surface to the centre." — HAWTHORNE in a letter to Bridge.

"Every true family is a solar system that outshines all the solar systems in space and time." — MRS. HAWTHORNE to Horatio Bridge.

Mrs. Hawthorne was a superior woman, and a sympathetic helper in her husband's literary career.

The Peabody Sisters. (Their father, a cultured Salem physician.)

Elizabeth, the philanthropist and "saintly abbess of Concord."

Sophia. A favorite pupil in the studio of Washington Allston.

Mary. Mrs. Horace Mann, who aided her husband considerably in his educational work, and wrote after his death an excellent memoir of him.

Consult Julian Hawthorne's *Hawthorne and His Wife.*

Edits the African Journal of his friend, Horatio Bridge.

Life in Concord at the Historic Manse.

"Created by Providence expressly for our use." "Our Eden."

Three years "devoted to literature and happiness;" troubled only by limited means because of the tardy payment of debts due him.

Neighbors. Emerson. Thoreau. The Alcotts. Ellery Channing.

Una Hawthorne born here.

Writes *Mosses from an Old Manse.* Describes his home in its Introduction.

Read Notes on the Manse, under Emerson's *Homes.*

Surveyor in the Salem Custom-House, at the time of Salem's importance as a seaport. 1846–1849.

The appointment to office "ended his poverty, but also his paradise."

Popular and faithful.

Begins *The Scarlet Letter*, and in its Introduction delineates strongly his fellow-officials.

A Second Loss of Office with change of political party.

When in his dejected mood he said to his wife, "I am removed from office," she replied by putting pen, ink, and paper before him, with the words, "Now you can write your book."

Removal to Lenox, Mass. One year's residence.

His "ugly little red farmhouse," destroyed by fire, and reproduced in 1893.

On the banks of a small lake, called Stockbridge Bowl.

Near the Plunkett House, Pittsfield (which contained Longfellow's "Clock on the Stairs"), the Bryant House at Barrington, Holmes's ancestral estate, the home of Fanny Kemble Butler, and that of the Sedgwicks.

Daughter Rose born at this time.

Rural Life. "We have become so intimately acquainted with every individual of them [the chickens], that it really seems like cannibalism to think of eating them."

Writes here *The House of Seven Gables, The Wonder Book for Boys and Girls* (three hundred pages written in seven weeks), and begins *The Blithedale Romance.*

See article, "The Hawthornes in Lenox," in *The Century Magazine* for November, 1894; also, "Reminiscences of Literary Berkshire," in the same magazine, August, 1895 (illustrated); Theodore Wolfe's *Literary Shrines.*

Brief Residence at West Newton, Mass., in the Horace Mann house.

Finishes here *The Blithedale Romance,* and writes *The Snow Image and Other Twice Told Tales.*

Return to Concord and Purchase of "The Wayside." 1852.

"I sat down to write by the wayside of life, like a man under enchantment, and a shrubbery sprang up around me, and the bushes grew to be saplings, and the saplings became trees, until no exit appeared possible through the entangling depths of my obscurity."

The grounds were beautified for him by Bronson Alcott and Thoreau.

Thoreau remarked to Hawthorne that the house was once occupied by a man who believed that he should never die. This suggested Hawthorne's story, *Septimius Felton.*

Writes a Campaign Document for Franklin Pierce when candidate for the Presidency.

"After a friendship of thirty years, it was impossible to refuse my best efforts in his behalf at this, the great pinch of his life."

Party-serving spirit unjustly attributed to him.

Consul at Liverpool from 1853 to 1857 ; then a high position.

Now for the first time in easy circumstances.

Shows at the expense of his inadequate income many kindnesses to unfortunate countrymen. (Note especially his friendly conduct toward Delia Bacon.)

Gathers material for his *English Note Books* and *Our Old Home.* Dedicates the latter to Pierce, to the consternation of its publisher.

Not a congenial life to him. "When my successor arrived, I drew the long, delightful breath which first made me thoroughly sensible what an unnatural life I had been leading."

Two Years' Travel with his family in Europe, mostly in Italy.

Acquaintance with Hiram Powers, the Brownings, the Storys, the Trollopes, and John Lothrop Motley.

Material for his *Italian Note Book* and *The Marble Faun.*

Closing Years in Concord, at The Wayside.

Family illnesses and national disturbances.

Sudden death (as desired by him), May 19, 1864, while asleep, at the Pemigewasset House, Plymouth, N. H., when travelling to the White Mountains for his health, accompanied by his devoted friend, Franklin Pierce, then a widower and childless.

See Pierce's descriptive letter in Bridge's *Recollections,* pp. 176–179.

"The memory of President Pierce has lost some stains through his lifelong devotion to his early friend."

Burial.

The unfinished MS. of *The Dolliver Romance* and a wreath of apple-blossoms from the Old Manse were laid upon his coffin.

Read Longfellow's poem, "Hawthorne."

Services. Conducted by the Rev. James Freeman Clarke, who had married him twenty-two years before.

Emerson, Longfellow, Lowell, Holmes, Whipple, Channing, Alcott, Agassiz, and Pierce were among the mourners present.

Resting Place. Sleepy Hollow, Concord, Mass. Ridge Path.

Under a group of pines. Near Emerson and Thoreau.

Grave fenced in 1891 because of mutilations for "relics."

For views, consult Bridge's *Recollections*, p. 180, *Harper* for October, 1872, or *The Ladies' Home Journal* for March, 1894.

His wife and Una lie buried in Kensal Green Cemetery, London, near Thackeray and Leigh Hunt. Fanny Kemble Butler, Hawthorne's friend and neighbor when in Lenox, lies in the same God's acre, by the side of her father, the actor.

Hawthorne's Family.

His Wife. Literary and artistic. Hawthorne became acquainted with her through her illustrations of his story, *The Gentle Boy.* She believed fully in his inspirations.

Children.

Una. Died unmarried. After her father's death she deciphered, with the help of Robert Browning, the MS. of *Septimius Felton*, and had it published in *The Atlantic Monthly.*

Rose. An artist. Married to George Parsons Lathrop, author of *Spanish Vistas, A Study of Hawthorne*, and several novels. Mr. and Mrs. Lathrop are members of the Church of the Paulist Fathers, New York.

Julian. A novelist, essayist, and author of a text-book on American literature. Julian's daughter Hildegarde is a writer of novelettes.

Autobiographic Glimpses of Hawthorne.

> *Note Books.* Introduction to *The Scarlet Letter.* The Old
> Manse in *Mosses from an Old Manse. The Gentle Boy.
> The Devil in Manuscript. Footprints by the Seashore.
> Blithedale Romance. Our Old Home.*

His Politics. (Like those of his father.)

> "A Democrat before the Rebellion, a War Democrat after it
> broke out." Ostracized from Salem society because of
> this.
>
> "I had no kindred with, nor leanings toward, the Abolition-
> ists."
>
> He thought the war might have been avoided; advocated a
> separation, an "amputation."
>
> His opinions were expressed in *The Atlantic Monthly* for
> July, 1862 ("Chiefly about War Matters").
>
> When, in Liverpool, he saw that the Civil War was inevitable,
> he told a friend that he "meant to go home and die with
> the Republic."
>
> Consult Bridge, pp. 155, 165–170.

Character.   .

> Taciturn, shy, melancholy (rarely laughed), distrustful of self,
> restless, gentle; a lover of solitude and of out-door life (he
> walked much and rapidly). "A November nature with a
> name of May." — LOWELL. "He is like a dim room with
> a little taper of personality burning on the corner of the
> mantel." — HOLMES.
>
> A charming playmate to his children.
>
> "His reserve was the reserve of self-respect, not of pride or
> timidity."
>
> "From the first moment of our acquaintance, I never knew
> him to utter an unmanly sentiment, or to do a mean or
> unkind act." — HORATIO BRIDGE.
>
> "The high qualities of his genius were well matched by those
> of character."

Manners.   .

> Self-respecting, reserved, gracious, kindly.

Appearance and Voice.

Erect, full, shapely, and commanding figure. Noticeably handsome. Expressive face with regular features. Massive forehead and brow. Dark locks. "The most wonderful eyes in the world, searching as lightning, and unfathomable as night."

"His bearing was modestly grand, and his voice touched the ear like a melody."

APPELLATIONS.

America's Prose Poet.

A Wordsworth in Prose.

A Romancer without a Peer.

A Profound Anatomist of the Heart.

A Literary Artist and Art Critic.

A Creator, not a Follower.

A Dweller Among Visions.

The Rarest Genius America has given to Literature.

The Patient and Masterful Observer and Chronicler.

The Greatest Imaginative Writer since Shakespeare.

An Allegorist of the Conscience.

Moralist of Moralists.

The Rembrandt of America's Word-Painters.

The Poussin of Our Unrhymed Poetry.

The Weaver of the Scarlet Web.

The Ideal Realist.

The Novelist of the Puritan.

The Last Wizard of Salem.

A Pioneer and Master of Realism.

The Delineator of Early New England Life.

Hawthorne the Only.

NOTES ON HIS WRITINGS.

Their Nature.
Intensely imaginative and weird.

"Hawthorne rarely gained any hint from any other imagination."

"Hawthorne had a predilection for the remote, the shadowy, the vague." He loved to deal with questions of conscience.

"His narratives are one-tenth matter and nine-tenths spirit."

The plot is always a subordinate feature.

"His writings are overcast with the pain of a heart held under a necessity to expose its inmost recesses to the world." — CONWAY.

Style.
. Pure, clear, harmonious, suggestive.

Whittier regarded Hawthorne as the greatest master of the English language.

An excellent model for study.

"It is the result of a great deal of practice. It is a desire to tell the simple truth as honestly and as vividly as one can." — HAWTHORNE.

"There was no conception so daring that he shrank from attempting it; and none that he could not so master as to state it, if he pleased, in terms of monosyllables." — HIGGINSON.

The Scarlet Letter. 1850. A romance of sin.
"The New England Epic."

Made the writer famous. (Hawthorne was then forty-five years of age.)

Written in Salem (when the author was living at 14 Mall Street).

Scene laid in Boston.

Unparalleled in imaginative prose writing.

As fiction, comparable in uniqueness only with Holmes's story, *Elsie Venner*. "Two great pieces of imaginative art in New England [*The Scarlet Letter* and *Elsie Venner*] came from the Bible when its altar-chain was broken."

Teaching of the tale. The effect of sin upon opposite natures.

Introduction. A graphic description of the inmates of the Salem
Custom-House when Hawthorne entered it. (Gave offence
to many residents of his native city.)

Note the sketch of himself as surveyor.

The germ of the romance is found in Hawthorne's short story,
Endicott and the Red Cross.

Such a symbol as the scarlet letter was once worn by a young woman
in the early days of New England's history.

The first edition, five thousand copies, sold in two weeks.

"The publisher speaks of it in tremendous terms of approbation.
So does Mrs. Hawthorne, to whom I read the conclusion last
night. It broke her heart, and sent her to bed with a grievous
headache, which I look upon as a triumphant success." — HAW-
THORNE.

Mrs. Hawthorne says that, before this story was finished, a knot was
visible in her husband's forehead, due to his intense thought.

Emerson exclaimed, upon finishing the book, "Ghastly!"

Dramatized in 1892. Arranged in operatic form by Walter Dam-
rosch, 1894.

Manuscript discovered by James T. Fields. (See Fields's *Yesterdays with Authors.*)

Read article in *The North American Review* for July, 1850.

An engraving of George H. Boughton's "Hester Prynne and Pearl"
may be seen in the *Appleton Art Journal* for 1877.

Illustrated edition. Artist, Mary Hallock Foote.

Darley's Twelve Compositions in Outline from *The Scarlet Letter.*
Folio size. ($10.00.)

> "I snatch the book, along whose burning leaves
> His scarlet web our wild romancer weaves."
>
> HOLMES.

The House of the Seven Gables. A romance of heredity. A story of
retribution.

Written in Lenox in about five months.

Scene laid in Salem.

Idea suggested by the curse invoked on John Hathorne by a faint-
ing witch.

Hawthorne considered this better than *The Scarlet Letter.*

This work contains more humor than the other tales.

"An impression of a summer afternoon in an elm-shadowed New
England town."

See article in *The North American Review*, January, 1853.

The Blithedale Romance. A story of the Brook Farm experiment.

   Written in West Newton.

   Scene laid at Roxbury.

   The tale of a man mastered by a theory.

   The catastrophe. Suggested by the suicide by drowning of Martha Hunt, — "an incident of the transcendental movement," — when Hawthorne was a member of the Farm community.

   Heroine. Zenobia, the romancer's finest woman creation. Possesses many of Margaret Fuller's traits.

   Hero. Miles Coverdale. Hawthorne himself.

   Consult *The North American Review*, January, 1853.

The Marble Faun; or, The Romance of Monte Beni.

   Product of life in Italy. "Hawthorne changed his skies, not his soul, when he crossed the sea."

   Written in Florence and England (Redcar, Yorkshire, and Leamington, Warwickshire).

   Scene laid in Rome. A good tourist's companion for one visiting that city.

   Published in England under the title, *Transformation.*

   The only one of Hawthorne's novels not American.

   Suggested by Praxiteles' "Faun," in the Capitoline Museum, Rome.

   Teaching. Sin may become a powerful factor in the development of mind and soul.

   Last chapter. Added after publication of the book, because of the many demands for an explanation of the mysteries in the story.

     "Don't read it; 'tis good for nothing. The story isn't meant to be explained; 'tis cloud-land." — HAWTHORNE, in a letter to Henry Bright.

"I like the misty way in which the story is indicated rather than revealed; the outlines are quite definite enough from the beginning to the end, to those who have imagination enough to follow you in your airy flights; and, to those who complain, I suppose that nothing less than an illustrated edition, with a large gallows on the last page, with Donatello in the most pensile of attitudes, — his ears revealed through a white night-cap, — would be satisfactory." — HENRY L. MOTLEY, in a letter to Hawthorne.

"Donatello belongs to the world of Caliban, Puck, and Ariel."

Somewhat allegorical in nature. Hilda personifies conscience; Miriam, imagination; Donatello, sense; Kenyon, reason.

Hilda. Resembles Miss Shepard, a governess in the Hawthorne
family when they were travelling in Europe.

Kenyon. The reputed original was Thomas Crawford, sculptor, and
father of the novelist, Marion Crawford.

Its criticisms on art. Invaluable.

Illustrated edition. Fifty photogravures of sculpture, painting, etc.,
and scenes in Rome. ($6.00.)

See *The Atlantic Monthly*, September, 1868; and *Scribner's Magazine*, September, 1871.

A statue of Praxiteles' "Faun" was given to Bowdoin College by
the class of 1881.

Notes on the Four Great Romances.

No two were written in the same home.

No two have their scenes laid in the same city.

Consult Julian Hawthorne's article on the scenes of these
romances, in *The Century Magazine*, July, 1884.

The number of characters in each is small — five in one, and but
four in the others.

Three are American stories; one, Italian.

" Poe did not find Ghostland itself a better artistic background than
Salem or Concord."

Posthumous Works. Edited by his wife and children.

English and Italian Note Books.

See *The Atlantic Monthly*, September, 1870; *Littell*, January-March,
1869.

Incomplete " Studies."

The Ancestral Footstep.

Dr. Grimshawe's Secret. 1882.

Septimius Felton ; a Romance of Immortality.

Scene laid at the Wayside.

Compare the hero with Goethe's Faust.

See note under Hawthorne's children.

Consult *The Atlantic Monthly* for October, 1872.

The Dolliver Romance.

The " unfinished Aladdin's Tower," of Longfellow's poem.

Note the humor in Hawthorne's letter to Fields about this tale,
Yesterdays with Authors, pp. 115, 116.

Most Characteristic Short Tales.

Drowne's Wooden Image. Young Goodman Brown. The Birthmark. Wakefield. Dr. Heidegger's Experiment. The Minis-

ter's Black Veil. (Mark its kinship to *The Scarlet Letter*.)
Graves and Goblins. Ethan Brand ("A Hawthorne micro-
cosm"). David Swan.

Most Realistic Tales.

Sights from a Steeple. A Rill from the Town Pump. Little
Annie's Ramble. Main Street.

Allegorical Stories.

The Great Stone Face. The Great Carbuncle. The Snow Image.
The Celestial Railroad. The Bosom Serpent. The Artist of
the Beautiful. A Rill from the Town Pump. The Sister
Years. Drowne's Wooden Image. Little Daffydowndilly.

Historical New England Sketches.

Endicott and the Red Cross. Old Ticonderoga. Legends of the
Province House. My Kinsman — Major Molineux. The May-
pole of Merrymount. Old News. John Eliot and His Indian
Bible. The Boston Massacre.

Stories of Earthly Immortality.

Septimius Felton. The Dolliver Romance.

Stories of the Elixir of Life.

Dr. Heidegger's Experiment. *Dr. Grimshawe's Secret.*

Stories for Children.

Grandfather's Chair.

Stories from New England history.

A Wonder Book for Girls and Boys.

Classic myths, — The Gorgon's Head, The Golden Touch, The
Miraculous Pitcher, and others. "Not content with the
Greek myths, Hawthorne created little incidents and im-
possible characters, that glance in and out with elfin grace."
— Mrs. Wright.

Two illustrated editions are published by Houghton, Mifflin, &
Co., and a pamphlet edition for school use.

True Stories from History and Biography.

Dr. Johnson, Benjamin West, Sir Isaac Newton, Benjamin
Franklin, *et al.*

Our Old Home.

Delightful sketches of England.

Made from his English note-books.

Compare with Emerson's *English Traits.*

Tanglewood Tales. A second Wonder Book.

> "I never did anything so well as those baby stories."

> "The writer, if he succeeds in pleasing his little readers, may
> hope to be remembered by them till their old age, — a far
> longer period of literary existence than is generally attained
> by those who seek immortality from the judgment of full-
> grown men." — Preface to *True Stories.*

Riverside Edition of His Works.

Thirteen volumes. Twelve etchings. Thirteen woodcuts and portraits.

NOTE. — All of Hawthorne's works, except *Mosses from an Old Manse,*
were published in Boston.

MISCELLANEOUS NOTES.

Tributes to Hawthorne.

"He was a beautiful, natural, original genius, and his life was singularly exempt from worldly preoccupation and vulgar efforts."
— HENRY JAMES.

"The Yankee mind has for the most part budded and flowered in pots of English earth, but you have fairly raised yours as a seedling in the natural soil." — HOLMES, in a letter to Hawthorne.

"Hawthorne uses words merely as stepping-stones, upon which, with a free and youthful bound, his spirit crosses and recrosses the bright and rushing stream of thought." — LONGFELLOW.

> "A frame so robust, with a nature so sweet,
> So earnest, so graceful, so solid, so fleet,
> Is worth a descent from Olympus to meet."
>
> J. R. LOWELL.

Poems by E. C. Stedman and H. W. Longfellow.
Verses in Lowell's *Fable for Critics.*

His Method of Writing.

"He uses his characters, like algebraic symbols, to work out certain problems with; they are rather more, yet rather less, than flesh and blood." — H. A. BEERS.

"He used habitually guarded under-statements and veiled hints."

Consult Rose Hawthorne Lathrop's article on the subject, in *The Ladies' Home Journal,* March, 1894.

His Own Description of His Method.

"The Devil himself always gets into my inkstand, and I can only exorcise him by penfuls at a time."

"I sternly shut myself up, and come to close grip with the romance I am trying to tear from my brain."

"I must breathe the fogs of Old England, or the east winds of Massachusetts, in order to put me in working trim."

His Aims in Writing.

"The only sensible ends of literature are, first, the pleasurable toil of writing; second, the gratification of one's family and friends; and, lastly, the solid cash."

" The bubble reputation is as much a bubble in literature as in war."

Literary Defects.

Occasional mannerisms.

Style not sufficiently varied. " His colors were too pale and monotonous, not the colors of flesh and blood."

A Wish of Hawthorne's.

" I wish God had given me the faculty of writing a sunshiny book." — Expressed in a letter to Fields.

His Mental Sight was both " panoramic and microscopic." " Every new experience was a fatality to him for good or evil."

The Ethics of His Stories.

" The morals of his tales are never obtrusive."

" Hawthorne was too great an artist to confuse for a moment the demands of ethics with those of pure art."

Writings that Reflect the Reforms of His Age.

The Blithedale Romance. The Hall of Fantasy. Earth's Holocaust. The New Adam and Eve.

Note the characterization, in Hawthorne and Lemmon's *American Literature*, p. 163, of the three last named above.

The Names of His Characters.

Many of them are found among those of early New Englanders; such as Hooper, Felton, Dolliver, Prynne, Maule.

Two English names — Chillingworth, Coverdale.

The Story, "The Gentle Boy."

" I chanced on a story called *The Gentle Boy*. . . . It is marked by so much grace and delicacy of feeling that I am very desirous to know the author, whom I take to be a lady." — MARGARET FULLER, in 1836.

" In this Hawthorne dangerously approached sentimentalism."

A Lost Work.

Soon after graduation from college, Hawthorne wrote a volume of stories, *Seven Tales of My Native Land*. The publisher engaged to bring it out was so dilatory that the writer sent for the manuscript, and, " in a mood half-savage and half-despairing," burned it. At that time he said, " I pass the days in writing stories, and the nights in burning them."

Choice of a Profession.

"I do not want to be a doctor, and live by men's diseases; nor a minister, to live by their sins; nor a lawyer, and live by their quarrels. So I do not see that there is anything left for me but to become an author." — *Letter to his mother in boyhood.*

Tribute to His Friend, Horatio Bridge.

"If anybody is responsible for my being at this day an author, it is yourself. I know not whence your faith came, . . . still, it was your prognostic of your friend's destiny that he was to be a writer of fiction."

Bits of His Philosophy.

"It may be superstition, but it seems to me that the bitter is very apt to come with the sweet; and bright sunshine casts a dark shadow."

"If, for any cause, I were bent upon sacrificing every earthly hope as a peace-offering toward heaven, I would make the wide world my cell, and good deeds of mankind my prayer."

"Let us hope, therefore, that all the dreadful consequences of sin will not be incurred, unless the act have set its seal upon the thought. Yet . . . man must not disclaim his brotherhood, even with the guiltiest, since, though his hand be clean, his heart has surely been polluted by the flitting phantoms of iniquity."

"I assure you that trouble is the next best thing to enjoyment, and that there is no fate in this world so horrible as to have no share in either its joys or its sorrows."

"I want a little piece of land that I can call my own, big enough to stand upon, big enough to be buried in. I want to have something to do with this material world."

"No sagacious man will long retain his sagacity if he live exclusively among reformers and progressive people, without periodically returning to the settled system of things, to correct himself by a new observation from that old standpoint."

"No; I desire not an earthly immortality. Were man to live longer on the earth, the spiritual would die out of him. . . . There is a celestial something within us that requires after a certain time the atmosphere of heaven to preserve it from ruin."

"All through my life I have had occasion to observe that what seemed to be misfortunes have proved in the end to be the best things that could possibly have happened to me."

" No one that needs a monument ever ought to have one."

For an article on " Hawthorne's Philosophy," consult *The Century Magazine*, May, 1886.

His Idea of the Judgment Day.

" At the last day, — when we see ourselves as we are, — man's only inexorable judge will be himself, and the punishment of his sins will be the perception of them."

Hawthorne and Emerson.

" On a day in Concord I saw two men whom Michael Angelo might have chosen as emblems of Morning and Twilight, to be carved over the gates of the New World." — CONWAY.

" Emerson feared the melancholy temperament of his most distinguished neighbor, but recognized his genius and his almost magical art. So long as Margaret Fuller frequented Concord, she was an element that enabled them to mingle."

See note, " Emerson and Hawthorne," under Emerson.

Irving, Cooper, and Hawthorne.

" Irving feels the heart of humanity ; Cooper, like Scott, magnifies the chivalric virtues, under new skies ; and Hawthorne goes to the depth of the soul in his search for the basal principles of human action." — RICHARDSON.

Irving, Poe, and Hawthorne Compared.

See Lathrop's *Study of Hawthorne*, chapter xii.

A Trio of Writers on the Puritan.

Milton, the poet of the Puritan ; Bunyan, the allegorist ; Hawthorne, the novelist.

Hawthorne's Friend and Publisher for many years. James T. Fields.

For a portrait of Fields, see *Harper's Magazine*, July, 1894, p. 230.

Hawthorne's First Hundred Dollars.

When his publisher, Mr. Fields, brought this sum to him, Hawthorne is said to have exclaimed, " Take it back ! I don't know what to do with it ! "

His Humor.

At times Hawthorne showed a quiet, slightly satiric humor. It was not so gentle as Irving's. " It was but sunshine breaking through, or lighting up, a sombre and ominous cloud."

Anecdotes. Consult Fields, Bridge, Lathrop.

The Material for Evangeline.

Hawthorne first had the opportunity to write a story on the Acadian exiles. "He promised not to treat the subject in prose till Longfellow had seen what he could do with it in verse." See note under Longfellow's *Evangeline*.

Suggestive Composition Themes.

Hawthorne's "Notes for Stories and Essays." See Julian Hawthorne's *Nathaniel Hawthorne and His Wife*, vol. i., pp. 488–505.

Relations to Delia Bacon, the Shakespeare-Baconian theorist.

He helped her in the publication of her book, *The Philosophy of Shakespeare's Plays Unfolded*, by writing an introduction for it, — "an unspontaneous bit of kindly hackwork," — and largely defrayed the expenses.

Despite his kindness, Miss Bacon became offended because Hawthorne was unwilling to accept her theory.

He wrote "Recollections of a Gifted Woman," an interesting sketch of Miss Bacon, in *Our Old Home*. The manuscript of this may be seen in Harvard's library.

Theodore Bacon's *Life of Delia Bacon* contains twenty letters written to her by Hawthorne.

Salem Associations with Hawthorne.   (He lived thirty-five years in Salem.)

House of birth, 27 Union Street.

Other homes. On Herbert, Mall, Chestnut, and Dearborn Streets.

"The Grimshawe House." 63 Charter Street.

The cemetery in which Judge Hathorne lies.

"The House of the Seven Gables."

The Ingersoll House? Foot of Turner Street. (See *Harper's Magazine*, June, 1894, p. 41.)

The Curwin House? Corner Essex and North Streets. "The Witch House." Mrs. Hathorne Curwin, builder, was an ancestor of Henry W. Longfellow.

The writer himself said he had no particular house in mind.

The Custom-House, and Hawthorne's room in it.

Hawthorne's desk, in the historic old meeting-house (the oldest in New England), on Essex Street.

See booklet, *Picturesque Salem*, published by Wm. H. Wiggin, Cambridge.

Houghton & Mifflin publish a "Salem Edition," pleasing and inexpensive, of Hawthorne's works.

Read Julian Hawthorne's article, "The Salem of Hawthorne," in *The Century Magazine*, May, 1884.

His Concord Homes.

The Old Manse.

"A little island of the past, standing intact above the flood of events."

The Ripley House and Emerson's ancestral home.

See note under Emerson's homes.

The Wayside.

On the highway to Boston, the road down which the British marched in April, 1775.

Bought of his friend, A. Bronson Alcott, father of Louisa Alcott. (Here Louisa Alcott had done her first writing.)

The Alcotts lived in the adjoining house, and on the other side of Hawthorne dwelt Ephraim Bull, the originator of the Concord grape.

Figures in *Septimius Felton*.

Hawthorne added a tower, for a retreat, like Alexander Dumas and T. B. Aldrich.   In the study of the tower hangs the motto from Tennyson, "There is no joy but calm."

Now owned by "Margaret Sidney," Mrs. Lothrop, widow of Daniel Lothrop, the late Boston publisher, and a charming writer of children's books.

On the crest of the ridge back of the house, the path worn by Hawthorne in his meditations is still visible.

NOTE. — For Hawthorne's several homes and views of them, consult *The New England Magazine* for November, 1893; G. W. Curtis's *Homes of American Authors*; *Harper's Magazine*, August, 1894, pp. 444, 445; Theodore Wolfe's *Literary Shrines*; *The Century Magazine*, August, 1895.

Like Cooper, Hawthorne did not wish his family to give the world biographical material relating to himself.

Hawthorne could not distinguish one melody from another, although he had a nice perception of rhythm, and was sensitive to the quality of the human voice.

Edgar Allan Poe considered *Howe's Masquerade* plagiarized from his own story, *William Wilson*.

"He waited twenty-five years to be appreciated."

Twice in his journal he speaks of wishing to write a novel upon the probable subsequent career of the rich young man in the Scriptures whom Jesus loved.

"Hawthorne had the art of not being 'embarrassed by his own ideas.'"

A copy of his first novel, *Fanshawe*, was found in Lewiston, Me., in 1896, in an old beanpot, and sold to a Bostonian for a hundred dollars.

Hawthorne believed that he could not have read through his own books had they been written by another.

"He had a spiritual insight, but it did not penetrate to the source of spiritual joy." — E. P. WHIPPLE.

Emerson believed that the world would sooner see another Shakespeare than another Hawthorne.

QUERY. — To what extent did environment mould Hawthorne's literary productions?

RALPH WALDO EMERSON.

RALPH WALDO EMERSON.

LECTURER, ESSAYIST, POET, PHILOSOPHER, REFORMER.

EXTRACTS.

Nor knowest thou what argument
Thy life to thy neighbor's creed hath lent.
All are needed by each one —
Nothing is fair or good alone.

EACH AND ALL.

Beauty through my senses stole —
I yielded myself to the perfect whole.

IBID.

If eyes were made for seeing,
Then beauty is its own excuse for being.

THE RHODORA.

Not from a vain or shallow thought
His awful Jove young Phidias brought.

THE PROBLEM.

The hand that rounded Peter's dome,
And groined the aisles of Christian Rome,
Wrought in a sad sincerity;
Himself from God he could not free;
He builded better than he knew; —
The conscious stone to beauty grew.

IBID.

THE word by seers or sibyls told,
In groves of oak, or fanes of gold,
Still floats upon the morning wind,
Still whispers to the willing mind.
One accent of the Holy Ghost
The heedless world hath never lost.

THE PROBLEM.

So nigh is grandeur to our dust,
So near is God to man,
When duty whispers low, "Thou must,"
The youth replies, "I can."

VOLUNTARIES.

WHAT are they all in their high conceit
When man in the bush with God may meet?   '

GOOD-BYE.

By the rude bridge that arched the flood,
Their flag to April's breeze unfurled,
Here once the embattled farmers stood,
And fired the shot heard round the world.

CONCORD HYMN.

WHAT care though rival cities soar
Along the stormy coast,
Penn's town, New York, and Baltimore,
If Boston knew the most?

BOSTON.

UNLESS to Thought is added Will,
Apollo is an imbecile.

THE POET.

If Thought unlock her mysteries,
If Friend's lip on me smile,

I walk in marble galleries,
I talk with kings the while.

WALDEN.

THE silent organ loudest chants
The master's requiem.

DIRGE.

APOTHEGMS FROM HIS ESSAYS.

HE serves all who dares be true.

The gentleman is quiet; the lady is serene.

There is always the best way of doing things, if it be but to boil an egg.

Insist on yourself; never imitate.

Proverbs are the sanctuary of the intuitions.

Language is fossil poetry.

If you put a chain around the neck of a slave, the other end fastens itself around your own.

No man ever prayed heartily without learning something.

All mankind love a lover.

America means opportunity.

Every opinion reacts on him who utters it.

Manners are the happy way of doing things.

A great man is always willing to be little.

The moment we indulge our affections the world is metamorphosed.

Every man alone is sincere. At the entrance of a second person hypocrisy begins.

Nothing great was ever achieved without enthusiasm.

A friend is a person with whom I may be sincere. Before him I may think aloud.

The world exists for the education of each man.

Hitch your wagon to a star.

A scholar is the favorite of heaven and earth — the happiest of men.

Faces are a record in sculpture of a thousand anecdotes of whim and folly.

I look upon the simple and childish virtues of veracity and honesty as the root of all that is sublime in character. Speak as you think, be what you are, pay your debts of all kinds.

We love any forms, however ugly, from which great qualities shine.

A VISIT TO STONEHENGE.

WE left the train at Salisbury and took a carriage to Amesbury, passing by Old Sarum, a bare, treeless hill, once containing the town which sent two members to Parliament — now, not a hut; and, arriving at Amesbury, stopped at the George Inn. After dinner we walked to Salisbury Plain. On the broad downs, under the gray sky, not a house was visible, nothing but Stonehenge, which looked like a group of brown dwarfs in the wide expanse, — Stonehenge and the barrows, which rose like green bosses about the plain, and a few hayricks. On the top of a mountain the old temple would not be more impressive. Far and wide a few shepherds with their flocks sprinkled the plain, and a bagman drove along the

road. It looked as if the wide margin given in this
crowded isle to this primeval temple were accorded by
the veneration of the British race to the old egg out of
which all their ecclesiastical structures and history had
proceeded. Stonehenge is a circular colonnade with a
diameter of a hundred feet, and enclosing a second and
third colonnade within. We walked around the stones
and clambered over them, to wont ourselves with their
strange aspect and groupings, and found a nook sheltered
from the wind among them, where Carlyle lighted his
cigar. It was pleasant to see that just this simplest of
all simple structures — two upright stones and a lintel
laid across — had long outstood all later churches and
all history, and were like what is most permanent on
the face of the planet; these, and the barrows — mere
mounds (of which there are a hundred and sixty within
a circle of three miles about Stonehenge), like the same
mound on the plain of Troy, which still makes good to
the passing mariner on Hellespont the vaunt of Homer
and the fame of Achilles. Within the enclosure grow
buttercups, nettles; and all around, wild thyme, daisy,
meadowsweet, goldenrod, thistle, and the carpeting grass.
Over us, larks were soaring and singing, — as my friend
said, "the larks which were hatched last year, and the
wind which was hatched many thousand years ago." We
counted and measured by paces the biggest stones, and
soon knew as much as any man can suddenly know of
the inscrutable temple. There are ninety-four stones, and
there were once probably one hundred and sixty. The
temple is circular and uncovered, and the situation fixed
astronomically, — the grand entrances, here and at Abury,
being placed exactly north-east, "as all the gates of the

old cavern temples are." How came the stones here? for these sarsens, or Druidical sandstones, are not found in this neighborhood. The sacrificial stone, as it is called, is the only one in all these blocks that can resist the action of fire, and, as I read in the books, must have been brought one hundred and fifty miles.

ENGLISH TRAITS.

The scholar, then, is unfurnished who has only literary weapons. He ought to have as many talents as he can: memory, arithmetic, practical power, manners, temper, lion-heart, are all good things, and if he has none of them he can still manage, if he have the mainmast — if he is anything. But he must have the resource of resources, and be planted on necessity. For the sure months are bringing him to an examination-day in which nothing is remitted or excused, and for which no tutor, no book, no lectures, and almost no preparation, can be of the least avail. He will have to answer certain questions, which, I must plainly tell you, cannot be staved off. For all men, all women, Time, your country, your condition, the invisible world, are the interrogators: Who are you? What do you? Can you obtain what you wish? Is there method in your consciousness? Can you see tendency in your life? Can you help any soul?

THE SCHOLAR.

REFERENCES.

Biographies by James E. Cabot, George W. Cooke, O. W. Holmes, Richard Garnett, and Alexander Ireland.

Stedman's *Poets of America.*

M. D. Conway's *Emerson at Home and Abroad.*

E. W. Emerson's *Emerson in Concord.*

A. B. Alcott's *Genius and Character of Emerson* and *Concord Days.*

D. G. Haskins's *Emerson's Maternal Ancestors.*

Correspondence of Thomas Carlyle and Ralph Waldo Emerson.

C. F. Richardson's *American Literature.* Vol. I., chap. ix., and vol. II., chap. v.

Stedman-Hutchinson's *Library of American Literature.* Vol. VI.

Welsh's *Development of English Literature and Language.* Vol. II.

Gilman's *Poets' Homes.*

H. T. Griswold's *Home Life of Great Authors.*

Shepard's *Pen Pictures of Modern Authors.*

Lowell's *Fable for Critics* and *My Study Windows.* (Chapter in the latter on Emerson as Lecturer.)

Margaret Sidney's *Old Concord: Her Highways and Byways.*

G. B. Bartlett's *Concord Guide Book.*

Theodore Wolfe's *Literary Shrines.*

Hawthorne's "The Great Stone Face" in *Twice-told Tales.* ("Ernest," the hero of this story, is said to be Emerson.)

George William Curtis's *Literary and Social Essays.*

E. P. Whipple's *Recollections of Eminent Men.*

Hermann Grimm's *Essay on Emerson.*

Griswold's *Poets of America* and *Prose Writers of America.*

Holmes's Address before the Massachusetts Historical Society, 1882.

E. E. Hale's *Lights of Two Centuries.*

Appleton's Cyclopædia of American Biography.

Text-books and Cyclopædias of American Literature.

Harpers' Magazine. September, 1882; February, 1884; August, 1894. (Howells's "My First Visit to New England.")

The Century Magazine. April, 1883.

The New England Magazine. December, 1890. (Article by Sanborn. Illustrated.) July, 1891.

Scribner's Monthly.   February, 1879.   (" Homes and Haunts of Emerson.")

The Literary World.   Emerson Number, May 22, 1880.

NOTE. — For additional references on Emerson's Philosophy, Optimism, Influence, Theism, and Writings, and for an indicated selection of his works, poetical and prose, see Miss Hodgkins's *Guide to the Study of Nineteenth Century Authors.*

OUTLINE OF HIS LIFE.

May 25, 1803.
April 24, 1882.

" Great geniuses have the shortest biographies." — EMERSON.

Born in Boston, corner of Summer and Chauncey Streets, near the site of Franklin's birthplace.

His birthday was the same as that of Edward Bulwer Lytton.

Ancestors.

He was descended from eight generations of ministers, — " the concentration of their spiritual and intellectual tendencies."

" An Academic race." — HOLMES.

Notable Ancestors.

Peter Bulkley, minister of the first church in Concord.

Rev. John Emerson, pastor of the First Parish Church, Gloucester, Mass., in the time of Cotton Mather.

Grandfather, William Emerson.

Minister at Concord at the time of the Revolution.

The first battle was fought close to the pastor's manse.

(" Let us stand our ground," William Emerson said ; " if we die, let us die here.")

Father.

Minister of the First Church, Boston.

An Overseer of Harvard College.

Editor of *The Monthly Anthology*, a precursor of *The North American Review*, and a factor in forming the literary taste of New England.

Died when Ralph Waldo was but seven years old.

Mother.

" A woman of great patience and fortitude, of the serenest trust in God, of a discerning spirit and the most courteous bearing."

Struggled victoriously with poverty.

Second of Five Sons.

> The youngest, Charles Chauncy, who died in early life, had shown literary talent not unlike Ralph Waldo's. Called by Holmes, "the calm, chaste scholar."

> In his boyhood, Ralph Waldo used to drive his mother's cow daily to the Common for pasture.

Education.

> Deeply impressed during his youth by the remarkable character of his aunt, Mary Moody Emerson.

> *Boston Latin School.* At the age of eleven, Emerson was putting Vergil into English.

> *Harvard College,* when Edward Everett was professor of Greek Literature there.

>> "President's freshman," messenger boy, and waiter at Commons.

>> Visited the library frequently.

>> Showed no unusual ability, but gained two Bowdoin prizes for dissertations, and the Boylston prize for declamation. (The thirty dollars received for the latter he carried home to his mother for the purchase of a shawl.)

>> Great enthusiasm for Montaigne. He felt that "he himself had written the essays in a former life."

>> Ambitious, on graduating, to be a professor of rhetoric and elocution.

>> Poet of his class. 1821.

>> Roomed three years in Hollis Hall. Nos. 5, 15, 9.

>> Classmates, Samuel J. Tilden and Dr. Wm. H. Furness.

Teaches five years in Boston and Chelmsford (Lowell).

Studies Theology, with Dr. W. E. Channing, founder of Unitarianism, at the Cambridge Divinity School.

Travels in the South for his Health.

Colleague, then Pastor, over the Second Church (Unitarian), Boston. 1829.

> His preaching was "simple, eloquent, effective."

> Resigned, in 1832, because he thought the sacrament of the Lord's Supper should be observed without symbols.

>> (See his sermon on its interpretation.)

Marriage to Ellen Tucker, "a bright revelation to me of the best nature of woman." 1829.

His wife died within three years, a victim to consumption.

Trip to Europe, in 1833, for health.

Meets Carlyle, Wordsworth, De Quincey, and Coleridge.

Friendship with Carlyle.

One of the most beautiful in literary annals.

Emerson visits Carlyle twice, and the latter likens these visits in his home to those of an angel.

Invites Carlyle to spend a year with him in Concord.

Corresponds with him thirty-six years, calling out the best of Carlyle's nature.

Edits Carlyle's works in America.

Introduces Charles Sumner and Longfellow to the philosopher.

Carlyle outlives Emerson but a year.

"The hatred of unreality was uppermost in Carlyle; the love of what is real and genuine, with Emerson." -- O. W. HOLMES.

NOTE. -- See the Emerson-Carlyle Correspondence, Lowell's comparison of the two men in *The Fable for Critics,* Haweis's in *American Humorists,* p. 87, and Welsh's in *The Development of English Literature.*

(Compare Emerson's *Representative Men* and Carlyle's *Heroes and Hero-Worship.*)

Life in Concord until his death.

Emerson makes Concord now the " Delphi of New England," " America's Literary Mecca."

"The fame of the philosopher attracts admiring friends and enthusiasts from every quarter, and the scholarly grace and urbane hospitality of the gentleman send them charmed away." — GEORGE W. CURTIS.

Second Marriage, 1835, to Lidian Jackson, of Plymouth, Mass., and purchase of a house, the " Emerson home," on the Lexington Road.

Their domestic life was simple, frugal, hospitable, genuine.

Mrs. Emerson survived her husband ten years.

Publishes, anonymously, Nature, an essay expressing his philosophy. 1836.

    Its sale for twelve years was an average of a copy once in ten days.

Delivers an Oration, "The American Scholar," before the Phi Beta Kappa Society at Harvard, 1837.

    "Our Yankee version of a lecture by Abélard." — LOWELL.

    "Our intellectual Declaration of Independence." — HOLMES.

Address before Divinity School, Cambridge.

    Creates a sensation in religious circles.

Lyceum Lecturer for Forty Years.

    "My pulpit is the lyceum platform."

    Emerson was the founder of this system of lecturing, popular in New England for many years because it furnished a supplementary education to that of the public schools. (Note the derivation and definition of "Lyceum," and read article, "The Rise and Decline of the New England Lyceum," in *The New England Magazine*, February, 1895.)

    Emerson gave courses of lectures in America, England, and Scotland.

    Subjects. — Biography, English Literature, Philosophy of History, Human Life, and Human Culture.

    Upon his hundredth lecture in Concord, the audience rose spontaneously when he appeared.

    Read Lowell's chapter on Emerson in *My Study Windows.*

Death of Waldo, his eldest son, at five years of age.

    See poem, "Threnody."

Publishes the first series of his essays, 1841; second series, 1844; poems, 1846.

Contributes to *The Atlantic Monthly* and *The North American Review.*

Edits *The Dial* from 1842 to 1844, succeeding Margaret Fuller, the "priestess and queen of transcendentalism."

    See notes on *Transcendentalism* and *Brook Farm.*

Supports, in Theory, the Brook Farm Experiment.

Advocates Anti-Slavery.

Opens his Boston church to Abolition speakers.

Addresses Anti-Slavery societies.

Makes a speech on Brooks's assault of Sumner.

His Proposal. To buy the slaves for two billions of dollars, and educate them morally.

Read his poem, " Freedom."

Visits England.

Meets Arthur Hugh Clough on the steamer coming home.

Makes a Trip to California. 1871.

" There was never a more agreeable travelling companion."

Meets Brigham Young at Salt Lake City.

Home Burned in 1872.

Goes to England and the Nile.

"*An American Myth.* When Emerson gazed at the Sphinx, she said to him, ' You're another.' "

See poem, " The Sphinx," and his book, *English Traits.*

Returns, to find the home rebuilt by his friends.

Nominated, with Disraeli, for the office of Lord Rector of Glasgow University.

Outlives His Mental Power, but lingers, honored by all.

Funeral Services.

Conducted by Dr. Furness, his classmate and friend.

Judge Hoar and James Freeman Clarke gave the addresses, and the flowers were arranged by Louisa Alcott.

Rhodoras were among the floral offerings.

Burial Place.

Near Hawthorne and Thoreau, in ground on which he had often walked and talked with them.

His grave was disturbed in the winter of 1889–1890. Site marked by a boulder of rose quartz. Tablet inserted, in 1894, bearing this couplet (from Emerson), —

> " The passive master lent his hand
> To the vast soul that o'er him planned."

View. See Wolfe's *Literary Shrines,* p. 78.

Character.

Retiring, simple, serene, hospitable, philanthropic ; a ready lis-
tener ; "intuitive rather than logical ;" "in his nature,
emotion seems to be less the product of the heart than of
the brain." He had a "genius for friendship." A good
citizen. "Goodness and truth were spontaneous to him."

" Beauty is at the heart of his nature ; he avoided instinctively
the ugly and the base."

" His personal humility was as great as his personal dignity."

Appearance.

" I have seen Emerson, the first man I have seen. — GEORGE
ELIOT'S Diary.

" Tall, slender, not robust. Sallow, aquiline nose, and eyes of
the strongest and brightest blue."

Majestic, calm, kindly. He frequently smiled, but never laughed.

" The most gracious of mortals."

Manners.

Dignified and simple.

Voice.

" The perfect music of spiritual utterance."

" The choir was coarse and discordant after his voice."

Family.   Four children.

Waldo.   Died young.

Edith, Mrs. J. M. Forbes, Brookline, Mass.

Edward.   A Concord physician, art student, and lecturer.

Ellen Emerson, who occupies the Concord house.   (1896.)

Poem, " To Ellen."

APPELLATIONS.

The Buddha of the West.

The Poet Philosopher.

The Worshipper of the Beautiful.

The Practical Idealist.

A John Crying in the Wilderness.

A Born Poet, but not a Born Singer.

An Intellectual Mystic.

America's most Original Writer.

The Apostle of Sincerity.

The Glorified Farmer.

The Poetic Seer.

A Hindoo Yankee.

The Concord Sage.

The Landlord and Waterlord of Walden.

An Incorrigible Spouting Yankee. (Self-given.)

The Paragon of a Gentleman.

The New World Transcendentalist.

A Philosopher without a System.

Our most Typical and Inspiring Poet.

A Pure Type of Human Innocence.

The Prince of Idealists.

The Intellectual Emancipator of America.

The Concord Sphinx.

New England's Gentle Iconoclast.

A Winged Franklin.

The Yankee Plato.

NOTES ON HIS WRITINGS.

General Comments.

"He lived and wrote by a sort of divine instinct."

"His poetry is filled with celestial imagery." (Expressive of its writer's lofty nature.)

Emerson said of himself, "I am not a great poet."

"His poetry is his serenest heaven, and his most convenient rubbish-heap."

"Emerson is distinguished as a writer for a singular union of poetic imagination with practical acuteness. . . . He seldom indulges in the expression of sentiment, and in his nature emotion seems to be less the product of the heart than of the brain. . . . His style is in the nicest harmony with the character of his thought. It is condensed almost to abruptness. . . . His merits as a writer consist rather in the choice of words than in the connection of sentences, though his diction is vitalized by the presence of a powerful creative element." — *The American Encyclopædia.*

Profuseness of Quotation. Although one of the most original of writers, Emerson quoted freely, and from many writers, — nearly nine hundred.

His Philosophy.

Obscure, mystical. "Home-bred."

It exalted the spiritual side of life and the principle of individuality. The universe was to him "but one vast symbol of God."

"I am part and particle of God."

Works that reveal it best.

Nature. The Over-Soul. Circles. The Conduct of Life.

His favorite philosopher. Plato.

NOTE. — For an explanation of his philosophy, and for a brief characterization of his representative poems, consult Hawthorne and Lommon's *American Literature,* pp. 126-130.

His only Autobiographical Writing. *English Traits.*

Parnassus.

A collection of poems edited by Emerson, consisting of verses he personally liked. The result of copying, from time to time, such poems into a "commonplace book."

Memoirs of Thoreau and Margaret Fuller are among Emerson's writings

The Mountain and the Squirrel.   (**Fable.**)

A poem that shows the possession of keen wit on the part of Emerson.

Boston Hymn.

Read by the author at an abolition jubilee held in Boston in celebration of Lincoln's Emancipation Proclamation.

A Posthumous Publication.   (1893.)

The Natural History of Intellect and Other Essays.

Sale of Works.

The first edition of *The Conduct of Life*, twenty-five hundred copies, sold in two days. Contrast this with the very slight demand for *Nature*, published twenty-seven years earlier.

Suggested Readings from Emerson.

Poetry. The Rhodora. (A woodcut of the flower may be seen in Appletons' *American Encyclopædia.*) The Snow Storm. Friendship. The Humble Bee. Each and All. The Concord Hymn. (Memorize the last-named.)

Prose. Essays on Friendship, Self-reliance, Compensation, and Manners. A chapter each from *English Traits, Representative Men,* and *The Conduct of Life.*

MISCELLANEOUS NOTES.

Tributes.

"If any one can be said to have given the impulse to my mind, it is Emerson. Whatever I have done the world owes to him."— PROFESSOR TYNDALL.

"Whenever I take up a volume [of Emerson] anew, it seems to me as if I were reading it for the first time."— HERMANN GRIMM.

"Emerson could no more help taking the hopeful view of the universe and its future than Claude could help flooding his landscapes with sunshine."— O. W. HOLMES.

"Emerson was a great man who wrote poems rather than a great poet."— C. F. RICHARDSON.

"Theodore Parker was wont to thank God for the moon, the stars, and Ralph Waldo Emerson."

Emerson was elected a member of the Moral Science section of the French Academy.

Hawthorne's *The Great Stone Face.*

Lowell's *Fable for Critics.* (Emerson is the first writer characterized by Lowell in this poem.)

Poems by F. B. Sanborn, Emma Lazarus, J. R. Lowell; A. Bronson Alcott's monody, Ion.

Emerson's Disciples.

In the pulpit, Theodore Parker.

In literature, Walt Whitman and John Burroughs.

In theory of living, Henry Thoreau and W. E. Channing, Jr.

Views on Woman's Suffrage.

(Uttered in 1856 at a Woman's Rights Convention.)

"It is for women, not men, to determine if women wish an equal share in affairs. If we refuse them a vote, we should refuse to tax them. . . . If the wants, the passions, the vices, are allowed a full vote, through the hands of a half-brutal, intemperate population, I think it but fair that the virtues, the aspirations, should be allowed a full voice as an offset, through the purest of the people."

Emerson and Hawthorne.

Good neighbors, but not intimate or sympathetic friends.

Emerson used to say that he always talked better when Hawthorne's eyes were fixed upon him.

Hawthorne says of the philosopher, "It was impossible to dwell in his vicinity without inhaling more or less of the mountain atmosphere of his lofty thought."

See note on the two men among the Hawthorne Notes.

Emerson and Longfellow Contrasted.

"In Longfellow, true poet though he was, art sometimes usurped the place of genius; in Emerson, genius too often refused the needed aid of art." — RICHARDSON.

Emerson's Rules for Reading.

Never read any book that is not a year old.

Never read any but famed books.

Never read any but what you like.

His Homes.

The Manse. Emerson's ancestral home, at Concord, Mass.

Occupied by Emerson at several different times.

Built in 1765 for Rev. Wm. Emerson, Ralph Waldo's grandfather. (His widow married the succeeding minister, Ezra Ripley. It was with the Ripleys that James Russell Lowell spent his period of college rustication.)

Scores of New England ministers have been entertained here, and thousands of sermons have been written in it.

The Study. A small square room over the dining-room.

Here Hawthorne wrote *Mosses from an Old Manse*, and Emerson wrote *Nature*.

From its north window Emerson's grandmother watched the Concord fight.

Read the Introduction to Hawthorne's *Mosses From an Old Manse*.

Views. See *Scribner's Magazine*, February, 1879; *The New England Magazine*, November, 1893.

The Emerson Home. On the Lexington road.

In a grove of pines; a garden of roses and hollyhocks in the rear.

Visited often by Thoreau, Theodore Parker, Margaret Fuller, the Alcott family, Elizabeth Peabody; entertained Frederika Bremer, Harriet Martineau, and Arthur Hugh Clough.

Views. *Scribner's Magazine*, February, 1879; *Concord Guide Books*; *Harper's Magazine*, August, 1894.

His Personality.

" In everything he thought, wrote, and did, we feel the presence of
a personality as vigorous and brave as it was sweet; and the
particular radical thought he at any time expressed, derived its
power to animate and illuminate other minds from the might
of the manhood which was felt to be within and behind it. To
'sweetness and light' he added the prime quality of fearless
manliness." — WHIPPLE.

Emerson on Genius.

" It is the nature of genius to spring, like the rainbow, daughter of
Wonder, from the invisible, to abolish the past and refuse all
history."

Emerson on Newspaper Reading.

"Newspapers have done much to abbreviate expression, and so to
improve style. . . . The most studious and engaged man can
neglect them only at his cost. But have little to do with them.
Learn how to get their best, too, without their getting yours.
Do not read them when the mind is creative; and do not read
them thoroughly, column by column. Remember they are made
for everybody, and don't try to get what is not meant for you.
. . . There is a great secret in knowing what to keep out of the
mind, as well as what to put in. . . . The genuine news is what
you want. Practice quick searches for it. Give yourself only
so many minutes for the paper. Then you will learn to avoid
the premature reports and anticipations, and the stuff put in for
people who have nothing to think."

The Apostle of Sincerity.

" Emerson preached sincerity as among the first of virtues. He
never hesitated to tell the poets, prose writers, reformers, ' fanat-
ics,' who were his friends and acquaintances, exactly what he
thought of them. . . . He could afford to be sincere, for everybody felt there was no taint of envy, jealousy, or malice in his
nature."

Curtis on Emerson.

" It is the peculiarity of Emerson's mind to be always on the alert.
He eats no lotus, but forever quaffs the waters which engender
immortal thirst. . . . His writings have no imported air. If
there be something Oriental in his philosophy and tropical in
his imagination, they have yet the strong flavor of his mother
earth — the underived sweetness of the open Concord sky, and
the spacious breadth of the Concord horizon."

Transcendentalism in New England.

"A new avatar of the old Puritan spirit."—H. A. BEERS.

References.

Conway's *Emerson*, chap. xxi. Cabot's *Emerson*, chap. vii.

O. B. Frothingham's "Transcendentalism in New England." *The Atlantic Monthly*, October and November, 1878.

Beers's *Initial Studies in American Literature*, pp. 96–103.

An Era of Agitation. 1830–1850. "A Modern Renaissance."

Philosophic Inquiry. "Transcendentalism."

Reforms. Temperance, Anti-slavery, Social Life.

New Religious Sects. Millerites, Second Adventists, Mormons, Spiritualists, Unitarians (Conservatives, followers of William Ellery Channing; Radicals, those of Theodore Parker).

Caused largely by Carlyle's writings.

Pulpit Representative of the movement.

Theodore Parker, a pupil of Emerson.

The Transcendental Club.

At first, "The Symposium." In 1849 it was succeeded by "The Town and Country Club."

Met in Boston, Concord, and other Massachusetts towns.

Founders. Dr. Channing and George Ripley.

Prominent Members. Emerson (its "prophet"), Channing, Alcott, Ripley, Parker, John S. Dwight, James Freeman Clarke.

Its Organ. *The Dial*, a quarterly, published from 1840 to 1844. Devoted to mooted points in philosophy, history, and literature.

"If I were a Bostonian, I think I would be a Transcendentalist."— CHARLES DICKENS.

On a meeting of the club, this "congress of oracles," in its incipient stage, read Curtis's *Literary and Social Essays*, pp. 24–26.

Definitions of Transcendentalism.

Emerson's. "Modern Idealism."

Other Definitions.

"A new philosophy maintaining that nothing is everything in general, and everything is nothing in particular."

"Intuitive religion."

"A belief that there is a power in man which transcends the senses and the understanding."

Its Reformatory Spirit. Well shown in the experiment at

Brook Farm. West Roxbury, Mass. 1841–1847.

>   The ideal commonwealth of the Transcendentalists.

>   (Compare with More's *Utopia*, Sidney's *Arcadia*, Bacon's *The New Atlantis*, and Bellamy's *Looking Backward*.)

>   " A remarkable outburst of Romanticism on Puritan ground."

>   " Plain living and high thinking."

>   " A strange mixture of culture and agriculture."

>   " Communities were to be established where everything should be common, save common sense." — LOWELL.

>   *Members.* George Ripley, Charles A. Dana, Margaret Fuller, Hawthorne, George William Curtis, John S. Dwight.

>   >   Emerson was not a member of the community, but visited it frequently, and sympathized with the earnest spirit of its supporters; in a humorous mood he described it as "a French Revolution in small, an Age of Reason in a patty-pan."

>   >   Hawthorne joined the company of experimenters, but lost money and health in the venture, and was not happy in it.

>   >   >   His *Blithedale Romance* is the best outcome of this attempt at social reform.

>   NOTE. — Interesting reading matter, in addition to the references given above, on this epoch of New England history, may be found in George T. Bradford's " Reminiscences of Brook Farm " (see *The Century Magazine*, November, 1892); T. W. Higginson's *Life of Margaret Fuller;* Cooke's *Emerson*, chap. viii.; Hawthorne's *American Notes;* the first pages of Lowell's essay on Thoreau in *My Study Windows;* and Willis Boughton's *Syllabus of University Extension Lectures on Brook Farm.*

HENRY DAVID THOREAU.

HENRY DAVID THOREAU.

NATURALIST, STOIC, SCHOLAR, TRANSCENDENTALIST.

EXTRACTS.

FROM "WALDEN."

I SHOULD not talk so much about myself if there were anybody else I knew so well.

I think that we may safely trust a great deal more than we do. We may waive just so much care of ourselves as we honestly bestow elsewhere.

We are eager to tunnel under the Atlantic, and bring the Old World some weeks nearer to the New; but perchance the first news that will leak through into the broad, flapping American ear will be that the Princess Adelaide has the whooping-cough.

Nations are possessed with an insane ambition to perpetuate the memory of themselves by the amount of hammered stone they leave. What if equal pains were taken to smooth and polish their manners ?

Those who would not know what to do with more leisure than they now enjoy, I might advise to work twice as hard as they do, — work till they pay for themselves and get their free papers.

I am convinced both by faith and experience that to maintain one's self on this earth is not a hardship, but a pastime, if we will live simply and wisely.

Books are the treasured wealth of the world, and the fit inheritance of generations and nations.

I think that, having learned our letters, we should read the best that is in literature, and not be forever repeating our a b abs, and words of one syllable, in the fourth and fifth classes.

Society is commonly too cheap. We meet at very short intervals, not having had time to acquire any new value for each other. . . . The value of a man is not in his skin, that we should touch him.

Only that day dawns to which we are awake.

If you would learn to speak all tongues and conform to the customs of all nations, if you would travel farther than all travellers, be naturalized in all climes, and cause the Sphinx to dash her head against a stone, obey the precept of the old philosopher, Explore thyself.

Drive a nail home and clinch it so faithfully that you can wake up in the night and think of your work with satisfaction, — a work at which you would not be ashamed to invoke the Muse. So will help you God, and so only.

A huckleberry never reaches Boston; they have not been known there since they grew on her three hills. The ambrosial and essential part of the fruit is lost with the bloom which is rubbed off in the market cart.

> Men say they know many things;
> But lo! they have taken wings, —

The arts and sciences,
And a thousand appliances;
The wind that blows
Is all that anybody knows.

Beware of all enterprises that require new clothes, and not rather a new wearer of clothes. If there is not a new man, how can the new clothes be made to fit? . . . All men want not something to *do with*, but something to *do*, or rather something to *be*.

FROM "EARLY SPRING IN MASSACHUSETTS."

No sooner has the ice of Walden melted, than the winds begin to play in dark ripples over the face of the virgin waters. It is affecting to see nature so tender, however old, and wearing none of the wriinkles of age. Ice dissolved is as perfect water as if it had been melted a million years. What if our moods could dissolve thus completely?

I cannot think or understand my thoughts unless I have infinite room. The cope of heaven is not too high, the sea is not too deep, for him who would unfold a great thought. It must feed me, warm me, clothe me. It must be an entertainment to which my whole nature is invited. I must know that the gods are my fellow-guests.

Nothing can be more useful to a man than the determination not to be hurried.

FROM "SUMMER."

Decay and disease are often beautiful, like the pearly tear of the shell-fish and the hectic glow of consumption.

Woe to him who wants a companion, for he is unfit to be the companion of himself.

Painters are wont, in their pictures of Paradise, to strew the field too thickly with flowers. . . . But a clover field in bloom is some excuse for them.

It seems natural that rocks that have lain under the heavens so long should be gray, as it were an intermediate color between the heavens and the earth.

FROM "WINTER."

I love nature partly because she is not man, but a retreat from him. In her midst I can be glad with an entire gladness. . . . Man makes me wish for another world; she makes me content with this.

To live in relations of truth and sincerity with men is to dwell in a frontier country.

Men wear their hats for use; women theirs for ornament.

If we try thoughts by their quality, not their quantity, I may find that a restless night will yield more than the longest journey.

The death of friends should inspire us as much as their lives.

In prosperity I remember God; in adversity I remember my own elevation, and only hope to see God again.

FROM HIS LETTERS.

CAN'T you extract any advantage out of that depression of spirits you refer to? It suggests to me cider-mills, wine-presses, etc. All kinds of pressure or power should be used, and made to turn some kind of machinery.

It is strange that men will talk of miracles, revelation, inspiration, and the like, as things past, while love remains.

Warm your body by healthful exercise, not by cowering over a stove. Warm your spirit by performing independently noble deeds, not by ignobly seeking the sympathy of your fellows, who are no better than yourself.

If you would convince a man that he does wrong, do right. But do not care to convince him. Men will believe what they see. Let them see.

Men and boys are learning all kinds of trades but how to make *men* of themselves.

A noble person confers no such gift as his whole confidence; none so exalts the giver and the receiver; it produces the truest gratitude. Perhaps it is only essential to friendship that some vital trust should have been reposed by the one in the other. I feel addressed and probed even to the remote parts of my being when one nobly shows, even in trivial things, an implicit faith in me. . . . What if God were to confide in us for a moment! Should we not then be gods?

My breath is sweet to me. Oh, how I laugh when I think of my vague, indefinite riches. No run on my bank can drain it; for my wealth is not possession, but enjoyment.

SCATTERED THOUGHTS.

How can we expect a harvest of thought who have not had a seed-time of character?

Sugar is not so sweet to the palate as sound to the healthy ear.

The bluebird carries the sky on his back.

Only he can be trusted with gifts who can present a face of bronze to expectations.

One wise sentence is worth the State of Massachusetts many times over.

I regard the horse as a human being in a humbler state of existence.

If one hesitates in his path, let him not proceed. Let him respect his doubts; for doubts, too, may have some divinity in them.

Love is a severe critic. Hate can pardon more than love. They who aspire to love worthily, subject themselves to an ordeal more rigid than any other.

I have but few companions on the shore :
   They scorn the strand who sail upon the sea;
Yet oft I think the ocean they've sailed o'er
   Is deeper known upon the strand to me.

THE FISHER'S BOY.

REFERENCES.

William Ellery Channing's *Thoreau: The Poet Naturalist.* ("A rhapsody rather than a biography.")

Frank B. Sanborn's *Henry D. Thoreau.*

Henry A. Page's *Thoreau: His Life and Aims.*

Familiar Letters of Henry D. Thoreau. (Edited by F. B. Sanborn.)

Ralph W. Emerson's *Memoir of Thoreau.* (Published as Preface to Thoreau's *Excursions*, and in *The Literary World*, March 26, 1881.)

Emerson's poem, *Woodnotes.*

T. W. Higginson's *Short Studies of American Authors.*

James R. Lowell's Essay on Thoreau in *My Study Windows.* ("The subtlest of Lowell's minor reviews." —STEDMAN.)

John Burroughs's *Indoor Studies.*

M. D. Conway's *Emerson* (chap. xxv.).

Henry A. Beers's *Initial Studies in American Letters.* (Pp. 110–114.)

Appletons' Cyclopædia of American Biography.

Duyckinck's *Cyclopædia of American Literature.* Vol. II.

Hawthorne and Lemmon's *American Literature.*

George B. Bartlett's *Concord Guide Book.* (Pp. 72–75.)

Theodore Wolfe's *Literary Shrines.*

Extracts from Thoreau's writings may be found in —
Stedman-Hutchinson's *Library of American Literature.* Vol. VII.
Beers's *Century of American Literature.*
F. H. Underwood's *American Authors.*
Masterpieces of American Literature.

The Atlantic Monthly. August, 1862. September, 1863 (Article by Louisa Alcott).

The North American Review. October, 1863. October, 1865.

The Century Magazine. July, 1882 (Article by John Burroughs).

The New England Magazine. December, 1890 ("Emerson and his Friends." Illustrated).

Harper's Magazine. August, 1894 (Howells's "My First Visit to New England").

Scribner's Magazine. March, 1895 ("Thoreau's Poems of Nature").

OUTLINE OF HIS LIFE.

July 12, 1817.
May 6, 1862.

His writings, prose and verse, are his best biography.

Birthplace.

    Concord, Mass. ("To him, Concord was the centre of the universe, and he seriously contemplated annexing the rest of the planet to Concord.")

    House, on the Virginia road, still standing.

    For view, see Margaret Sidney's *Old Concord: Her Highways and Byways.*

    "Thoreau was the best topographer of his birthplace."

    He never left Concord except for a lecturing tour or a pedestrian excursion.

Grandfather.

    A Frenchman, who married in Boston a woman of Scotch birth.

    Thoreau's speech bore a slight French accent, and his pronunciation of the letter " r " was always peculiar.

Early Home.

    One of simplicity and poverty.

    A gathering-place for the early Abolitionists, and a refuge for fugitive slaves.

Education.

    School life in Concord and Boston.

    At Harvard. Degree in 1837. (He refused his diploma, considering it not worth five dollars.)

        Made possible by the special efforts of his family and aunts.

        Independent. Made no friends. Roomed in Hollis Hall.

    A lifelong student of the classic literatures.

Acquaintance with Emerson, fourteen years his senior.

    The most valuable and intimate of his acquaintances.

    Dated from his college days.

Emerson wrote a letter of recommendation for him as teacher.

At one time Thoreau was an inmate of Emerson's household.

An unconscious disciple of the Concord seer.

Begins to Lecture. 1838.

Various Occupations.

Manufactured lead pencils (he stopped doing so when he had made a perfect one).

Taught in the Concord Academy. Tutored in the family of Emerson's brother at Staten Island. Surveyed land for Concord farmers.

Builds his " Hermitage " (1845), on land belonging to Emerson, by the shore of Walden Pond, — "God's Drop," "a gem of the first water that Concord wears in her coronet."

View. Selected Proofs, Century Co., No. 46. Duyckinck, Vol. II., p. 602.

> " Who liv'st all alone,
> Close to the bone,
> And where life is sweetest,
> Constantly eatest."
>
> *The Old Marlborough Road.*

Erected by Himself at the cost of less than thirty dollars.

Ten feet by fifteen ; garret, closet, door, and window ; no lock or curtain.

"There is some of the same fitness in a man's building his own house that there is in a bird's building her own nest."

Spent for food about twenty-seven cents a week.

Lived here for two years, in order to read, write, and study nature. Abandoned the life when his object was accomplished. Did not recommend any one to try the same experience unless he had "a good supply of internal sunshine."

"I am no more lonely than Walden Pond itself. What company has that, I pray? And yet it has not the blue devils, but blue angels in it, in the azure tint of its waters."

Kept a calendar of the flowers of the neighborhood (knew the day of blossoming for each one).

Many and various Visitors sought him out in this retreat.

Here Ellery Channing and Thoreau practised "the art of taking walks."

Site is marked by a cairn of stones, which every pilgrim to the spot makes higher by his contribution from the shore of the pond. For view, see Margaret Sidney's *Old Concord*, and *The New England Magazine*, November, 1893, p. 300.

The furniture of the hut and other Thoreau relics may be seen in the "Antiquarian House," Concord.

Publishes   A Week on the Concord and Merrimac Rivers.   1849.

"A collection of essays tied together by a slight thread of travel." — BURROUGHS.

It abounds in excellent quotations, particularly from the minor Elizabethan poets.

Publishes Walden; or, Life in the Woods. ("A sermon on economy.") 1854.

"The only book printed in America, to my thinking, that bears an annual perusal." — HIGGINSON.

"Few authors since Shakespeare have been less anxious to print their works."

"Capital reading, but very wicked and heathenish." — WHITTIER.

"Like many reformers, he carried his views to an extreme."

"In no other book can one come so close to Nature's heart. We hear in it the weird cry of the loons over the water; we watch the frolics of the squirrels; we observe the thousand phenomena of the wonderful little lake; we listen to the forest sounds by day and by night; we study the tell-tale snow; we watch, with bated breath, a battle to the death between two armies of ants. For minute and loving descriptions of the woods and fields, *Walden* has had no rival." — F. L. PATTEE.

"If every quiet country town in New England had a son who, with a lore like Selborne's and an eye like Buffon's, had watched and studied its landscape and history, and then published the result, as Thoreau has done, in a book as redolent of genuine and perceptive sympathy with nature as a clover-field of honey, New England would seem as poetic and beautiful as Greece." — G. W. CURTIS.

Persons referred to in the book.

See Wolfe's *Literary Shrines*, pp. 72, 73.

Death from Consumption.

Buried in Sleepy Hollow, Concord.

Character and Temperament.

"Hypæthral."

"Like his native air in winter, — clear, frosty, inexpressibly pure and bracing." Stoical, sturdily independent, a consistent believer in individualism. "His affections were more deep than expansive."

"His religion was that of Transcendentalism, and his spirit that of other-worldliness."

Self-centred. — "May I love and reverence myself above all the gods that man ever invented." ("This egotism of his is a Stylites pillar, after all, a seclusion which keeps him in the public eye." — LOWELL.)

Renunciatory. — "He was bred to no profession ; he never married (his celibacy was due to the fact that he surrendered his love in favor of his brother) ; he lived alone ; he never went to church ; he never voted ; he refused to pay a tax to the State (was imprisoned for doing so) ; he ate no flesh, he drank no wine, he never knew the use of tobacco ; and, though a naturalist, he used neither a trap nor gun." — EMERSON.

"Thoreau seemed to me a man who had experienced Nature as other men are said to have experienced religion." — E. P. WHIPPLE.

Appearance.

Average height ; spare build ; sloping shoulders, long arms ; large hands and feet. "His aspect suggested a faun, one who was in the secrets of the wilderness."

Features marked. — Roman nose, large overhanging brows, deep-set, expressive blue eyes, prominent lips.

Abundant dark-brown hair. Plain in dress.

Resembled Emerson in features, expression, and tones of voice.

A woodcut of his face may be found in *Harper's Magazine,* August, 1894, p. 448, and in the *Cyclopædia of American Biography.*

Habits.

Solitary. Kept "Fact-Books" assiduously and very systematically. ("He recorded the state of his personal thermometer thirteen times a day.") Read with a pen in his hand. (Left thirty manuscript volumes at his death.) Ignored the conventionalities of life. Could walk thirty miles a day for weeks together. ("Thoreau knew the world, having 'travelled' many years in Concord.") Could go without food and water longer than the Indians. Knew the notes of all birds, insects, and animals. He did not read novels or stories.

Ambition and Purpose.

"To reduce existence to the lowest terms." To cultivate the power of understanding and enjoying nature.

"Give me the obscure life, the cottage of the poor and humble, the work-days of the world, the barren fields ; the smallest share of all things but poetical perception." "I would fain improve every opportunity to wonder and worship, as the sunflower welcomes the light."

Reputation.

Thoreau was not appreciated in his lifetime.

"I have now a library of nearly nine hundred volumes, over seven hundred of which I wrote myself." (Referring to the first edition of *A Week*, which consisted of a thousand copies.)

In England, Thoreau was not known at all when he died ; now one of his biographers, H. A. Page, is an Englishman.

"His fame has survived two of the greatest dangers that can beset reputation, — a brilliant satirist for critic [Lowell] and an injudicious friend for biographer [Channing]." — HIGGINSON.

APPELLATIONS.

CONCORD'S RECLUSE.

THE BACHELOR OF THOUGHT AND NATURE.

A MASTER OF THE SHORT EPIGRAMMATIC SENTENCE.

A FREE AND JUST MAN.

THE INFLEXIBLE THOREAU.

A BORN PROTESTANT.

A KING IN THE WILDERNESS.

A MODERN JAQUES.

A SCHOLASTIC AND PASTORAL ORSON.

THE NEW ENGLAND ESSENE.

AN OBSERVER OF THE RAREST, CLOSEST KIND.

THE POET-NATURALIST.

AN ANGLO-SAXON REVERSAL TO THE TYPE OF THE RED INDIAN.

A LOVER OF NATURE RATHER THAN OF MAN.

"THOREAU WAS A VERGIL, WHITE OF SELBORNE, ISAAK WALTON, AND YANKEE SETTLER ALL IN ONE." — *A. B. Alcott.*

THE CHAMPION OF INDIVIDUALISM.

NEW ENGLAND'S STOIC.

CONCORD'S PAN.

> "This Concord Pan would oft his whistle take,
>   And forth from wood and fen, field, hill, and lake,
>   Trooping around him in their several guise,
>   The shy inhabitants their haunts forsake."
>
>   A. B. ALCOTT.

MISCELLANEOUS NOTES.

Tributes to Thoreau.

"The only man who thoroughly loved both Nature and Greek." — J. G. KING.

"His soul was made for the noblest society; he had in a short life exhausted the capabilities of this world; wherever there is knowledge, wherever there is virtue, wherever there is beauty, he will find a home." — EMERSON.

> "To hill and sky his face was known,
> It seemed the likeness of their own."
> EMERSON.

"His metaphors and images are always fresh from the soil. . . . As we read him, it seems as if all outdoors had kept a diary and become its own Montaigne." — LOWELL.

"In his own house he was one of those characters that may be called household treasures." — CHANNING.

> "Modest and mild and kind,
> Who never spurned the needing from thy door —
> (Door of thy heart, which is a palace-gate);
> Temperate and faithful, — in whose word the world
> Might trust, sure to repay; unvexed by care,
> Unawed by Fortune's nod, slave to no lord,
> Nor coward to thy peers, — long shalt thou live!"
> CHANNING.

Alcott's sonnet and Louisa Alcott's poem on Thoreau.

Thoreau as Poet.

His poems are short, vigorous, not polished in style; they are "moralized descriptions of nature."

His Themes.

Smoke. Haze. Mist. Mountains. Sympathy. True Love. Inspiration.

Made Translations from a number of the classic poets, including two of Æschylus' tragedies.

"He possessed the essential element of the poet, a soaring imagination, but he lacked the art of musical expression."

His Theory of Poetry.

"It is not important that the poet should say some particular thing, but that he should speak in harmony with nature. The tone and pitch of his voice is the main thing."

His Favorite Poets and Poems.

Homer and Vergil, Chaucer, Milton, Ossian.

The Robin Hood Ballads.

Carlyle was his only favorite among modern writers.

His Prose Writings.

A Week on the Concord and Merrimack Rivers. Walden. Excursions in Field and Forest. The Maine Woods. Cape Cod. Letters to Various Persons, with nine poems. *A Yankee in Canada. Early Spring in Massachusetts. Summer. Autumn, Winter.*

Only the first two works were published in his lifetime.

"Homeliness is almost as great a merit in a book as in a house, if the reader would abide there." — THOREAU.

His Friends.

Emerson, Margaret Fuller, William E. Channing, A. Bronson Alcott, Hawthorne, John Brown, Horace Greeley.

Thoreau and Emerson.

"While Thoreau was to a certain degree stamped by the more powerful mind of Emerson, it is certain that the latter was much influenced by Thoreau. Emerson was blind to less obvious processes of nature till Thoreau opened his eyes." — F. L. PATTEE.

"Among the pistillate plants kindled to fruitage by the Emersonian pollen, Thoreau is thus far the most remarkable."

His Several Concord Homes.

Described in the first chapter of Wolfe's *Literary Shrines.*

Lowell on Thoreau.

"It is not so much the True that he loves as the Out-of-the-Way. . . . He valued everything in proportion as he fancied it to be exclusively his own. . . . His whole life was a rebuke of the waste and aimlessness of our American luxury, which is an abject enslavement to tawdry upholstery. . . . His works give one the feeling of a sky full of stars, — something impressive and exhilarating certainly, something high overhead and freckled thickly with spots of isolated brightness; but whether these have any mutual relation with each other, or have any concern with our mundane affairs, is for the most part matter of conjecture,— astrology as yet, and not astronomy."

———

"Thoreau believed that one of the arts of life was to make the most out of it."

"Thoreau chose to be rich by making his wants few and supplying them himself."

"He preferred the Indian to the civilized man, and indigenous plants to imported ones."

"I leave this world without a regret."　(Said in his last illness.)

———

Suggested Readings.

Chapter on Friendship in *A Week on the Concord and Merrimack Rivers*.

On Reading the Classics, and The Battle of the Ants, from *Walden*.

Question for Debate.

Was Thoreau's life a success?

EDGAR ALLAN POE.

EDGAR ALLAN POE.

ROMANCER, POET, CRITIC.

EXTRACTS.

IT was many and many a year ago,
  In a kingdom by the sea,
That a maiden there lived whom you may know
  By the name of Annabel Lee;
And this maiden she lived with no other thought
  Than to love and be loved by me.

ANNABEL LEE.

AND the Raven, never flitting, still is sitting, still is sitting
On the pallid bust of Pallas just above my chamber door;
And his eyes have all the seeming of a demon's that is
    dreaming,
And the lamp-light o'er him streaming throws his shadow
    on the floor;
And my soul from out that shadow that lies floating on
    the floor,
            Shall be lifted — nevermore!

THE RAVEN.

  HEAR the sledges with the bells —
      Silver bells!
What a world of merriment their melody foretells!
    How they tinkle, tinkle, tinkle
      In the icy air of night!

While the stars that oversprinkle
All the heavens, seem to twinkle
    With a crystalline delight;
Keeping time, time, time,
In a sort of Runic rhyme,
To the tintinnabulation that so musically wells
    From the bells, bells, bells, bells,
        Bells, bells, bells —
    From the jingling and the tinkling of the bells.

                                    THE BELLS.

AND now, as the night was senescent
    And the star-dials pointed to morn —
    As the star-dials hinted of morn —
At the end of our path a liquescent
    And nebulous lustre was born,
Out of which a miraculous crescent
    Arose with a duplicate horn —
Astarte's bediamonded crescent
    Distinct with its duplicate horn.

                                    ULALUME.

AROUND, by lifting winds forgot,
Resignedly beneath the sky
The melancholy waters lie.

                        THE CITY IN THE SEA.

Is all that we see or seem
But a dream within a dream?

                        A DREAM WITHIN A DREAM.

THOU wast that all to me, love,
    For which my soul did pine —

A green isle in the sea, love,
　A fountain and a shrine,
All wreathed with fairy fruits and flowers,
　And all the flowers were mine.

To One in Paradise.

Ah, broken is the golden bowl! the spirit flown forever!
Let the bell toll!—a saintly soul floats on the Stygian
　river;
And Guy de Vère, hast thou no tear?—weep now or
　never more!
See! on yon drear and rigid bier low lies thy love, Lenore!—
An anthem for the queenliest dead that ever died so
　young—
A dirge for her, the doubly dead in that she died so young.

Lenore.

It is an evil growing out of our republican institutions,
that here a man of large purse has usually a very little
soul which he keeps in it. The corruption of taste is a
portion or a pendant of the dollar-manufacture.

Philosophy of Furniture.

There is one dear topic, however, on which my memory
fails me not. It is the person of Ligeia. In stature she
was tall, somewhat slender, and, in her latter days, even
emaciated. I would in vain attempt to portray the majesty, the quiet ease, of her demeanor, or the incompre-
hensible lightness and elasticity of her footfall. She came
and departed as a shadow. I was never made aware of
her entrance into my closed study, save by the dear music
of her low sweet voice, as she placed her marble hand
upon my shoulder.

Ligeia.

Never shall I forget the sensations of awe, horror, and admiration with which I gazed about me. The boat appeared to be hanging, as if by magic, midway down, upon the interior surface of a tunnel vast in circumference, prodigious in depth, and whose perfectly smooth sides might have been mistaken for ebony, but for the bewildering rapidity with which they spun around, and for the gleaming and ghastly radiance they shot forth, as the rays of the full moon, from that circular rift among the clouds which I have already described, streamed in a flood of golden glory along the black walls, and far away down into the inmost recesses of the abyss.

A Descent into the Maelstrom.

There are chords in the hearts of the most reckless which cannot be touched without emotion. Even with the utterly lost, to whom life and death are equally jests, there are matters of which no jest can be made.

The Masque of the Red Death.

The chest had been full to the brim, and we spent the whole day, and the greater part of the next night, in scrutiny of its contents. There had been nothing like order or arrangement. Everything had been heaped in promiscuously. Having assorted all with care, we found ourselves possessed of even vaster wealth than we had at first supposed. In coin there was rather more than four hundred and fifty thousand dollars, estimating the value of the pieces, as accurately as we could, by the tables of the period. There was not a particle of silver. All was gold of antique date and of great variety, — French, Spanish, and German money, with a few English guineas, and some counters, of which we had never seen specimens before. There were several very large and heavy coins, so worn that we could make nothing of their inscriptions. There was no American money. The value of the jewels we found more difficulty in estimating. There were diamonds — some of them exceedingly large and fine — a hundred and ten in all, and not one of them small; eighteen rubies of remarkable brilliancy; three hundred and ten emeralds, all very beautiful; and twenty-one sapphires with an opal. These stones had all been broken from their settings, and thrown loose in the chest. The settings themselves, which we picked out from among the other gold, appeared to have been beaten up with hammers, as if to prevent identification. Besides all this, there was a vast quantity of solid gold ornaments, — nearly two hundred massive finger and ear rings; rich chains (thirty of these, if I remember); eighty-three very large and heavy crucifixes; five gold censers of great value; a prodigious golden punch-bowl, ornamented with richly chased vine-leaves and bacchanalian figures; with two sword-handles exquisitely embossed, and many other smaller articles which I cannot recollect. The weight of these valuables exceeded three hundred and fifty pounds avoirdupois; and in this estimate I have not included one hundred and ninety-seven superb gold watches, three of the number being worth each five hundred dollars, if one. Many of them were very old, and as timekeepers valueless, the works having suffered more or less from corrosion; but all were richly jewelled and in cases of great worth. We estimated the entire contents of the chest, that night, at a million and a half of dollars; and upon the subsequent disposal of the trinkets and jewels (a few being retained for our own use), it was found that we had greatly undervalued the treasure.

When, at length, we had concluded our examination, and the intense excitement of the time had, in some measure, subsided, Legrand, who saw that I was dying with impatience for a solution of this most extraordinary riddle, entered into a full detail of all the circumstances connected with it.

"You remember," said he, "the night when I handed you the rough sketch I had made of the scarabæus. You recollect also, that I became quite vexed at you for insisting that my drawing resembled a death's-head. When you at first made this assertion I thought you were jesting; but afterward I called to mind the peculiar spots on the back of the insect, and admitted to myself that your remark had some little foundation in fact. Still the sneer at my graphic powers irritated me, — for I am considered a good artist, — and therefore, when you handed me the scrap of parchment, I was about to crumple it up, and throw it angrily into the fire."

"The scrap of paper, you mean," said I.

"No: it had much the appearance of paper, and at first I supposed it to be such; but when I came to drawing upon it, I discovered it at once to be a piece of very thin parchment. It was quite dirty, you remember. Well, as I was in the very act of crumpling it up, my glance fell upon the sketch at which you had been looking; and you may imagine my astonishment, when I perceived, in fact, the figure of a death's-head just where, it seemed to me, I had made the drawing of a beetle. For a moment I was too much amazed to think with accuracy. I knew that my design was very different in detail from this, although there was a certain similarity in general outline. Presently I took a candle, and, seating myself at the other end of the room, proceeded to scrutinize the parchment more closely. Upon turning it over, I saw my own sketch upon the reverse, just as I had made it. My first idea now was mere surprise at the really remarkable similarity of outline, — at the singular coincidence involved in the fact, that, unknown to me, there should have been a skull upon the other side of the parchment, immediately beneath my figure of the scarabæus, and that this skull, not only in outline, but in size, should so closely resemble my drawing. I say, the singularity of this coincidence absolutely stupefied me for a time. This is the usual effect of such coincidences. The mind struggles to establish a connection, — a sequence of cause and effect, — and, being unable to do so, suffers a species of temporary paralysis. But, when I recovered from this stupor, there dawned upon me gradually a conviction which startled me even far more than the coincidence. I began distinctly, positively, to remember that there had been no drawing upon the parchment when I made my sketch of the scarabæus. I became perfectly certain of this; for I recollected turning up first one side and then the other, in search of the cleanest spot. Had the skull been there, of course I could not have failed to notice it. Here was indeed a mystery which I felt it impossible to explain; but, even at that early moment, there seemed to glimmer faintly, within the most remote and secret chambers of my intellect, a glowworm-like conception of that truth which last night's adventure brought to so magnificent a demonstration. I arose at once, and putting the parchment securely away, dismissed all further reflection until I should be alone."

THE GOLD BUG.

DIVIDING the world of mind into its three most immediately obvious distinctions, we have the Pure Intellect,
Taste, and the Moral Sense. I place Taste in the middle,
because it is just this position which, in the mind, it
occupies. It holds intimate relations with either extreme;
but from the Moral Sense is separated by so faint a difference that Aristotle has not hesitated to place some of
its operations among the virtues themselves. Neverthe-
less, we find the *offices* of the trio marked with a sufficient
distinction. Just as the Intellect concerns itself with
Truth, so Taste informs us of the Beautiful, while the
Moral Sense is regardful of Duty. Of this latter, while
Conscience teaches us the obligation, and Reason the expediency, Taste contents itself with displaying the charms;
waging war upon Vice solely on the ground of her de-
formity — her disproportion — her animosity to the fitting,
to the appropriate, to the harmonious — in a word, to
Beauty.

An immortal instinct, deep within the spirit of man, is
thus plainly a sense of the Beautiful. This it is which
administers to his delight in the manifold forms, and
sounds, and colors, and odors, and sentiments amid which
he exists. And just as the lily is repeated in the lake,
or the eyes of Amaryllis in the mirror, so is the mere oral
or written repetition of these forms, and sounds, and
colors, and odors, and sentiments, a duplicate source of
delight. But this mere repetition is not poetry. He who
shall simply sing, with however glowing enthusiasm, or
with however vivid a truth of description, of the sights,
and sounds, and odors, and colors, and sentiments, which
greet *him* in common with all mankind — he, I say, has
yet failed to prove his divine title. There is still a some-

thing in the distance which he has been unable to attain.
We have still a thirst unquenchable, to allay which he has
not shown us the crystal springs. This thirst belongs to
the Immortality of Man. It is at once a consequence and
an indication of his perennial existence. It is the desire
of the moth for the star. It is no mere appreciation of
the Beauty before us, but a wild effort to reach the
Beauty above. Inspired by an ecstatic prescience of the
glories beyond the grave, we struggle, by multiform com-
binations among the things and thoughts of Time, to
attain a portion of that Loveliness whose very elements,
perhaps, appertain to Eternity alone. And thus when by
Poetry — or when by Music, the most entrancing of the
Poetic moods — we find ourselves melted into tears, we
weep then — not as the Abbaté Gravina supposes, through
excess of pleasure, but through a certain petulant, im-
patient sorrow at our inability to grasp *now*, wholly, here
on earth, at once and forever, those divine and rapturous
joys of which through the poem, or through the music,
we attain to but brief and indeterminate glimpses.

· The struggle to apprehend the supernal Loveliness —
this struggle, on the part of souls fittingly constituted —
has given to the world all that which it (the world) has
ever been enabled at once to understand and to *feel* as
poetic. . . .

That pleasure which is at once the most pure, the most
elevating, and the most intense, is derived, I maintain,
from the contemplation of the Beautiful. In the contemplation of Beauty, we alone find it possible to attain that
pleasurable elevation or excitement *of the soul* which we
recognize as the Poetic Sentiment, and which is so easily
distinguished from Truth, which is the satisfaction of the

Reason, or from Passion, which is the excitement of the heart. I make Beauty, therefore, — using the word as inclusive of the sublime, — I make Beauty the promise of the poem, simply because it is an obvious rule of Art that effects should be made to spring as directly as possible from their causes; no one as yet having been weak enough to deny that the peculiar elevation in question is at least *most readily* attainable in the poem. It by no means follows, however, that the incitements of Passion, or the precepts of Duty, or even the lessons of Truth, may not be introduced into a poem, and with advantage; for they may subserve incidentally, in various ways, the general purposes of the work : but the true artist will always contrive to tone them down in proper subjection to that *Beauty* which is the atmosphere and the real essence of the poem.

THE POETIC PRINCIPLE.

REFERENCES.

George E. Woodberry's *Life of Poe*.

T. W. Higginson's *Short Studies of American Authors*.

Stedman's *Poets of America*.

Andrew Lang's *Letters to Dead Authors*.

J. G. Wilson's *Bryant and His Friends*.

Memoirs by R. H. Stoddard, 1880; by Ingram (London, 1880).

Lowell's *Fable for Critics*.

H. T. Griswold's *Home Life of Great Authors*.

Beers's *Initial Studies in American Letters*.

Hawthorne and Lemmon's *American Literature*.

Richardson's *American Literature*. Vol. II. chap. iv.

Appletons' Cyclopædia of American Biography.

Duyckinck's *Cyclopædia of American Literature*.

Lippincott's Biographical Dictionary.

Allibone's *Dictionary of Authors*.

Stedman-Hutchinson's *Library of American Literature*. Vol. VI.

C. F. Briggs's Sketch in *The New York Independent*. June 24, 1884.

The Literary World. Dec. 16, 1882.

The New England Magazine. March, 1894 ("Pioneers of Southern Literature." Illustrated).

Harper's Magazine. September, 1872 ("Poe at Fordham." Illustrated).

Scribner's Magazine. October, 1875. August, 1894 ("Lowell's Letters to Poe").

The Century Magazine. August, 1894 ("Poe in the South." Selections from his correspondence. Two illustrations). September, 1894 ("Poe in Philadelphia"). October, 1894 ("Poe in New York").

Prefaces to Editions of Poe's Works.

OUTLINE OF HIS LIFE.

January 19, 1809.
October 7, 1849.

Born in Boston, of parents who were members of the Federal Street Theatre company.

Ancestors.
> *Great-grandfather.* A descendant of one of Cromwell's officers.
> *Grandfather.* A patriot of the Revolution and of the War of 1812.
> *Father.* Educated for the legal profession; adopted the stage, and married in Boston a pleasing English actress, Elizabeth Arnold.

Early Left an Orphan.

Adopted by John Allan, a tobacco merchant of Richmond, Va.; christened Edgar Allan.
> Home of luxury and every advantage.
> At six years of age the boy could read, sing, and dance.
> He was especially fond of animals, flowers, and books.
> Passionately devoted to Mrs. Allan.

Taken to England with the Allans. 1815.
> Five years in the school at Stoke Newington, near London.
> Experiences recorded in his tale, *William Wilson,* in which both the boys represent Poe.

Private School in Richmond.

One Year at the University of Virginia.
> (Founded by Jefferson. For view, see article on Poe, in Duyckinck's *Cyclopædia of American Literature.*)
> Fair student. Contracted gambling-debts.
> Removed, and put into Mr. Allan's counting-room.

Leaves Richmond to seek his fortune.

    Intended to aid the Greeks (like Byron) in their war for independence (Halleck's poem, " Marco Bozzaris," had recently appeared.) Known to have appeared in St. Petersburg, and to have fallen into difficulty there over a passport.

Publishes, in Boston, *Tamerlane and other Poems.*

    " By a Bostonian." (Note, later, Poe's antipathy to Boston and its people.)

    Only two copies of this edition are now in existence, one in the British Museum.

Enlists as a Private in the U. S. Army, and attains the rank of sergeant-major.

Cadetship at West Point.

    At first he excelled in French and mathematics.

    Later he purposely neglected study and ignored the regulations. Consequent expulsion.

Banished from the Home of the Allans.

    " He forfeited his home-right more recklessly than Esau."

    (Compare " Uncle Contarine's " experience with Oliver Goldsmith.)

Journalistic Life in Baltimore, Richmond, Philadelphia, and New York.

    Remarkably conscientious as contributor and as editor.

    Poe did good pioneer work for American journalism.

    " A Pegasus in harness."

    Obtained two prizes of $100 each. *A Manuscript Found in a Bottle. The Gold Bug.*

    (His first prize story secured for him the friendship of John P. Kennedy.)

    Development as an unsparing critic.

Marries His Child-Cousin, Virginia Clemm, in whose family he had lived for several years.

    His wife was the ideal of a number of his poems. (See note under Poe's writings.)

"I can wish you no better wish than that you may derive from
your marriage as substantial happiness as I have derived
from mine." — POE, *in a letter to J. R. Lowell.*

Mutual and lifelong devotion between Poe and his mother-in-
law, Mrs. Clemm.

Gives anonymously to the Public "The Murders of Rue Morgue."

The idea of the story was stolen by two rival French periodicals;
a consequent lawsuit revealed the true author. From this
time on, Poe's works commanded an admiring public in
the French people.

In this, "Poe may be said to have originated the modern detec-
tive story."

Pleasure and Success in the Study of Cryptography.

The Gold Bug called forth a multitude of letters appealing to
Poe's skill in this direction, all of which he laboriously
worked out.

Publishes a Prediction of Dickens's Story, "Barnaby Rudge," after the appearance of the first few chapters.

"A feat that filled Dickens with amazement."

"Tales of the Grotesque and Arabesque." 1840.

Publication of "The Raven." 1845.

Immediate popularity.

"The Adventures of Arthur Gordon Pym" makes Poe known in England.

Removal to a Cottage at Fordham, N. Y.

Illness. Intemperance and the opium habit. Great poverty.
(A friend's public appeal resented by Poe.)

> "Here lived the soul enchanted
>   By melody of song;
> Here dwelt the spirit haunted
>   By a demoniac throng;
> Here sang the lips elated;
> Here grief and death were sated;
> Here loved, and here unmated
>   Was he, so frail, so strong."
>
> *Poe at Fordham.* By J. H. BONER.

See *Harper's Magazine* for September, 1872.

The Fordham cottage is now owned by the New York Shakespeare Society, and is always open to visitors.

Death of Mrs. Poe, from the rupture of a blood-vessel when singing.
(She had always been a semi-invalid.)

All but fatal illness on the part of her husband.

After the decease of his wife, Poe seemed to find death less
horrible than before.

Friendship with Sarah Helen Whitman, a poetess and a superior
woman, of Providence, R. I.

See poem " To Helen," which was inspired by the poet's first
sight of her when among the roses of her garden by
moonlight.

After Poe's death, Mrs. Whitman became his champion in a
work entitled, *Edgar Allan Poe and His Critics.*

Death from Delirium Tremens in a Baltimore hospital on the night
before his prospective marriage to Mrs. Shelton, a widow
in Richmond, whom he had loved in his youth.

His last words. " Lord, help my poor soul ! "

Grave unmarked until 1875, when the school-teachers of Baltimore
erected a monument over it.

Temperament and Character.

Sensitive, morbid, imaginative, intellectually proud, passionate; imperious, self-indulgent; judgments biased largely
by his feelings. An impressive talker. He lacked high
motives.

" His domestic life was well-nigh faultless."

" The defect in Poe was in character, — a defect which will
make itself felt in art as in life."

" In the place of moral feeling, he had the artistic conscience."
— BEERS.

" He created no character because he was deficient in the
human element."

" The heart somehow seems all squeezed out by the mind." —
LOWELL.

Appearance.

> Slight and erect figure; medium height; well proportioned; large forehead; dark and curling hair; handsome, intellectual face; winning smile; hands fair and delicate.

Manners.

> Fascinating and polished.

Voice.

> A low, rich baritone; responsive to his friends; highly effective in recitation, as he thus occasionally used it when lecturing.
> He inherited from his parents declamatory power.

His own Summary of His Life.

> " My life has been whim — impulse — passion — a longing for solitude — a scorn of all things present, in an earnest desire for the future."

Three " Problematic Characters " in American Literature.

> Poe. Hawthorne. Emerson.

APPELLATIONS.

A Poet among Poetasters.

A Subtle Artist in the Realm of the Weird and the Fantastic.

America's Unique Poet.

A Careful Artist rather than an Inspired Poet.

The Imp of the Perverse. (Borrowed from the title of one of his tales.)

The Forerunner of our Chief Experts in Form and Sound.

The Most Isolated and Exceptional of America's Poets and Pioneers.

A Dreamer.

A Genius Tethered to the Hackwork of the Press.

Our Stygian American.

The Hamlet of America.

Poetically the Most Gifted of America's Sons.

A Brilliant Exotic among America's Native Wild Flowers.

A Poet of Assonance and Alliteration, of Refrain and Repetend. ("The Jingle Man." — *Emerson.*)

A Disciple of Coleridge.

A Master in Tombland and Ghostland.

A Poet of Mysticism, Melancholy, Morbidness.

A Melodist.

The Poet of a Single Mood.

Our Greatest Southern Writer.

An Unfortunate Child of Genius.

A Lyrist Pure and Simple.

An Analyst of Great Power.

The First American Critic Who Made Criticism an Art.

NOTES ON HIS WRITINGS.

"His works are more remarkable for their ability than for
their contents."

His Favorite Themes.

Death.

Prose. — Ligeia. The Premature Burial. A Manuscript found
in a Bottle.

Poetry. — The City in the Sea. The Sleeper. Annabel Lee.
Lenore, and other poems.

Insanity.

Prose. — The Fall of the House of Usher.

Poetry. — The Haunted Palace. (A poem found in the story
above.)

Pestilence.

Prose. — The Masque of the Red Death. King Pest.

Conscience.

Prose. — William Wilson. The Tell-Tale Heart. The Imp of
the Perverse. The Black Cat.

Poetry. — The Raven.

Ratiocination.

Prose. — The Gold Bug. The Murders of the Rue Morgue. The
Mystery of Marie Roget. The Purloined Letter.

"Vagueness was the hue in which he painted." — WOODBERRY.

HIS POEMS.

Style.

Remarkable for its mechanism, art, and finish.

Number.

About forty.

Nature.

"Though his poems are all sombre in hue, — mere cries of despair, —
there is a haunting beauty in their melody which makes them
cling in the memory, even against the will." — F. L. PATTEE.

His Theory of Poetry.

"Aim not to convey an idea, but to make an impression."

"Poetry is the rhythmical creation of the Beautiful."

"Narration is unsuited to poetry, and is admissible only when given in the dramatic form."

"I hold that a long poem does not exist. . . . The phrase, 'a long poem,' is simply a flat contradiction in terms."

Well illustrated in Poe's own poetic writings.

"Poetry has been with me a passion, not a purpose."

Causes of his Artistic Effects.

Sonorousness. Refrains. Repetition of the same vowel sound. New expressions of the same thought. Simple measures. Brevity.

"The limitations of his poems serve as a foil for their peculiar merits."

NOTE. — To Poe the most poetic subject possible was the death of a beautiful woman. (Beauty and death appealed most powerfully to his mind.)

See his essays, "The Poetic Principle," "The Rationale of Verse," and "The Philosophy of Composition."

The Raven.

Published at first anonymously.

One of the most popular lyric poems in all literature.

"No great poem ever established itself so immediately, so widely, and so imperishably in men's minds."

"The Raven became in some sort a national bird, and the author the most notorious American of the hour." — WOODBERRY.

"As grotesque as the gargoyles seen by moonlight on the *façade* of the Notre Dame." — STEDMAN.

"Poe's raven is the very genius of the Night's Plutonian Shore."

Illustrated edition (Doré). Published by Harper.

"There comes Poe with his raven, like Barnaby Rudge.
Three-fifths of him genius, and two-fifths sheer fudge."

LOWELL.

See Ingram's *The Raven*, with Literary and Historical Commentary.

Its Structure. (Described in Poe's "Philosophy of Composition.")

The theme should be both beautiful and sad.

The length should be about one hundred lines.

A refrain, of a single word, should be prominent.

"Nevermore," the most suitable and effective.

A human being (a lover) and a bird of ill-omen.

Space circumscribed ("like a frame to a picture") — a chamber.

Chiaroscuro. The black raven and the "pallid bust of Pallas."

Development of the metaphorical, the raven becoming "emblematic of mournful and never-ending Remembrance."

"Its spirit is the spirit of Poe's life, — a vain struggle against the inevitable."

"It inspired Rossetti's poem, 'The Blessed Damozel.'"

Ulalume. Annabel Lee. To One in Paradise.

In memory of his wife.

The Bells.

A fine illustration of onomatopœia.

Compare it in this quality with Dryden's *Alexander's Feast.*

The original draft consisted of but eighteen lines.

The Haunted Palace.

"The parable of a ruined mind."

HIS TALES.

Characteristics.

They bear striking titles.

Their introductory sentences are usually apt, and command attention at once.

They are all short. (Their brevity conduces to the intensity of impression made.)

They contain but two or three characters (rarely those of flesh and blood), and only one action.

"In his tales, Poe meant not to tell a story, but to produce an effect."

Ligeia.

Suggested by a dream in which the eyes of the heroine produced the powerful effect described in the story.

Its theme is the conquest of death through the power of will.

The tale dearest to Poe.

"Upon this story he lavished all his poetic, inventive, and literary skill, and at last perfected an exquisitely conceived work, and made it, within its own laws, as faultless as humanity can fashion." — WOODBERRY.

The Gold Bug.

Poe's most successful tale.

Scene laid on Sullivan's Island, near Charleston, S.C., and the cipher made to concern Captain Kidd's buried treasure.

The Fall of the House of Usher.

Intensely dramatic.

One of the most powerful depictions of insanity to be found in literature.

William Wilson.

Autobiographic.

Suggestive of Stevenson's *Dr. Jekyll and Mr. Hyde.*

Narrative of A. Gordon Pym.

" In this tale all the horrors of the deep are brought in and huddled up together."

Eureka.

" A speculative analysis of the universe."

" A remarkably ingenious piece of fiction."

"A puzzle to the critics."

The Masque of the Red Death.

" A legend fearful in its beauty, and beautiful in its fear."

See A. E. Sterner's picture in *The Century,* August, 1894.

Poe's Best Tales.

The Gold Bug. The Fall of the House of Usher. Ligeia.

As Critic, Poe was bold, severe, not always honest; "prejudiced, yet often saying a true thing."

"The sketches in his *Literati* are waspish and unfair, though not without touches of magnanimity."

He denounced Longfellow as a " plagiarist," and called Hawthorne "peculiar, but not original."

In his lifetime he was more widely known in America as critic than poet or romancer.

In this department of writing he contrasts painfully with our master critic, J. R. Lowell.

Consult Richardson's *American Literature,* Vol. I., pp. 404–409.

Illustrated Edition of Poe's Complete Works. (Stedman and Woodberry.)

Ten volumes ($15). (Kimball, New York.)

MISCELLANEOUS NOTES.

"Though his writings are *un*moral, they cannot be called in any sense *im*moral. His poetry is as pure in its unearthliness as Bryant's in its austerity." — H. A. BEERS.

Poe's writings are more popular in France than in any other country.

"He idealized women, and secretly worshipped them."

"Women inspire most of his poems, but do not appear as characters in his romances."

When editor of *The Southern Literary Messenger,* he brought out in it Mitchell's *Reveries of a Bachelor.*

Poe had no sympathy with Emerson and the other Transcendentalists. He belonged to the New York school of writers, — Bryant, Cooper, Irving, Halleck, and Paulding, — rather than to the New England.

Poe was among the first to recognize Hawthorne's genius.

He wrote and re-wrote his sentences very carefully, but never learned to punctuate. (In the latter particular, he resembled Shelley, Byron, and Scott.) In his poems, "some of his most haunting melodies were the result of the most exacting effort."

His genius was closely akin to insanity.

He lacked humor because he held himself so aloof from his fellowmen. His few literary attempts in this direction were not successful; "to him the humorous was merely the incongruous."

In patriotism, also, Poe was apparently lacking; he did not live at all in touch with the national life.

A Dweller among Visions.

"Through all his disappointments Poe lived much in that dream-world which had always been so real to him, and much of his best work found there its inspiration. His exquisite story, *Ligeia,* came to him first in a dream. This world, so unreal to many, was to Poe as real as his actual life. . . . No other American has ever brought from the dream-world such beautiful creations, which charm and mystify at the same time, and force the most unimaginative reader to believe for the time in the existence of this elusive realm of faery." — MRS. WRIGHT.

Hawthorne and Poe.

Compared. Both are highly imaginative, keenly analytic, isolated in their lives, unique in their genius.

Contrasted. Hawthorne's imagination busied itself with the development of human character; Poe's with the supernatural and unearthly, with problems of the intellect. Hawthorne is spiritually analytic, Poe intellectually so. Hawthorne is morally fascinating, Poe sensuously so.

"Poe is a kind of Hawthorne and *delirium tremens.*" — LESLIE STEPHEN.

Poe His Own Worst Enemy.

"Poe was a worse enemy to himself than any one else could be. The fine enamel of his genius is all corroded by the deadly acid of his passions. The imperfections of his temperament have pierced his poetry and prose, shattered their structure, and blurred their beauty." — GEORGE PARSONS LATHROP.

His Character and His Genius.

"Poe was the victim of the disproportion between his character and his genius. His nature was passionate, but narrow and of little depth; his character was selfish, and undisciplined by his will. On the other hand, his intellect was of exceptional force and capacity, as is evidenced by his power of close and cogent reasoning, his retentive and ready memory, his quick (though not intuitive) insight into complicated problems, the scope — wide, though not profound — of his attainments, and the fickleness characteristic of an active mind unrestrained by personal weight. . . . Had Poe possessed a small, bright intellect, proportioned to his nature, he would have been a happy and successful man, but unknown. Had he possessed a nature commensurate with his intellect, he would have been one of the greatest of the human race." — HAWTHORNE AND LEMMON.

Tributes to His Genius.

Tennyson considered Poe America's greatest genius. (Poe called Tennyson "the greatest poet that ever lived.")

"Poe ranks next to Hawthorne in strength of personality." — T. W. HIGGINSON.

A memorial bust to Poe was placed, in 1885, in the Poets' Corner of the Metropolitan Museum of Art, New York, by the actors of that city. Edwin Booth made the dedicatory address, and William Winter's fine tributary poem was read. Its inscription reads, " Poe was great in his genius; unhappy in his life; wretched in his death; but in his fame he is immortal."

" Had you lived a generation later, honor, wealth, applause, success in Europe and at home, would all have been yours." — ANDREW LANG in his *Letters to Dead Authors.*

" Through many a night of want and woe
His frenzied spirit wandered wild,
Till kind disaster laid him low,
And love reclaimed its wayward child.

Through many a year his fame has grown —
Like midnight, vast; like starlight, sweet, —
Till now his genius fills a throne,
And homage makes his realm complete."

WILLIAM WINTER.

HENRY WADSWORTH LONGFELLOW.

POET, TRANSLATOR, ROMANCER, ESSAYIST.

EXTRACTS.

THEN pealed the bells more loud and deep,
"God is not dead nor does he sleep!
    The Wrong shall fail,
    The Right prevail,
With peace on earth, good will to men!"

CHRISTMAS BELLS.

AND the night shall be filled with music;
    And the cares that infest the day
Shall fold their tents like the Arabs,
    And as silently steal away.

THE DAY IS DONE.

LIKE Dian's kiss, unasked, unsought,
Love gives itself, but is not bought.

ENDYMION.

No one is so accursed by fate,
No one so utterly desolate,
    But some heart, though unknown,
    Responds unto his own.

IBID.

THE hooded clouds, like friars,
Tell their beads in drops of rain.

MIDNIGHT MASS.

187

In the elder days of Art,
  Builders wrought with greatest care
Each minute and unseen part,
  For the gods see everywhere.
                            THE BUILDERS.

TRUST no Future, howe'er pleasant!
  Let the dead Past bury its dead!
Act, — act in the living Present!
  Heart within, and God o'erhead!
                         THE PSALM OF LIFE.

THERE is no flock, however watched and tended,
  But one dead lamb is there!
There is no fireside, howsoe'er defended,
  But has one vacant chair.
                              RESIGNATION.

THERE is a Reaper, whose name is Death,
  And, with his sickle keen,
He reaps the bearded grain at a breath,
  And the flowers that grow between.
                  THE REAPER AND THE FLOWERS.

THE lovely stars, the forget-me-nots of the angels.
                              EVANGELINE.

WHEN she had passed, it seemed like the ceasing of exquisite music.
                                   IBID.

As unto the bow the cord is,
So unto the man is woman;
Though she bends him, she obeys him,
Though she draws him, yet she follows,
Useless each without the other.
                              HIAWATHA.

Thou, too, sail on, O Ship of State !
Sail on, O Union, strong and great !
Humanity with all its fears,
With all its hopes of future years,
Is hanging breathless on thy fate !
THE BUILDING OF THE SHIP.

O FEAR not in a world like this,
    And thou shalt know erelong, —
Know how sublime a thing it is
    To suffer and be strong.
THE LIGHT OF STARS.

FOR age is opportunity no less
Than youth itself, though in another dress ;
And, as the evening twilight fades away,
The sky is filled with stars, invisible by day.
MORITURI SALUTAMUS.

WHENE'ER a noble deed is wrought,
Whene'er is spoken a noble thought,
    Our hearts in glad surprise
    To higher levels rise.
SAINT FILOMENA.

O THOU sculptor, painter, poet !
    Take this lesson to thy heart :
That is best which lieth nearest ;
    Shape from that thy work of art.
GASPAR BECERRA.

HE did not feel the driver's whip,
    Nor the burning heat of day ;
For Death had illumined the Land of Sleep,

And his lifeless body lay
A worn-out fetter, that the soul
Had broken and thrown away.

The Slave's Dream.

Then stay at home, my heart, and rest;
The bird is safest in its nest;
O'er all that flutter their wings and fly
A hawk is hovering in the sky;
To stay at home is best.

Song.

Then fell upon the house a sudden gloom,
A shadow on those features fair and thin;
And softly from that hushed and darkened room
Two angels issued where but one went in.

The Two Angels.

THE STORY OF THE LANDLADY'S DAUGHTER.

The next stopping-place was the little tavern of the Star, an out-of-the-way corner in the town of Salzig. It stands on the banks of the Rhine; and directly in front of it, sheer from the water's edge, rise the mountains of Liebenstein and Sternenfels, each with its ruined castle. These are the Brothers of the old tradition, still gazing at each other, face to face; and beneath them, in the valley, stands a cloister, — meet emblem of that orphan child they both so passionately loved.

In a small flat-bottomed boat did the landlady's daughter row Flemming "over the Rhine-stream, rapid and roaring wide." She was a beautiful girl of sixteen, with black hair, and dark, lovely eyes, and a face that had a story to tell. How different faces are in this particular! Some of them speak not. They are books in which not a line is written, save perhaps a date. Others are great Family Bibles, with the Old and New Testament written in them. Others are Mother Goose and nursery tales; others, bad tragedies, or pickle-herring farces; and others, like that of the landlady's daughter at the Star, sweet love-anthologies, and songs of the affections. It was on that account that Flemming said to her, as they glided out into the swift stream, —

"My dear child! do you know the story of the Liebenstein?"

"The story of the Liebenstein," she answered, "I got by heart when I was a child."

And here her large, dark, passionate eyes looked into Flemming's, and he doubted not that she had learned the story far too soon and far too well. The story he longed to hear, as if it were unknown to him; for he knew that the girl, who had got it by heart when a child, would tell it as it should be told. So he begged her to repeat the story, which she was but too glad to do; for she loved and believed it, as if it had all been written in the Bible. But, before she began, she rested a moment on her oars, and, taking the crucifix which hung suspended from her neck, kissed it, and then let it sink down into her bosom, as if it were an anchor she was letting down into her heart. Meanwhile her moist, dark eyes were turned to heaven. Perhaps her soul was walking with the souls of Cunizza, and Rahab, and Mary Magdalen. Or perhaps she was thinking of that nun, of whom St. Gregory says in his *Dialogues*, that, having greedily eaten a lettuce in a garden without making the sign of the cross, she found herself soon after possessed with a devil.

The probability, however, is that she was looking at the ruined castles only, and not to heaven, for she soon began her story, and told Flemming how, a great, great many years ago, an old man lived in Liebenstein with his two sons; and how both young men loved the Lady Geraldine, an orphan, under their father's care; and how the elder brother went away in despair, and the younger was betrothed to the Lady Geraldine; and how they were as happy as Aschenpüttel and the Prince. And then the holy Saint Bernard came and carried away all the young men to war, just as Napoleon did afterwards; and the young lord went to the Holy Land, and the Lady Geraldine sat in her tower and wept, and waited for her lover's return, while the father built the Sternenfels for them to live in when they were married. And when it was finished, the old man died; and the elder brother came back and lived in the Liebenstein, and took care of the gentle lady. Erelong there came news from the Holy Land that the war was over; and the heart of the gentle lady beat with joy, till she heard that her faithless lover was coming back with a Greek wife, — the wicked man! — then she went to a convent and became a holy nun. So the young Lord of Sternenfels came home, and lived in his castle in great splendor with the Greek woman, who was a wicked woman, and did what she ought not to do. But the elder brother was angry for the wrong done the gentle lady, and challenged the Lord of Sternenfels to single combat. And, while they were fighting with their great swords in the valley of Bornhofen behind the castle, the convent bells began to ring, and the Lady Geraldine came forth with a train of nuns all dressed in white. and made the brothers friends again, and told them she was the bride of Heaven, and happier in her convent than she could have been in the Liebenstein or the Sternenfels. And when the brothers returned they found that the false Greek wife had gone away with another knight. So they lived together in peace, and were never married. And when they died —

"Lis'beth! Lis'beth!" cried a sharp voice from the shore, "Lis'beth! where are you taking the gentleman?"

This recalled the poor girl to her senses; and she saw how fast they were floating down-stream. For, in telling the story, she had forgotten everything else, and the swift current had swept them down to the tall walnut-trees of Kamp. They landed in front of the Capuchin Monastery. Lisbeth led the way through the little village, and, turning to the right, pointed up the romantic, lonely valley which leads to the Liebenstein, and even offered to go up. But Flemming patted her cheek, and shook his head. He went up the valley alone.

HYPERION.

MR. CHURCHILL'S DREAM.

In the night Mr. Churchill had a singular dream. He thought himself in school, where he was reading Latin to his pupils. Suddenly all the genitive cases of the first declension began to make faces at him, and to laugh immoderately; and, when he tried to lay hold of them, they jumped into the ablative, and the circumflex accent assumed the form of a great moustache. Then the little village schoolhouse was transformed into a vast and endless schoolhouse of the world, stretching forward, form after form, through all the generations of coming time; and on all the forms sat young men and old, reading and transcribing his Romance (which now in his dream was completed), and smiling and passing it onward from one to another, till at last the clock in the corner struck twelve and the weights ran down with a strange, angry whirr, and the school broke up; and the schoolmaster awoke to find this vision of fame only a dream, out of which his alarm-clock had aroused him at an untimely hour.

KAVANAGH.

REFERENCES.

W. S. Kennedy's *Life of Longfellow*. (A Longfellow bibliography is appended to this.)

F. H. Underwood's *Life of Longfellow*.

E. S. Robertson's *Longfellow*.

Samuel Longfellow's *Henry Wadsworth Longfellow* and *Final Memorials of Longfellow*.

George Lowell Austin's *Life of Longfellow*.

Stedman's *Poets of America*.

Richardson's *American Literature*. Vol. II., chap. iii.

Hazeltine's *Chats about Books*.

E. E. Hale's *Lights of Two Centuries*. (Dr. Hale was a pupil of Longfellow at Harvard.)

Hattie T. Griswold's *Home Life of Great Authors*.

G. W. Curtis's *Homes of American Authors*, and his *Literary and Social Essays*.

R. H. Stoddard's *Poets' Homes*.

Stedman-Hutchinson's *Library of American Literature*. Vol. VI.

Shepard's *Pen Pictures of Modern Authors*.

William Winter's *Old Shrines and Ivy*.

Andrew J. Lang's *Letters on Literature*.

Poe's *Literati*. (Caustic. Underwood answers Poe's adverse criticisms in his *Life of Longfellow*.)

Griswold's *Poets of America*.

Lowell's *Fable for Critics*.

Whipple's *Essays*.

Allibone's *Dictionary of Authors*.

Appletons' Cyclopædia of American Biography.

Text-books, cyclopædias, and histories of American Literature.

Chappel's *Portrait Gallery of Eminent Americans*. Vol. II. (Sketch by Duyckinck.)

Samuel Adams Drake's *Old Landmarks of Middlesex*.

Paige's *History of Cambridge*.

The Atlantic Monthly. December, 1863 (G. W. Curtis's review of some of Longfellow's poems). June, 1882 (Article by O. B. Frothingham). May, 1886 (Article by Samuel Longfellow).

Scribner's Magazine. September, 1878. November, 1878 (This contains Wyatt Eaton's portrait of Longfellow).

The Century Magazine. October, 1883 (E. C. Stedman's Essay). April, 1876 ("Glimpses of Longfellow in Social Life").

The North American Review. April, 1867 (Howells on Longfellow).

Harper's Magazine. January, 1876 ("Cambridge on the Charles." Illustrated). June, 1882 (Article by G. W. Curtis).

Riverside Edition of Longfellow's Works.

The Longfellow Number of *The Literary World.* Feb. 26, 1881.

Munsey's Magazine. June, 1893 (A short illustrated article on "Longfellow's Places and People").

Lippincott's Magazine. January, 1896 (R. H. Stoddard's Reminiscences of Longfellow).

Biographical sketch in the Cambridge Edition of Longfellow's Poetical Works.

NOTE. — For classifications of many of Longfellow's poems, consult Miss Hodgkins's *Guide to the Study of Nineteenth Century Authors,* and W. C. Gannett's *Studies in Longfellow* (Riverside Literature Series).

OUTLINE OF HIS LIFE.

February 27, 1807.
March 24, 1882.

Paternal Ancestry.

William Longfellow came to Newbury, Mass., in the middle of the seventeenth century.

The homestead is only about five miles from Whittier's at Haverhill. Visited but once by the poet, with Charles Sumner as companion; the two then drove to Amesbury, and made a call on Whittier.

One ancestor lost his life in the expedition of Sir William Phips against Quebec.

Father.

A Harvard man, classmate of Dr. Channing and Judge Hoar.

Lawyer. Member of Congress.

"A cordial, courteous, high-spirited gentleman of the old school."

Mother.

Zilpah Wadsworth, descendant of John Alden.

(Bryant also could claim the same Puritan ancestor.)

A beautiful woman; fond of music, poetry, nature, and social life.

Her father, General Wadsworth, was a distinguished officer in the Revolutionary War.

Birth at Portland, Me.; corner of Fore and Hancock Streets.

(Portland was also the birthplace of the poet N. P. Willis.)

House used now as a tenement-house; for view, see Kennedy's *Longfellow*; and *Harper's Magazine*, May, 1894, p. 820.

Second Son in a family of eight children.

Named for his maternal uncle, a lieutenant in the American navy, who, when nineteen years of age, perished gallantly at Tripoli, preferring death to slavery.

Home of His Youth.

Congress Street, Portland.

The mother's ancestral home.

Presented by the poet's sister to the Maine Historical Society on condition that two rooms be forever kept as Longfellow Memorial Rooms.   Many relics have been gathered here.

For view, see Samuel Longfellow's *Life of the Poet*, and *Harper's Magazine* for May, 1894.

. For a description of the Portland of Longfellow's early days, consult Kennedy, pp. 19–24.

A happy childhood.

Read his poem, " My Lost Youth."

First Book that interested Him.

Irving's *Sketch-Book*.

Education.

Bowdoin College.   Class of 1825.   (His father was a trustee of Bowdoin.)

Classmate of Nathaniel Hawthorne.   (See note under Hawthorne's classmates.)

A close student.   Ranked second in a class of thirty-seven.
Usually studied until midnight, and rose at six o'clock.

Popular with both professors and students.

His translation, in the sophomore year, of one of Horace's odes secured later a professor's chair for him in his Alma Mater.

Sent poems, from time to time, to *The Literary Gazette*, Boston, for which he received a dollar each.

Subject of his Commencement oration, "Our Native Writers."

Professor Packard's remembrance of him.   " An attractive youth, with auburn locks, clear, fresh, blooming complexion, and, as might be expected, of well-bred manners and bearing."

(A view of Bowdoin College is shown in Duyckinck, II., p. 193. See, also, note under Hawthorne's education.)

Studied Law a short time in his father's office.

Appointment at Bowdoin (the first) Professor of Modern Languages, a position largely created for him.   (At the age of nineteen.)

Preliminary Travel of four years in France, Spain, Italy, and Germany.   (A month's voyage-out in a packet-ship.)

· His *Outre-Mer*, a literary product.

Taught four modern languages, and prepared his own text-books in French, Spanish, and Italian.

"He wrote his text-books at an age when most poets go a-gypsy-ing."

Five years of teaching here. Salary, a thousand dollars.

Becomes a Contributor to The North American Review.

Marriage to Mary Storer Potter, the "Being Beauteous." 1831.

Keeps a Scrap-book of notices of his writings, calling it "Puffs and Counter-blasts."

Called to Harvard, as Smith Professor of Modern Languages and Belles-lettres. (Succeeds George Ticknor, the historian of Spanish literature, and is followed later by James Russell Lowell.)

Second Residence Abroad, for study of the Scandinavian tongues and further acquaintance with Germany.

Visits Carlyle, through Emerson's letter of introduction.

Death of Wife, at Rotterdam. 1835.

See poem, "Footsteps of Angels" (written many years afterward), and allusions in the first part of *Outre-Mer.*

Adopts his Life Motto. (Found under Miscellaneous Notes.)

("An early sorrow is often the truest benediction of the poet.") — WASHINGTON IRVING.

Continues his journey to the region of the Rhine.

Meets Bryant at Heidelberg, whose influence proves both soothing and strengthening.

Becomes acquainted, at Interlachen, with Miss Frances Appleton (travelling with her family), sister of Thomas Gold Appleton, the Boston *littérateur,* who inspires the writing of his romance, *Hyperion.* In this, Miss Appleton appears as Mary Ashburton.

Return to America. 1837.

Publishes "Hyperion" and "Voices of the Night." 1839.

Written in "Washington's south-east chamber" of the famous Craigie House.

"The public plighted its faith to the new poet, and no meddling critics have since been able to break the alliance."

Life in Cambridge, at the Craigie House, Brattle Street.

Arduous College Work. Seventy lectures a year.

"He was scrupulously faithful to his duties, and even went through the exhausting process of marking French exercises with exemplary patience."

Always courteous to his pupils. "Let's hear Longfellow, for he always treats us as gentlemen!" (Exclaimed at a time of uprising among the students.)

Member of a Mutual Admiration Society. "The Five of Clubs."

Charles Sumner, Cornelius C. Felton, George S. Hillard, Henry Cleveland, and the poet Longfellow.

All gifted men, and possessed of literary tastes.

Friendship with Sumner.

The two were distantly connected by marriage.

Sumner was a lecturer in the Harvard Law School when Longfellow came to Cambridge.

When near Boston, Sumner spent every Sabbath with the poet.

Longfellow followed enthusiastically all of the orator's public speeches.

Wrote two poems on Sumner.

His poems on slavery were largely due to Sumner's urgency that he should express himself on the subject.

Occupies the professor's chair seventeen years, and then leads a retired life.

Read Lowell's "Cambridge Thirty Years Ago:" *Fireside Travels.*

(For an illustrated historical sketch of Harvard's college buildings and Cambridge as a university town, consult *Harper's Magazine* for January, 1876.)

Marriage to Frances Appleton, and Purchase of the Craigie House. 1843.

(See note on the House under Miscellaneous Notes.)

"His home, if deeply saddened in recent years, was always the House Beautiful."

Children. Five.

Charles Appleton. Severely wounded in the Civil War.

Ernest Wadsworth. Artist.

> Has illustrated, with fifty-one designs, a collection of twenty of his father's poems.

Three daughters. The "blue-eyed banditti" of his "Children's Hour."

Alice.

> Occupies the Craigie House, and invites to it annually a number of working-girls from Boston.

> One of the three committee women of Cambridge.

Annie *Allegra*, Mrs. Thorpe.

> Mr. Thorpe's sister married the violinist, Ole Bull, who appears as the musician in the poet's *Tales of a Wayside Inn*.

Edith, Mrs. Richard H. Dana, Jr.

> Mr. Dana is a grandson of the poet Dana.

Thomas Buchanan Read's portrait of the trio hangs in the dining-room of the Longfellow house.

Contributes Frequent Poems to The Atlantic Monthly.

Tragic Death by Fire of Mrs. Longfellow. July 9, 1861.

Buried on the anniversary of her wedding-day.

The poet was too severely injured in trying to subdue the flames to attend the funeral.

No direct mention of his loss appeared in his later poetry, but this bears a sadder tone.

His translation of Dante became the poet's solace. (Recall Bryant's turning to the translation of *The Iliad* upon the death of his wife.)

Remark to a friend in after years. " I was too happy, I might fancy the gods envied me — if I could fancy heathen gods."

See posthumous poem, " In the long, sleepless watches of the night " (The Cross of Snow).

Trip to England. His fourth journey to Europe.

LL.D. from Cambridge. D.C.L. from Oxford.

Elected a Member of the Historical and Geographical Society of Brazil ; of the Scientific Academy of St. Petersburg ; of the Royal Academy of Spain ; of the Massachusetts Historical Society ; and of the Mexican Academy of Arts and Sciences.

Delivers " Morituri Salutamus."   (See note under Writings.)

Celebration of Seventy-fifth Birthday throughout the schools of
the country.

Read Whittier's poem, "The Poet and the Children."

Death in Cambridge, and Burial at Mt. Auburn.

A palm branch and a passion-flower were laid upon the casket.

At the service, verses from "Hiawatha" were read, beginning

"He is dead, the sweet musician!"

Fields, Holmes, Emerson, Lowell, and Whittier were among the
mourners present.

Public Memorials to Longfellow.

A monument at Portland, 1888.

Bust in Westminster Abbey, in the Poets' Corner.

(The first American author thus distinguished.)

See view in *Appletons' Cyclopædia of American Biography,*
and in *Final Memorials of Longfellow,* p. 408.

The Longfellow Park in Cambridge.

Land opposite the Craigie House, secured by the Longfellow
Memorial Association.

Commands the poet's favorite view of the Charles.

No statue has yet been erected here (1895).   •

Character.

Introspective, exact, methodical, symmetrical, impressionable,
buoyant; liberal in his judgments; "full of the modesty
that generally characterizes great genius;" had a pronounced taste for linguistic study and for travel.

Generous to fellow-poets. — "Where others were cold, or satirical, or contemptuous, he was kind and cordial, and full of
cheer."

Fond of children, and especially kind to them.

"Liked little girls best," he told Lowell, adding —

"What are little girls made of?
Sugar and spice
And all things nice, —
That's what little girls are made of."

" Pure, kindly, and courteous, simple yet scholarly, he was never
otherwise than a gentleman." — WHITTIER.

Appearance, Voice, and Manner.

" His natural dignity and grace, and the beautiful refinement of
countenance, together with his perfect taste in dress, and
the exquisite simplicity of his manners, made him the
absolute ideal of what a poet should be. His voice, too,
was soft, sweet, and musical; and, like his face, it had the
innate charm of tranquillity. His eyes were bluish-gray,
very bright and brave, changeable under the influence of
emotion (as afterward I saw), but mostly calm, grave, at-
tentive, and gentle. The habitual expression of his face
was not that of sadness ; and yet it was pensive. He had
conquered his own sorrows thus far, but ' the sorrows
of others threw their shadows over him.' " — WILLIAM
WINTER.

" His face was the mirror of his harmonious and lovely mind."

" I do not think I ever saw a finer human face." — CHARLES
KINGSLEY.

" The charm of a well-bred manner asserts itself over every
other personal attribute."

" His gentle tact and exquisite courtesy remind one of that fine
compliment paid to Villemand, — which is a fine definition
of politeness, — ' when he spoke to a lady one would think
he had offered her a bouquet.' "

Autobiographic Glimpses.

Outre-Mer. Hyperion.

The Village Blacksmith. The Bridge. To the River Charles.
Footsteps of Angels. In the Long, Sleepless Watches of
the Night. The Two Angels. (See note on this poem
under the death of Maria White Lowell.) The Children's
Hour. Morituri Salutamus. From My Arm-chair. Old
St. David's at Radnor. Kéramos. The Rope-walk. (The
last two poems were evoked by the pottery and the rope-
walk in Portland, Me., familiar to the poet's boyhood.)
L'Envoi (The Poet and His Songs). My Books. Weariness.

APPELLATIONS.

A Poet of the Affections.
Our New World Academic Singer.
The American Poet Laureate.
The Most Scholarly of American Poets.
The Clerkly Singer.
A Craftsman of Unerring Taste.
Our Pilgrim Poet.
The Poet of the Sea.
The St. John of our American Apostles of Song.
The Least National of our Poets.
A Universal Poet.
A Painstaking Literary Artist.
An Artist of the Beautiful.
Our Best Beloved Poet.
Swan of the Charles.
Our American Minnesinger.
The Children's Poet.
A Good Borrower.
A Poet of Grace and Sentiment.
A Born Romanticist.
A Metrical Expert.
A very Benvenuto of Grace and Skill.
A Poet of the Niche and Alcove.
The Catholic Singer of Sympathy and of Art.
Our Chief Representative of Continental Culture.
An Impartial Judge of Himself, and of his Writings.
Our Earliest Maker of Exquisite Verse.
The Poet of Peace and Repose.
A Teller of Bewitching Tales.
A Swallow that has built under the Roof of Legend.
Fortune's Favorite.

The Man of the Million.
The Christian Gentleman.
Leader of the American Choir.
Our Benignant Poet.
The Most Popular of University Poets.
A Lovable Man and Artist.
A Devotee to One Calling.
The Laureate of the Common Human Heart.

NOTES ON HIS WRITINGS.

PROSE.

Travel. *Outre-Mer.*

Fiction. *Hyperion* and *Kavanagh.*

Criticism. *Poets and Poetry of Europe.*

Essays. *Driftwood.* (Collected from his contributions to *The North American Review;* includes his favorable review of Hawthorne's first book.)

Outre-Mer.

"A young poet's sketch-book."

Written before European travel was generally known to Americans.

Copyright sold to Harper Brothers for five hundred dollars.

In the first twenty years but seventy-five hundred copies were sold.

"All the world was Arcady,—a land of beauty and romance."— STEDMAN.

"The work is picturesque, antiquarian; golden and mellow as the shield of its Lion d'Or, full of quiet *causerie* about mediæval legends, *trouvères,* and old chansons."— KENNEDY.

Hyperion ; a Romance.

"The work of an idyllist."   "An agreeable love-tale."

"The companion of all romantic pilgrims to the Rhine."

Superior to its successor, *Kavanagh,* in power and in style.

Partly written in the picturesque ruined tower of Unspunnen, in the beautiful valley of the Lauterbrunnen.

Somewhat autobiographical in nature. (Paul Flemming, "what I thought I might have been.")

Contains appreciative criticisms of German authors, translations from gems of German literature, descriptions of nature.

"*Hyperion* did great service in its day, and certainly shared with Carlyle's essays the merit of directing the attention of English-speaking people to the wealth of German literature."

"No traveller can fully enjoy Quebec without Howells's *Wedding Journey,* or Heidelberg without *Hyperion.*"

Read Curtis's description of the romance in *Literary and Social Essays*, pp. 190, 191.

Key-note of the Book. — "The setting of a great hope is like the setting of the sun. . . . Then stars arise, and the night is holy."

Kavanagh, a Tale.

Written in Pittsfield, the home of Mrs. Longfellow's mother.

The poet's "brief and nearest approach to a novel."

"An exact *daguerreotype* of New England life."

Its Lesson. Purpose should crystallize into action.

"We are so charmed with elegance in an American book that we could forgive more vices than are possible to you." — EMERSON, to the author (in 1849).

POETRY.

Voices of the Night.

The volume that established his name as a poet.

When Longfellow was once driving in England, a hod-carrier came up to the carriage, and asked if he might take the hand of the man who had written *Voices of the Night*.

Its most popular poem is —

The Psalm of Life.

"What the heart of the young man said to the Psalmist."

Written three years after the death of the poet's first wife.

Never paid for by the magazine that published it.

Contrast with the fact that, in later years, an English firm paid £1,000 for the privilege of publishing the advance proofs of one of Longfellow's works, "New England Tragedies."

This poem, during the siege of Paris, saved a Frenchman from committing suicide.

Translated into many languages, including Chinese and Marathi. The Chinese translator had a fan made with his translation on it, and sent it to Longfellow. An interesting retranslation of this version into English is given in Kennedy's *Life*, p. 64.

"The very heart-beat of the American conscience." — G. W. CURTIS.

Compare this poem with Whittier's " My Psalm."

Evangeline.   1847.

"The flower of American idyls."

Longfellow's representative poem, and his favorite among his own writings.

Persons have been known to study the English language in order to be able to read this poem in the original.

Story of the expulsion of the Acadians from Nova Scotia by order
of George III., 1755. (An historical introduction is prefixed to
Houghton & Mifflin's annotated version of the idyl.)

Material. Furnished by Hawthorne and his friend, Rev. H. L.
Conolly. (Consult Fields's *Yesterdays with Authors*, pp. 64, 65;
Shepard's *Pen Pictures*, pp. 129–132; and Kennedy's *Longfellow*,
pp. 73, 74.) Whittier intended to write a poem on this theme,
until he learned that Hawthorne and Longfellow were both
considering it.

Hawthorne took great pleasure in the success of the poem.

Its Metre. Rhymeless dactylic hexameter. (Consult the Analysis
of Versification.)

"The velvety verse that Evangeline trod." — HOLMES.

A bold innovation in English versification.

Employed afterward by Arthur Hugh Clough, Matthew Arnold,
Charles Kingsley, and William D. Howells.

Lowell, Higginson, and Stoddard approve its use in English
poetry.

"It is easy for you to read *Evangeline* because it was so hard
for me to write it."

On its fitness, consult Stedman's *Poets of America*, pp. 195–200;
Richardson, II., pp. 73–78, Parsons's *English Versification*,
chap. xii., and Lowell's lines in the *Fable.*

Other Longfellow poems in this measure.

The Courtship of Miles Standish. Elizabeth, the Theologian's Tale. To the Driving Cloud. The Children of
the Lord's Supper.

Comments on the Poem.

'That rare, tender, virgin-like pastoral, *Evangeline.*
That's not ancient nor modern, its place is apart,
Where time has no sway, in the realm of pure Art;
Tis a shrine of retreat from Earth's hubbub and strife,
As quiet and chaste as the author's own life."

                                                    LOWELL.

"I read it as I should have listened to some exquisite sym-
phony." — HOLMES.

"The characters and the scenes are of the Western world; but
the love and pathos, like all great works of the sort, belong
to universal humanity." — RICHARDSON.

Longfellow was never in Nova Scotia. (Scott had never seen
Melrose by moonlight when he wrote his well-known lines.)

Whittier's essay on Evangeline is found in Vol. II. of his prose works.

Compare the poem in matter and in form with Goethe's *Hermann and Dorothea.*

Thomas Faed's picture of Evangeline. *Munsey's Magazine*, June, 1893.

Boughton's Evangeline. Cassell's *Some Modern Artists and their Works.*

(Emerson's first collection of poems appeared the same year as "Evangeline.")

Hiawatha; an Indian Edda. 1855.

America's national epic poem. (Compare the choice of theme with Tennyson's selection of the Arthur legends.)

" A Civilizer and Savior myth."

"Like Arthur, Hiawatha seeks to redeem his kingdom from savagery, and to teach the blessing of peace."

First successful treatment of the Indian legends.

(Goldsmith, Campbell, and Southey had attempted Indian poems.)

"Destined to give to coming generations their idea of the race of red men."

Ten thousand copies sold within four weeks of publication.

Won immediate European fame.

Translated into nearly all of the modern languages and into Latin.

"The story of the reception of the poem is one of the curiosities of American literature."

"To be ranked with such productions as the Anglo-Saxon epic of Beowulf and the old French song of Roland."

"These cantos remind us that poetry is the natural speech of primitive races."

"The very names are jewels which the most fastidious muse might be proud to wear." — HOLMES.

"The poet's most genuine addition to our native literature."

Longfellow never explored the Hiawatha region (southern shore of Lake Superior).

Its Metre. Unrhymed trochaic tetrameter. (Consult the Analysis of Versification.)

Unusual. Adapted to the theme.

The same as that used in *Kalevala*, the national epic of the Finns.

"A forest-poem; it is fragrant with the woods, fresh with the sky and waters of the breezy north."

"In *Hiawatha* the reader sees not only the representative of a westward-moving people, but also an allegorical picture of one's own progress onward." — RICHARDSON.

Sources of the Poem. Schoolcraft's *Hiawatha Legends.*

Selections. The Peace-pipe, I.   Hiawatha's Childhood, III.   His Sailing, VII.   His Wooing, X.   His Departure, XXII.

See *The North American Review* for January, 1856 (Article by E. E. Hale).

Other Indian Poems.

The Burial of the Minnesink.   To the Driving Cloud.

The Revenge of Rain-in-the-Face.

The attack upon General Custer and his party.

This Sioux chief, Rain-in-the-Face, a fine specimen of the red man, was exhibited in Chicago at the World's Columbian Exposition, 1893.

Compare with Whittier's Indian poems.

The Courtship of Miles Standish.   1858.

"The Plymouth Idyl."

Twenty-five thousand copies sold within a month of publication.

Bits of "frolicsome humor" throughout the poem.

George Boughton's picture, Puritans going to Church, is shown in *Munsey's Magazine*, June, 1893; his Priscilla, in *The New England Magazine*, September, 1889; his Rose Standish, in Cassell's *Some Modern Artists.*

"The bucolic wedding-scene at the close is a fine subject for the pastoral canvas."

Illustrated articles on the Pilgrims, Scrooby, Leyden, Plymouth, may be found in *The New England Magazine* for September, 1893.

Excelsior.   ("Higher.")

Written at one sitting, on the back of a letter from Charles Sumner.
The manuscript is kept in the Art Room of Harvard's Library.

Holmes's preference among Longfellow's poems.

Has been parodied more, probably, than any other poem in the language.

Longfellow's Explanation of the Poem.

"My intention was to display in a series of pictures the life of a man of genius. . . . He passes through the Alpine village, — through the rough, cold paths of the world, — where

the peasants cannot understand him, and where his watch-
word is 'an unknown tongue.' He disregards the happiness
of domestic peace, and sees the glaciers, — his fate, — before
him. . . . The monks of St. Bernard are the representa-
tives of religious forms and ceremonies, and with their oft-
repeated prayer mingles the sound of his voice, telling them
that there is something higher than forms or ceremonies.
Filled with these aspirations, he perishes without having
reached the perfection he longed for; and the voice heard
in the air is the promise of immortality and progress ever
upward."

The Skeleton in Armor.

Skeleton exhumed at Fall River, Mass.; by poetic license Longfellow connects it with the famous Round Tower at Newport.
(The skeleton was destroyed soon after its discovery, before it
was pronounced Scandinavian or Indian.)

"Full of the true Viking dash and fire."

The Wreck of the Hesperus.

Norman's Woe, a reef off the coast of Gloucester, Mass.

Origin of the Poem. — An issue of *The Boston Advertiser* in December, 1839, reported a wrecked vessel off this reef with a woman's
form lashed to the mast. About a fortnight later, after a
violent storm, Longfellow rose in the middle of the night, and
wrote the poem in less than an hour.

This ballad has been set to music.

The writer received twenty-five dollars for it.

The Old Clock on the Stairs.

The original clock is now in the home of Mr. Thomas Appleton, No.
10 Commonwealth Avenue, Boston.

Tales of a Wayside Inn.

Longfellow's longest work.

The poems appeared from time to time during a period of ten years.

Three Series. 1862. 1872. 1873.

Introduction. "A splendid piece of painting." — WHITTIER.

Plan. Similar to that of Boccaccio's *Decameron*, and Chaucer's
Canterbury Tales. "A series of short poems, mostly gathered
from older literatures, translated into Longfellow's varying and
crystalline verse, and linked together by a running commentary
of the poet's own." — STEDMAN.

√   One only, "The Birds of Killingworth," is wholly original with the
writer.

Narrators. Seven. "A cluster like the Pleiades."

The Poet. T. W. Parsons, translator of Dante.

The Sicilian. Luigi Monti, Dr. Parsons's brother-in-law.

The Musician. Ole Bull.

The Student. Dr. Henry Wales, a friend of Harvard College.

The Theologian. Professor Daniel Treadwell of Harvard.

The Spanish Jew. Israel Edrehi, a Boston dealer in Eastern
goods.

The Landlord. Squire Lyman Howe.

For an illustrated article on "The Landlord," consult *The New
England Magazine* for May, 1894.

Parsons, Monti, and Treadwell used to pass the summer season
together at the Sudbury Inn. Dr. Parsons has written verses
on "The Old House at Sudbury."

King Robert of Sicily.

Translated into Portuguese by the Emperor of Brazil, Dom
Pedro II., and a manuscript copy sent by the translator to
the poet.

Four Colonial Tales.

In the series above.

√   *Paul Revere's Ride.*

"The North Church." Christ Church, Salem Street, Boston.
A brick church, still standing ; original tower was blown
down in 1804, but the new one reproduced it. (Its chime of
eight bells, brought from England, is the oldest in America.)

Compare with other rides famous in literature.

Browning's "How they Brought the Good News from
Ghent to Aix," Cowper's "John Gilpin," Read's "Sher-
idan's Ride," Adelaide Procter's "Legend of Bregenz,"
Whittier's "Skipper Ireson's Ride."

Elizabeth.

Compare the heroine with Longfellow's other Puritan maiden,
Priscilla.

Furnished the title for Beatrice Harraden's popular story, *Ships
that Pass in the Night.* Canto iv., first verse.

Lady Wentworth.

Place the thought of the poem in juxtaposition with that of
Whittier's "Maud Muller" and of his "Mabel Martin."

The Rhyme of Sir Christopher.

NOTE. — *The Inn.* The Red Horse Inn at Sudbury, Mass., twenty-three miles from Boston, on the old road to Worcester. More than two hundred years old. Built by the Howe family, — "The Howe Tavern."

The room once occupied by Major Molineux is shown.

For view, see frontispiece of *The New England Magazine* for November, 1887 ; Lee and Shepard's *Our Colonial Homes ;* Kennedy's *Life*, p. 93.

Described in Wolfe's *Literary Shrines.*

(Another famous Red Horse Inn. At Stratford, England.)

Morituri Salutamis.

"The title a stroke of genius."

Written for the jubilee reunion of Bowdoin's Class of 1825. Eleven members present, and one instructor, Professor Packard, alluded to in the poem.

"One of the grandest hymns to age ever written."

"Never did poet more nobly say *ave atque vale* than did Longfellow in this poem." — RICHARDSON.

"How good Longfellow's poem is ! A little sad, but full of 'sweetness and light.' " — WHITTIER.

Contains a number of classic allusions, and an entire tale from the *Gesta Romanorum.*

Metre. Rhymed iambic pentameter.

Recall Gérôme's painting of the Roman Arena.

Sandalphon.

The author received for this poem a year's subscription to the paper that published it.

My Lost Youth.

"The utterance of a man who in middle age looked into his own heart to write, and found it warm and true."

A *fac-simile* of this poem, with illustrations, is printed in *The New England Magazine* for July, 1890.

The Sermon of St. Francis.

Henry Stacy Marks's picture, St. Francis Preaching to the Birds, is seen in Cassell's *Some Modern Artists.*

"Panoramic" Poems.

The Building of the Ship.

Note its literal and its symbolic interpretation.

(Compare with Schiller's "Song of the Bell" and his "Walk.")

Observe the expressiveness of the varying length of verse throughout the poem.

In 1850 Mrs. Kemble gave in Boston a memorable public reading of it.

"This poem was never read during the struggle of the Civil War
without raising the audience to a passion of enthusiasm."

President Lincoln was deeply touched upon hearing it read for
the first time, and remarked, "It is a wonderful gift to be
able to stir men like that."

The Hanging of the Crane. A domestic idyl.

Called forth by a visit of the poet to Thomas B. Aldrich and
his newly married wife in their home on Pinckney Street,
Boston.

Once presented in tableaux on the stage of the Fifth Avenue
Theatre, New York.

The New York Ledger paid four thousand dollars for the poem,
right to its publication in book-form being exclusive of this.

Kéramos. ("Potter's clay.")

Translated into his native language by a member of the Japa-
nese legation.

An annotated version of it is given in Swinton's *Studies in English Literature.*

Rain in Summer.

The Rope-Walk.

Dramatic Poems.

The Spanish Student.

A readable three-act play of "cheery grace."

The popular song, "Stars of the Summer Night," occurs in this.

Poe criticised the work with great hostility of spirit.

Christus. A Trilogy.

The poet worked more than twenty years on this production.

A disappointment to the writer.

Three Parts. Connected by two Interludes and a Finale.

    a. *The Divine Tragedy.* (1871.)

    b. *The Golden Legend.* (1851.) The best of the poet's
dramas.

"A bundle of poems tied by a silken string, carrying us
into the very heart of the Middle Ages."

A story of the power of love through self-sacrifice. Its
characters, — a peasant, a prince, and Lucifer.
(Compare with Goethe's *Faust.*)

Scene laid in Strasburg. "The Bells of Strasburg Cathedral" has been set to music by Franz Liszt.

The first draught of the "Legend" was made in four
weeks ; but six months were spent in "correcting
it and cutting it down."

"Longfellow, in 'The Golden Legend,' has entered
more closely into the temper of the monk, for good
and for evil, than ever yet theological writer or historian, though they may have given their life's labor
to the analysis." — RUSKIN.

Blackwood's Magazine, February, 1852. *Fraser's Magazine*, April, 1853.

  c. *New England Tragedies.*

   I. "John Endicott." A story of Quaker persecution.
   II. "Giles Corey of the Salem Farms." A story of
witchcraft.

A fourth part was planned by the poet, a painting of the life of
the Moravian Sisters at Bethlehem, Pa.

A brief description of the trilogy is given in Richardson, II., pp.
87–89.

Judas Maccabæus.

The Masque of Pandora.

Its story is that of Hawthorne's "Paradise of Children," in the
Wonder Book.

Acted at one time on the Boston stage, but not a success.

(Look up the nature of Masques, and their position in the history
of the English Drama.)

Michael Angelo. Posthumous.

A finely illustrated edition of this poem has been published.

Old St. David's at Radnor.

Scene laid near Philadelphia.

Mad Anthony Wayne is buried in the churchyard.

The poet's visit to the spot at the time of the Philadelphia Centennial suggested the writing of the poem.

In the Harbor.

A posthumous volume of poems.

The Name. Selected by the poet before his death, appropriately
following that of the preceding volume, *Ultima Thule.*

From My Arm-Chair.

A poem of acknowledgment to the school-children of Cambridge.

After the chair, made from the "spreading chestnut-tree," had
been placed in his home, the poet commanded that no child who
wished to see it should be denied the pleasure.

A woodcut of this chair with a history is shown in Kennedy's *Life of Longfellow*, p. 119.

✓ Sonnets.

Longfellow's sonnets are among the best in modern poetry.

"Uniformly sound and good; and some of them are perfect in degree, though inferior in spiritual exaltation to the great sonnets of Wordsworth, Milton, and Shakespeare."

Selected Sonnets. The Three Silences of Molinos (to Whittier). In the Churchyard at Tarrytown (on Irving). Wapentake (to Tennyson). Woodstock Park. Holidays. President Garfield. Dante (note the feminine endings in some of the verses). Venice. The Evening Star. The Sound of the Sea, and others.

NOTE.—A *fac-simile* of Wapentake ("Touch-Arms") and one of Tennyson's note of response to the poem, may be seen in *The New England Magazine* for December, 1892.

A noble series is found in his translation of Dante.

Structure of a Sonnet. Consult the Analysis of Versification.

Some Lyrics known to Old and Young.

The Rainy Day. The Arrow and the Song. The Day is Done. Maidenhood. The Bridge. The Old Clock on the Stairs. Something Left Undone. A Psalm of Life.

Poems of Friendship.

The Two Angels. Hymn for My Brother's Ordination (his biographer brother, Samuel). Bayard Taylor (at his death). Preludes and Interludes to Tales of a Wayside Inn. Hawthorne (on his burial). Charles Sumner (in memoriam). The Three Silences of Molinos. The Burial of the Poet (Richard Henry Dana). From My Arm-Chair (to the school-children of Cambridge). Auf Wiedersehen (in memory of James T. Fields). Three Friends of Mine (Felton, Agassiz, Sumner). Wapentake. The Fiftieth Birthday of Agassiz. Noël (to Agassiz). The Open Window. The Fire of Driftwood. The Herons of Elmwood (in Lowell's absence from America).

Poems of the Sea.

The Wreck of the Hesperus. Seaweed. The Secret of the Sea. The Building of the Ship. Sir Humphrey Gilbert. The Lighthouse. The Fire of Driftwood. The Sailing of the Mayflower. The Phantom Ship (compare its thought with the legend of the "Flying Dutchman"). My Lost Youth. The Brook and the

Wave. The Bells of Lynn. The Sound of the Sea. A Summer Day by the Sea. The Tides. The Tide Rises, The Tide Falls. A Ballad of the French Fleet. The City and the Sea.

Verses born of European Travel.

The Belfry of Bruges. Nuremberg. Cadenabbia. Monte Cassino. Amalfi. The Old Bridge at Florence. Castles in Spain. Song. Venice. Boston (St. Botolph's Town). St. John's, Cambridge. Woodstock Park. To the River Rhone.

Translations.

The Children of the Lord's Supper. From the Swedish.

Poems from many German writers.

Verses from many different languages.

The Divine Comedy.

A masterpiece of translation.

The Translator's Theory. " A literal and lineal rendering."

" He discarded the rhymes altogether, while striving to convey the rhythm and deeper music of the sublime original." — STEDMAN.

Its strict fidelity to the original, the careful scholarship which had literally scrutinized every word, the frequent combination of a life-giving spirit with the exact letter of utterance, gave this version a place which it is not likely to lose, at the head, on the whole, of English translation of Dante." — RICHARDSON.

Consult *The North American Review*, July, 1867 (Article by C. E. Norton).

" None of his translations equal his original work."

Longfellow introduced the legends of Old World places and literature into America.

Works Edited by Longfellow.

Poems of Places. Thirty-one volumes, arranged according to countries.

The Poets and Poetry of Europe. A large anthology.

Selections from three hundred and sixty authors, including translations from ten different languages.

The introductions, biographical sketches, criticisms, and many of the translations, are by Longfellow himself. (Read Longfellow as Critic under Miscellaneous Notes).

Posthumous Poetry.

In the Harbor. Mad River. Decoration Day.

Poems of Longfellow set to Music.

> The Arrow and the Song. The Bridge. The Day is Done. The Psalm of Life. My Lady Sleeps. The Reaper and the Flowers. She is Fooling Thee. The Village Blacksmith, and others.

> Ditson & Company, Boston, have published about forty. In Scotland, also, music has been composed for a number of them.

Evidences of the Poet's Popularity.

> His poems, complete or in part, have been translated into German, Dutch, Swedish, Norwegian, Danish, Italian, Portuguese, Spanish, Polish, Russian; one poem, "Hiawatha," into Latin; one, "Excelsior," into Hebrew; one, "The Psalm of Life," into Marathi, Chinese, and Sanscrit; one, "Kóramos," into Japanese. Of the *Longfellow Birthday Book*, nineteen thousand copies were sold during the year following its issue.

His Poetic Measure.

> Varied.

> "In the use of unrhymed hexameter and unrhymed trochaic tetrameter [the former an uncommon and difficult metre in English] he has virtually neither rivals nor successors." — RICHARDSON.

> *Poems in Trochaic Metre.*

>> Hiawatha. The Legend Beautiful. The Emperor's Glove. Bayard Taylor. Amalfi. Songo River. A Psalm of Life. Footsteps of Angels. To the River Charles. Nuremberg. Something Left Undone. The Builders. The Children's Crusade.

> *Poems in Anapestic Metre.*

>> Sandalphon. The Children's Hour. Helen of Tyre.

> *Other interesting Studies in Verse and Stanza Structure.*

>> Hymn to the Night. The Skeleton in Armor. Endymion. Maidenhood. Rain in Summer. Afternoon in February. To an Old Danish Song-Book. Curfew. Evangeline. Birds of Passage. Catawba Wine. Daybreak. Enceladus. Snowflakes. Aftermath. Palingenesis. Christmas Bells. The Chamber Over the Gate. From My Arm-Chair. Robert Burns. The Sifting of Peter. Loss and Gain.

> Longfellow liked best the metre of his poem, The Day is Done.

His Poetic Style.

> Graceful, polished, melodious, artistic.

Character of His Poetry.

Longfellow is not, as a poet, deep or intellectual, like Browning and Tennyson, musical like Poe, impassioned like Whittier, original and philosophic like Emerson, humorous like Lowell and Holmes; but his writings breathe a tender, sympathetic, human, serene spirit, and are acceptably ethical.

"His sweet and pure and tender genius has hallowed all domestic relations and events, and there is no emotion which does not readily and fitly express itself in his verse." — CURTIS.

Its Scholarly Nature. "His verse is embroidered with allusions and names and illustrations wrought with a taste so true and a skill so rare that the robe, though it be cloth of gold, is as finely flexible as linen, and still beautifully reveals, not conceals, the living form." — G. W. CURTIS.

Literary Faults Attributed to Him.

Didacticism, bookishness, and formal imagery.

("A lifelong moralizer, he shunned cant as the twin-devil of hypocrisy.")

Brief Comments from Stedman.

"Like greater bards before him, he was a good borrower."

"The world of books was to him the real world."

"Longfellow's impulse was to make a poem, above all, interesting."

"He was a lyrical artist whose taste outranked his inspirations."

"Superlative joy and woe were alike foreign to the verse of Longfellow. It came neither from the height nor out of the depths, but along the even tenor of a fortunate life."

MISCELLANEOUS NOTES.

Tributes to Longfellow.

"His poetry is a gospel of good-will set to music." — F. H. UNDER-
WOOD.

"Longfellow has made 'the songs of a people.' His works are
household words wherever the English language is spoken." —
CARDINAL WISEMAN.

"You sang me out of all my worries." — LOWELL, to the poet.

"Longfellow links moral truth to intellectual beauty." — E. P.
WHIPPLE.

"Nothing lasts like a coin and a lyric." — HOLMES, on Longfellow's poetry.

"His life and works together were an edifice fairly built, — the
House Beautiful, whose air is peace, where repose and calm are
ministrant, and where the raven's croak, symbol of the unrest of
a more perturbed genius, is never heard. . . . He convinces
the people that loveliness and righteousness may go together."
— E. C. STEDMAN.

"Of Longfellow's life, there is nothing to know but good; and his
poetry testifies to it, — his poetry, the voice of the kindliest and
gentlest heart that ever poet bore." — ANDREW LANG.

"While the magnetism of Longfellow's touch lies in the broad humanity of his sympathy, which leads him neither to mysticism
nor cynicism, and which commends his poetry to the universal
heart, his artistic sense is so exquisite that each of his poems is
a valuable literary study." — GEORGE W. CURTIS.

"There is no blot on the crystal purity of his writings." — J. G.
WHITTIER.

"He was the natural friend and earnest advocate of every good cause
and right idea." — WILLIAM WINTER.

"It is impossible to study so pure a life as this volume commemo-
rates, without receiving some of its lustre and perfume into one's
own nature." — W. S. KENNEDY in the Preface to his *Life of
Longfellow*.

"Longfellow has taught more people to love poetry than any other
English writer, however great." — MEIKLEJOHN.

"What he misses in intellectual greatness he possesses in heartfulness." — RICHARDSON.

> "His heart was pure, his purpose high,
>> His thought serene, his patience vast;
>> He put all strifes of passion by,
>> And lived to God, from first to last."
>
> WILLIAM WINTER.

Poems by Lowell, Holmes, Edith Thomas, Austin Dobson, Margaret Preston, Katherine Lee Bates, and others.

NOTE. — For other tributes, consult *The Literary World*, Feb. 26, 1881, and Kennedy's *Life of Longfellow*.

The Craigie House.

Brattle Street, Cambridge.

Longfellow's home for forty years.

Originally the Vassal House. (The tombstone of one of the family of Vassals called forth Longfellow's poem, "In the Churchyard at Cambridge.")

Built in 1759. Fine example of colonial architecture.

"Guarded by stately poplars." Commands a fine view of the Charles River.

"The most historic building in New England save Faneuil Hall."

Washington's headquarters for nine months after the Battle of Bunker Hill.

Talleyrand and Lafayette slept in the house.

Home for years of Thomas Tracy, "a sort of American Vathek;" bought of him by Andrew Craigie.

Jared Sparks, President of Harvard, kept house in it.

Half a mile from the college; three-quarters' from Elmwood, Lowell's home.

Longfellow, Jared Sparks, Edward Everett, and Joseph E. Worcester, the lexicographer, lodged here with the widow of Mr. Craigie, before Longfellow's marriage. (For Mrs. Craigie's eccentricities, see Stoddard, Kennedy, H. T. Griswold.)

Generous hospitality. — Here the poet received cordially his most distinguished foreign visitors and the humblest child admirer. "He was the most gracious of men in his own home." — PROFESSOR NORTON.

Possesses many interesting and curious treasures.

Esther Wynn's "Love Letters" were found in this house by Longfellow, — the basis of one of Saxe Holm's stories. They were letters addressed to the husband of Mrs. Craigie.

Its Study. — Contains, among other things, the original MSS. of the
poet's works in bound volumes, Coleridge's inkstand, a Cellini
cup, and "the children's arm-chair." A good view is given in
Final Memorials of Longfellow, p. 400.

For views of the house, consult Stoddard's *Poets' Homes*; *Harper*,
January, 1876, and June, 1894; Kennedy's *Life*; Wolfe's *Literary
Shrines*.

NOTES. — Brattle Street has recently been rescued by public-spirited
citizens from the encroachments of an electric railway.

Longfellow had a summer home at Nahant.

First Published Poem.

"The Battle of Lovell's Pond." Not extant.

Appeared in the poet's corner of a Portland newspaper the winter
before its writer went to college.

Three American "Swan-Songs."

Longfellow's "Morituri Salutamus," Holmes's "The Iron Gate,"
Bryant's "The Flood of Years."

Longfellow's Last Public Appearance. Dec. 28, 1880.

With Holmes, on the platform of Sanders Theatre, at the celebration of the two hundred and fiftieth anniversary of the founding
of Cambridge.

A thousand grammar-school children were among the audience, and
the poet gave every one of them who wished it his autograph.

Last Written Lines. (Nine days before his death.)

"Out of the shadows of night,
The world rolls into light;
It is daybreak everywhere."

The Bells of San Blas.

A *fac-simile* of the stanza is shown in Samuel Longfellow's *Longfellow*, Vol. II.

The poem was written after the destruction of a convent on the
Pacific slope.

The writings of the poet's advanced age equalled those of his prime.

Life Motto. (Adopted after the early death of his wife.)

"Look not mournfully into the Past, it comes not back again;
wisely improve the Present, it is thine; go forth to meet the
shadowy Future without fear and with a manly heart."

(Used as prefatory lines in *Hyperion* [quoted].)

A Critical Worker.

The poet is said to have re-written wholly *The Divine Tragedy*
after it was in type.

He could not compose for occasions, distrusting his own power; he
declined a thousand dollars for a poem on Garfield, offered by
a Boston paper at the time of the President's assassination,
although he had in his pocket the first draught of his sonnet
on Garfield.

As Critic.

"He belonged, by nature and choice, to the expository school; he
was unfitted for severe, destructive, or brilliantly critical work;
and his ability lay chiefly in his power to describe justly and
attractively the things he liked. . . . Too learned to commend
trash, too gentle to wield a critical scourge, his work of instruction and stimulus was done at a time when it was very effective." — RICHARDSON.

Longfellow and Transcendentalism.

The poet was friendly with the transcendental thinkers, but lived
outside their circle. He was "as untouched by this faith as
Charles Lamb by the wars of Napoleon."

His Early Friends.

Charles Sumner. George S. Hillard. Cornelius C. Felton. Samuel
Ward, Mrs. Howe's brother. Nathaniel Hawthorne.

Later Friends.

Louis Agassiz. J. R. Lowell. Richard H. Dana. Whittier. James
T. Fields. O. W. Holmes. Charles Eliot Norton.

Longfellow's Copy of Horace is kept at Bowdoin College, and bears the
owner's signature, together with that of Professor Calvin E. Stowe
(husband of the novelist, Harriet Beecher Stowe), and the date
"1824."

A Poet's Pun.

When Longfellow was introduced to Mr. Nicholas Longworth of
Cincinnati, allusion was made to the likeness of the first syllable
of their names. Longfellow quoted at once Pope's line,

"Worth makes the man, and want of it the fellow."

NOTE. — "Our poet's genial song, 'Catawba Wine,' is understood to
have been written on the receipt of a case of that delicate
liquor from his Cincinnati friend." — KENNEDY.

Anecdotes.

See Hale, H. T. Griswold, Shepard, Stoddard, and Lives of the poet.

Longfellow on the Study of Language.

"By every language you learn, a new world is opened before you. It is like being born again."

Income from His Pen.

Tennyson is said to have realized more money from poetry than any other English-writing poet; Longfellow and Whittier stood not far behind him.

His Autograph.

Probably no famous man was ever more besieged by autograph hunters. His patience was inexhaustible. Only the week before his death he received a call from four Boston schoolboys, and wrote in their albums.

He kept a store of autographs at hand with which to meet requests.

An Idealized Puritan.

"Child of New England, and trained by her best influences; of a temperament singularly sweet and serene, and with the sturdy rectitude of his race, refined and softened by wide contact with other lands and many men; born in prosperity, accomplished in all literatures, and himself a literary artist of consummate elegance, — he was the fine flower of the Puritan stock under its changed modern conditions. Out of strength had come forth sweetness. The grim iconoclast, 'humming a surly hymn,' had issued in the Christian gentleman. Captain Miles Standish had risen into Sir Philip Sidney." — GEORGE W. CURTIS.

Longfellow's Mission.

"He helped to utter the emotions of the universal human heart. It is when a writer speaks for us what were else unspoken — setting our minds free, and giving us strength to meet the cares of life and the hour of death — that he first becomes of real value. Longfellow has done this for thousands of human beings, and done it in the language of perfect simplicity, — never bald, never insipid, never failing to exalt the subject, — which is at once the most beautiful and the most difficult of all the elements of literature." — WILLIAM WINTER.

Longfellow, Whittier, Emerson, Poe.

"Like Whittier, Longfellow is beloved; like Emerson, he is honored for his poetic evangel; and, like Poe, he is studied as an artist in words and metrical effects."

Longfellow and Whittier Contrasted.

Longfellow.	*Whittier.*
Ideal.	Real.
Artistic.	Natural.
Symmetrical.	Of limited culture.
Elegant.	Vigorous.
Reposeful.	Vehement.
Attractively moral.	Intensely moral.
Cosmopolitan.	A New England product.
Literary.	Pastoral.

Longfellow and Lowell.

"Longfellow — less brilliant than Lowell, whether as a poet or a student, but his superior in patient industry and evenness of taste." — STEDMAN.

Some Studies in Longfellow.

The countries and times to which he turned for his poetic themes. The secret of his popularity. Evangeline and Priscilla. His metrical expertness. His poems of friendship.

See W. C. Gannett's *Studies in Longfellow.* (Riverside Literature Series.)

Illustrated Editions of Longfellow. (Houghton, Mifflin & Co.)

Complete Works. Subscription Edition. Three quarto volumes.

Poems. Four one-volumed editions.

Individual Works.

Christus. Hiawatha. Evangeline. The Building of the Ship. The Hanging of the Crane. Michael Angelo.

Twenty Poems. Birthday Book. Prose Birthday Book.

Annotated Editions. (By the same firm.)

Complete Works. New Riverside Edition. Eleven volumes.

Individual and Selected Works.

a. In "Riverside Literature" form. Evangeline. The Courtship of Miles Standish. Lyrics and Ballads (twenty-one in number). Hiawatha. The Golden Legend. Tales of a Wayside Inn.

b. In "American Poems." Evangeline. The Courtship of Miles Standish. The Building of the Ship.

c. In "Masterpieces of American Literature." Evangeline.

d. Translation of the Divina Commedia of Dante.

Anthologies by American Authors.

> Bryant's *Library of Poetry and Song*. Emerson's *Parnassus*.
> Longfellow's *Poets and Poetry of Europe*. Whittier's *Songs of
> Three Centuries*. Charles A. Dana's *Household Book of Poetry*.

A Group of Writers on the Indian.

James F. Cooper.	The Romancer of the Indian.
Henry W. Longfellow.	The Poet of the Indian.
Francis Parkman.	The Historian of the Indian.
Helen Hunt Jackson.	The Novelist of the Indian.

JAMES RUSSELL LOWELL.

JAMES RUSSELL LOWELL.

Poet, Critic, Diplomat, Editor, Abolitionist.

————

EXTRACTS.

Those love her [Truth] best who to themselves are true,
And what they dare to dream of, dare to do.

Harvard Commemoration Ode.

'Tis not the grapes of Canaan that repay,
'Tis the high faith that fails not by the way.

Ibid.

Be noble! and the nobleness that lies,
In other men, sleeping, but never dead,
Will rise in majesty to meet thine own.

Sonnet IV. Edition of 1865.

'Tis heaven alone that is given away,
'Tis only God may be had for the asking.

Vision of Sir Launfal.

The gift without the giver is bare;
Who gives himself with his alms feeds three, —
Himself, his hungering neighbor, and me.

Ibid.

Earth's noblest thing, a woman perfected.

Irené.

Life is a leaf of paper white
Whereon each one of us may write
His word or two, and then comes night.

For an Autograph.

Not failure, but low aim, is crime.

For an Autograph.

To learn such a simple lesson,
Need I go to Paris and Rome,
That the many make the household,
But only one the home ?

The Dead House.

She doeth little kindnesses,,
Which most leave undone or despise ;
For naught that sets one heart at ease,
And giveth happiness or peace,
Is low-esteemèd in her eyes.

My Love.

Man is more than Constitutions; better rot beneath the
    sod,
Than be true to Church and State while we are doubly
    false to God !

On the Capture of Fugitive Slaves.

'Tis ours to save our brethren, with peace and love to win
Their darkened heart from error, ere they harden it to sin;
But if before his duty man with listless spirit stands,
Ere long the Great Avenger takes the work from out his
    hands.

Ibid.

God hates your sneakin' creturs that believe
He'll settle things they run away and leave.

The Biglow Papers.

Ez fer war, I call it murder, —
There you hev it plain and flat ;
I don't want to go no furder
Than my Testyment fer that.

Ibid.

An' she'd blush scarlit, right in prayer,
When her new meetin'-bunnet
Felt somehow thru' its crown a pair
Of blue eyes set upon it.

THE COURTIN'.

THERE'S a narrow ridge in the graveyard
Would scarce stay a child in his race,
But to me and my thought it is wider
Than the star-sown vague of space.

AFTER THE BURIAL.

EACH age must worship its own thought of God.

THE CATHEDRAL.

ONCE to every man and nation comes the moment to decide,
In the strife of Truth with Falsehood, for the good or
evil side ;
Some great cause, God's new Messiah, offering each the
bloom or blight,
Parts the goats upon the left hand, and the sheep upon
the right,
And the choice goes by forever 'twixt that darkness and
that light.

THE PRESENT CRISIS.

GOD scatters love on every side,
Freely among his children all,
And always hearts are lying open wide,
Wherein some grains may fall.

There is no wind but soweth seeds
Of a more true and open life,
Which burst, unlooked for, into high-souled deeds,
With wayside beauty rife.

AN INCIDENT IN A RAILROAD CAR.

SOMEWHERE is comfort, somewhere faith,
　Though thou in outer dark remain;
One sweet, sad voice ennobles death,
And still, for eighteen centuries saith
　Softly, — " Ye meet again ! "

PALINODE.

SHOULD a man discover the art of transmuting metals, and present us with a lump of gold as large as an ostrich egg, would it be in human nature to inquire too nicely whether he had stolen the lead ?

ESSAY ON CHAUCER.

CHAUCER had been in his grave one hundred and fifty years ere England had secreted choice material enough for the making of another great poet.

IBID.

GOD is the only being who has time enough; but a prudent man, who knows how to seize occasion, can commonly make a shift to find as much as he needs.

ESSAY ON LINCOLN.

EVERY mortal man of us holds stock in the only public debt that is absolutely sure of payment, and that is the debt of the Maker of this Universe to the Universe he has made. I have no notion of selling out my stock in a panic.

ON A CERTAIN CONDESCENSION IN FOREIGNERS.

As for associations, if one have not the wit to make them for himself out of his native earth, no ready-made ones of other men will avail him much. Lexington is none the worse to me for not being in Greece, nor Gettysburg that its name is not Marathon.

IBID.

JUST so many misdirected letters every year and no more! Would it were as easy to reckon up the number of men on whose backs fate has written the wrong address, so that they arrive by mistake in Congress and other places where they do not belong.

ON A CERTAIN CONDESCENSION IN FOREIGNERS.

BUT then it is a fact in the natural history of the American, long familiar to Europeans, that he abhors privacy, knows not the meaning of reserve, lives in hotels because of their greater publicity, and is never so pleased as when his domestic affairs (if he may be said to have any) are paraded in the newspapers. Barnum, it is well known, represents perfectly the average national sentiment in this respect.

IBID.

THE robins are not good solo singers; but their chorus, as, like primitive fire-worshippers, they hail the return of light and warmth to the world, is unrivalled. There are a hundred singing like one. They are noisy enough then, and sing, as poets should, with no afterthought.

MY GARDEN ACQUAINTANCE.

ONE is far enough withdrawn from his fellows if he keeps himself clear of their weaknesses. He is not so truly withdrawn as exiled, if he refuses to share in their strength.

ESSAY ON THOREAU.

A MAN may surpass himself or fall short of himself, but he cannot change his nature.

ESSAY ON SHAKESPEARE'S RICHARD III.

THE pluralizing in his single person, by the Editor of the Newspaper, of the offices once divided among the Church, the University, and the Courts of Law, is one of the most striking phenomena of modern times in demo-cratized countries, and is calculated to inspire thoughtful men with some distrust.

THE PROGRESS OF THE WORLD.

ONCE in my life I have heard a funeral elegy which was wholly adequate. It was the long, quavering howl of a dog under a window of the chamber in which his master had at that moment died. It was Nature's cry of grief and terror at the first sight of Death. That faithful creature was not trying to say something; so far from it, that even the little skill in articulation which his race has acquired was choked in the gripe of such disaster. Consolation would shrink away abashed from the presence of so helpless a grief.

ESSAY ON ISAAC WALTON.

I WAS reminded of him [one of Emerson's listeners] by those hearty cherubs in Titian's "Assumption," that look at you as who should say, "Did you ever see a Madonna like that? Did you ever behold one hundred and fifty pounds of womanhood mount heavenward before like a rocket?"

EMERSON THE LECTURER.

"IF a man does anything good, the world always finds it out sooner or later; and, if he doesn't, the world finds *that* out too."

LETTER TO A FRIEND.

REFERENCES.

F. H. Underwood's *Biographical Sketch of Lowell*, and *The Poet and the Man.*

Letters of James Russell Lowell.

G. E. Woodberry's *Life of Lowell.*

E. E. Brown's *Life of Lowell.*

Stedman's *Poets of America.*

Hattie T. Griswold's *Home Life of Great Authors.*

R. H. Stoddard's *Poets' Homes.*

G. W. Curtis's *Homes of American Authors.*

H. R. Haweis's *American Humorists.*

E. P. Whipple's *Outlooks on Society.*

Sarah K. Bolton's *Famous American Authors.*

Shepard's *Pen Pictures of Modern Authors.*

Stedman-Hutchinson's *Library of American Literature.* Vol. VII.

Appletons' Cyclopædia of American Biography.

C. F. Richardson's *American Literature.*

Duyckinck's *Cyclopædia of American Literature.*

Allibone's *Dictionary of Authors.*

Penniman's *Syllabus of University Extension Lectures on American Authors.*

Theodore Wolfe's *Literary Shrines.*

The Century Magazine. May, 1882. August, 1893.

The Review of Reviews. October, 1891 (Five articles on Lowell).

The Arena. May, 1894 ("The Religion of Lowell's Poems." By Minot J. Savage).

The Literary World. June 27, 1885.

The Critic. Lowell Number. Feb. 20, 1889.

The Critic. Aug. 15, Aug. 22, Aug. 29, Oct. 12, 1891. Feb. 25, 1893.

The Cambridge Tribune. Lowell Number. Feb. 20, 1892.

The Atlantic Monthly. January, 1892. (Lowell in London.)

The New England Magazine. October, 1891 (Three articles). November, 1891 (Two articles; one illustrated).

Harper's Magazine. January, 1876 ("Cambridge on the Charles." Illustrated). January, 1881 (Article by F. H. Underwood. Illustrated). June, 1894 (Howells's "My First Visit to New England").

Harper's Weekly. June 20, 1885.

Beers's, Hawthorne and Lemmon's, Morgan's, and other text-books of American Literature.

Notes. — For a classification of his poems, see Miss Hodgkins's *Guide to the Study of Nineteenth Century Authors.*

For critical references, consult Welsh's *English Masterpiece Course.*

OUTLINE OF HIS LIFE.

February 22, 1819.
August 12, 1891.

Born the same year with Charles A. Dana, Walt Whitman, Mrs. Julia Ward Howe, Dr. J. G. Holland, W. W. Story, T. W. Parsons, George Eliot, Charles Kingsley, and John Ruskin.

Ancestors.

"Distinguished in every generation."

Eight generations in this country.

Percival Lowell (Lowle) of Bristol, England, settled in Newbury, Mass., in 1639.

The city of Lowell, Mass., was named for one of them.

Grandfather, Judge John Lowell, caused the phrase, "All men are created free and equal," to be inserted in the Constitution of Massachusetts. "A good sort of grandfather for the author of the Biglow Papers." — DR. HALE.

"Public spirit was the natural inheritance of the Lowells."

Father.

Charles Lowell, a Unitarian clergyman in Boston, settled for fifty years over the West Church.

Mother.

Gifted musician and linguist.

Lowell inherited from her his poetic and **imaginative** faculty.

Her family was descended, according to tradition, from Sir Patrick Spens, of ballad fame.

Lost her mental powers. See poem, "The Darkened Mind."

Youngest of five children.

Youth.

"Nurtured with romance and minstrelsy.'

As a boy Lowell used well his father's library.

"He could have passed a better examination, probably, in Scottish ballads, Hakluyt's *Voyages*, Froissart's *Chronicles*, and old plays, than in conic sections or Greek prosody."

Home.

"Elmwood," Cambridge, Mass. Near Mt. Auburn Cemetery.

Lowell's only home save when living abroad.

Old Tory mansion built just before the American Revolution by a "stamp" distributer.

Set in spacious grounds, and surrounded by fine English elms and beautiful ash-trees, planted by the poet's father.

Its birds and trees have been made familiar to us through *My Garden Acquaintance*.

Not far from Craigie Cottage, Longfellow's home.

Formerly occupied by Elbridge Gerry, Vice-President of the United States.

Its Motto, brought from the ancestral home at Newbury, Mass.

"In necessariis, unitas ; in non necessariis, libertas ; in omnibus, caritas."

See Longfellow's poem, "The Herons of Elmwood."

For view, consult the *Art Journal*, 1878, and Stoddard's *Poets' Homes*. Read, also, Wolfe's *Literary Shrines*.

For a woodcut of Lowell in his study, see frontispiece of *The New England Magazine* for October, 1891.

Education.

Harvard, class of 1838.

At this time he used to say, "he read almost everything except the text-books prescribed by the Faculty."

Classmates. William W. Story and George P. Loring.

(Dr. E. E. Hale was a member of the following class.)

Class Poem. Written during "rustication" at Concord. A witty attack on the Abolitionists (whose cause he soon learned to champion), on Carlyle, Emerson, and the Transcendentalists then prominent at Concord.

Lowell alludes to his rustication in the second series of *The Biglow Papers*, "Mason and Slidell."

Read his essay, "Cambridge Thirty Years Ago," in *Fireside Travels*.

Admission to the Bar.

His story, "My First Client," is the only record of his practice.

Publication of His First Volume of Poems.

A Year's Life. 1841.

Dedicated to "Una," Maria White.

The "Shepherd of Admetus," "The Heritage," and others.

Edits three numbers of a literary magazine, *The Pioneer*.

Hawthorne, Whittier, Poe, and Miss Barrett (Mrs. Browning) were contributors. Poe's "Lenore" first appeared here.

(See illustrated article in *The New England Magazine*, October, 1891.)

Marriage to Maria White (1844) of Watertown, sister of a classmate.

"It was ideally beautiful, and nothing was wanted to perfect happiness but the sense of permanence." — UNDERWOOD.

Miss White was beautiful, accomplished, and a poet.

"She made a Garrisonian Abolitionist of her lover."

Died in October, 1853, the same night a child was born to Longfellow.

See Longfellow's poem "The Two Angels."

"And softly from that hushed and darkened room,
Two angels issued where but one went in."

Four Children.

All of them died in infancy save one, Mabel, alluded to in the touching poem, "The First Snow-Fall." Read the poems, "The Changeling," and "She Came and Went;" also, Mrs. Lowell's poem, "The Alpine Sheep" (found in Underwood's *Biographical Sketch of Lowell*, p. 56).

Early Stand for Abolition.

"Lowell's patriotic verse lightens every part of our national chronicle."

Publications of the Year 1848.

The Vision of Sir Launfal. The Fable for Critics. The Present Crisis. Incident in a Railroad Car. The Biglow Papers.

Lecturer before the Lowell Institute, Boston.

Delivers twelve lecturers on British Poets.

The Institute was founded by an uncle of the poet, John Lowell, Jr., who made his will when on the summit of the great pyramid, bequeathing $250,000 for annual courses of free lectures. (See article on the subject, in *The New England Magazine*, February, 1895.)

Professor of Modern Languages and Belles-Lettres at Harvard, succeeding Longfellow. 1855.

Two years of preparatory European travel and study, the latter chiefly in Dresden.

Returned unexpectedly early because he kept no account of his bank drafts, and received notification from his bankers that his balance was reduced to a certain sum. (Discovered later to be a mistake.)

Lectures, also, in the Harvard Law School.

A popular professor.

" He not only knew, but loved, what he taught."

" It was difficult for Lowell to give a low mark to a good-looking or a well-mannered fellow."

Second Marriage, to Miss Frances Dunlap, of Portland, Maine, who had been an instructor of his daughter when Lowell was in Europe.

First Editor of The Atlantic Monthly. 1857–1862.

Salary, $3,000.

Lowell was willing to be its editor on condition that Dr. Holmes should be a contributor.

(Lowell was succeeded by James T. Fields.)

Editor, for Ten Years, with Charles Eliot Norton, of The North American Review.

Essays published in this, collected under *Among My Books*, and *My Study Window*.

Two Years in Europe.

Third visit.

Degree of D.C.L. from Oxford, and of LL.D. from Cambridge.

Presidential Elector.

Minister to Spain under President Hayes.

" During his stay there he made himself the friend of everybody who was engaged in the improvement and uplifting of Spain."

Transferred to England. 1880–1885.

His patriotism noteworthy.

Very popular in social and public life.

"The sparkle of his talk was perennial." "His after-dinner speeches filled those who heard them with despairing envy."

He won the respect and admiration of the English nation.

"The islands seemed brighter for his coming."

Made the address on Coleridge when a bust of the poet was unveiled at Westminster Abbey.

Speeches published in "Democracy and other Essays."

Gladstone's adoption of his Home Rule policy was hastened by Lowell's influence over him when in England.

Death of Mrs. Lowell.

Retired Life with his only daughter, at Southboro, Mass.

Lectures Again before the Lowell Institute.

On English Dramatists.

Return to Elmwood. 1889.

Valuable worker in the campaign for the Copyright Law. President of the League.

Death at Elmwood.

Burial from Appleton Chapel, Cambridge.

Phillips Brooks, the officiating clergyman.

O. W. Holmes and Judge Hoar, among the pall-bearers.

Resting-Place.

Mt. Auburn Cemetery. Near Longfellow.

Literary Executor.

Charles Eliot Norton.

Lowell's "Under The Willows" is dedicated to Professor Norton.

Memorial Service in Westminster Abbey.

"Two worlds their wreaths of honor have entwined About an open grave."

Memorial Window in the Chapter House, Westminster Abbey. 1893.

See *The Critic*, Dec. 2 and Dec. 23, 1893.

Character.

> Cultured, knightly, aristocratic, kind to the humble, humorous ;
> a pleasing letter-writer ; personally magnetic ; a lover of
> nature ; a keen observer of men and things. Lowell, like
> Bryant and Holmes, had a special fondness for trees. (See
> poems, "Under the October Maples," "The Birch-tree,"
> "The Oak," "A Mood," "To a Pine-Tree.")

> > "I in June am midway to believe
> > A tree among my far progenitors,
> > Such sympathy is mine with all the race."

> > > *Under The Willows.*

> "To his family and near friends, he was the most delightful
> and sunshiny being that ever came from the Author of joy."
> In politics, an Independent Republican.
> Lowell carried out his own injunction, —

> > "The epic of a man rehearse,
> > Be something better than thy verse."

Appearance.

> Robust and vigorous. "A broad-shouldered, full-bearded,
> strong, and cheery Anglo-Saxon." Sinewy and active.
> Chestnut hair and beard. Eyes reflecting his moods. Fine
> facial expression. Fastidious in his toilet.

Voice and Speech.

> "His voice had as great fascination for me as his face. The
> vibrant tenderness and crisp clearness of the tones, the
> perfect modulation, the clear enunciation, the exquisite ac-
> cent, the elect diction, — these were the graces of one from
> whose tongue our rough English came as music, such as I
> should never hear from any other.

> "In his speech there was nothing of our slipshod American
> slovenliness, but a truly Italian conscience, and an artistic
> sense of beauty in the instrument." — W. D. HOWELLS.

Surviving Brother.

> R. T. S. Lowell, an Episcopal clergyman at Schenectady, N.Y.,
> and author of several works of fiction.

Only Surviving Child.

> A daughter, Mrs. Edward Burnett.

APPELLATIONS.

A Typical New England Protestant.
The Cambridge Apollo.
Our Finest Representative Man of Letters.
The Literary Educator of America.
An Earnest Advocate of the Rights of Man.
The Author of the American Hudibras.
A Poet of Out-of-Doors and of To-Day.
The Songster of Elmwood.
The Best-launched Poet of His Time.
Our Poet-Ambassador.
The Scholar in Politics.
The Milton of an Epoch which had in Lincoln its Oliver
    Cromwell.
The Most Distinguished Editor of New England Mag-
    azines.
A Character-Forming Poet.
A Latter-Day Prophet.
A Yankee Idyllist.
Our Foremost Critic.
Prize Poet of the Vernacular.
The Blithest, most Unstudied Songster on the Old Bay
    Shore.
Disperser of the Ancestral [Puritan] Gloom.
The Matthew Arnold of America.
Our New Theocritus.
The Fine Flower of American Society.
Poet of Freedom, of Nature, and of Human Nature.
A Poet of the Eternal Mystery of Life and Death.

PSEUDONYMS.

HOMER WILBUR.   HOSEA BIGLOW.

NOTES ON HIS WRITINGS.

General Comments.

"Lowell's range of poetry is phenomenal, from *The Biglow Papers* to ' She Came and Went.' "

"His poetry has the strength, the tenderness, and the defects of the Down-East temper." — E. C. STEDMAN.

"He was intimately in touch with his social surroundings, and always needed some outside impulse of sympathy or indignation to call out his best powers."

"With Lowell, poetry was the utterance of fortunate moments, rather than the passion of a lifetime."

"His political and moral convictions appear chiefly in his verse. His prose, with the exception of some graceful sketch-work, bits of travel, and reminiscence, has been restricted to criticism."

" It does me good to see a poet who knows a bird or flower as one friend knows another, yet loves it for itself alone." — STEDMAN.

" He never lost the youthful thrill at being out-of-doors."

Howells speaks of "the constant glow of Lowell's incandescent sense."

His Own Characterization of His Poetry.

"There's Lowell, who's striving Parnassus to climb
With a whole bale of *isms* tied together with rhyme;
He might get on alone, spite of brambles and boulders,
But he can't for the bundle he has on his shoulders.
The top of the hill he will ne'er come near reaching
Till he learns the distinction 'twixt singing and preaching;
His lyre has some chords that would ring pretty well,
But he'd rather by half make a drum of the shell,
And rattle away till he's as old as Methusalem,
At the head of a march to the last new Jerusalem.

Fable for Critics.

POETRY.

The Vision of Sir Launfal.

The Legend of the Holy Grail.

Two pairs of pictures, Summer and Winter.

" Lowell is *par excellence* the poet of June, as Bryant is of autumn."
— F. L. PATTEE.

Exquisitely artistic. Lowell's most popular poem.

It "transcribes the mysticism of the past into the vital charity of the present."

"A frenzy of creative impulse."

Written in forty-eight hours, — no food or sleep.

Several illustrated editions have been published.

The Fable for Critics.

Appeared anonymously. Begun without thought of publication.

"A humorous yet just characterization of contemporary authors."

"One hardly knows whether to be more amazed at the audacity or the brilliancy of this elaborate *jeu d'esprit*." — UNDERWOOD.

"Written in the 'touch-and-go' style."

"Fantastic prose preface."

Courage to praise Whittier and Theodore Parker.

Women portrayed.

Miranda. Margaret Fuller.

Philoclea. Mrs. Lydia Maria Child.

An edition with outline portraits of the authors mentioned in the poem has been published.

The Present Crisis.

Published anonymously, and at first attributed to Whittier.

The "crisis" was that created by the annexation of Texas.

Note the "long, leaping metre."

Incident in a Railroad Car.

The effect of Burns's poetry upon laboring men.

The Biglow Papers.

(Consult its analysis by Haweis and by Underwood.)

"A masterpiece in wit, scholarship, and penetrating knowledge."

"Lowell reached in this the highwater mark of American humor."

"From this time on, it was respectable to be on the side of freedom."

"An important event in the history of the world's literature."

"Its dialect suggests the Ayrshire dialect of Burns in its keenness and suppleness."

"Every couplet contains some felicitous absurdity or hard hit."

"Never sprang the flower of art from more unpromising soil."

"The accompanying prose is often as amusing and as brilliant as the verse."

First Series. 1846. The Mexican War.

    First published in *The Boston Courier.*

Second Series. 1867. The Civil War.

    Exceeded the first in power.

Written by "Hosea Biglow," a typical Yankee.

Edited by "Parson Wilbur," a "deliciously humorous and absurdly
learned character."

Charles Sumner admired *The Biglow Papers,* but wished that their
author "could have used good English."

"The future student of American literature will be ever grateful
for this preservation of the Yankee dialect by New England's
greatest poet." — MRS. WRIGHT.

Harvard Commemoration Ode. 1865.

Dedicated "to the ever sweet and shining memory of the ninety-
three sons of Harvard College who have died for their country."

The classic poem of our Civil War.

"Deep comprehension of the greatness of the struggle, magnanimity
in victory, the solemn memory of the dead, admiration of their
heroic valor and self-sacrifice, and the lofty patriotic resolve
that their death shall not have been vain, mark the ode as the
one great poem which the war evoked."

"The best American poem of occasion."

"The most noble and massive of American lyrics."

"The ode is no smooth-cut block from Pentelicus, but a mass of
rugged quartz, beautiful with prismatic crystals, and deep-
veined here and there with virgin gold." — STEDMAN.

Contains a fine portrait of Lincoln. (Memorize the lines.)

His friend, William Wetmore Story, came from Rome to be present
on the occasion of its reading.

Delivered near the college grounds, after an address by General
Meade, the hero of Gettysburg.

Lowell lost three favorite nephews in the war, and another relative,
Colonel Shaw, who led the colored troops in the assault on Fort
Wagner.

> "Wut's words to them whose faith and truth
>   On War's red techstone rang true metal,
> Who ventured life an' love an' youth
>   For the gret prize o' death in battle ?
> To him who, deadly hurt, agen
>   Flashed on afore the charge's thunder,
> Tippin' with fire the bolt of men
>   Thet rived the Rebel line asunder ?"

Other **National Poems.**

    The Concord Ode.   The Centennial Ode.   Under the Old Elm.

The Cathedral.

    A philosophical poem.

    Suggested by a visit to Chartres.

    Written in blank verse.

    "A poem worthy of Browning."

Poems to His Wife.

    My Love, Sonnets, The Dead House, After the Burial.

Legend of Brittany.

    Pronounced by Poe, when it appeared, the noblest poem yet written
        by an American.

    Written in the Ottava Rima.   (See Analysis of Versification.)

The Courtin'.

    "This bucolic Idyl is without a counterpart.   No richer juice can be
        pressed from the wild grape of Yankee soil."

    Written to fill a vacant page in *The Biglow Papers.*

Fitz Adam's Story.

    An incomplete poem.   The first of a series of Chaucerian tales, to
        be called "Nooning."

Extreme Unction.

    "This poem changed my life." — W. T. STEAD.

Ambrose.

    A beautiful legend, that teaches forcibly the lesson of religious
        toleration.

Rhoecus.

    "Almost Grecian in its perfect art."

Hunger and Cold.

    A "revolutionary poem."

    The most democratic of Lowell's writings.

The First Snow-Fall.

    "Print that as if you loved it.   Let not a comma be blundered. . . .

    May you never have the key which shall unlock the whole meaning
        of the poem to you." — Letter to Sydney Gay from Lowell.

    Other Lyrics of Grief.   Threnodia.   The Changeling.   Auf Wieder-
        sehen.   After the Burial.   The Dead House.

Beaver Brook.

    A landscape poem, "rich enough in its suggestions to serve as an
        object-lesson upon poetic art." — UNDERWOOD.

"The brook is spiritualized, and sets machinery going in the brain
as well as in the mill."

Beaver Brook is a small valley a few miles from Elmwood, and was
a favorite haunt of the poet.

For view, see Underwood's *Sketch of Lowell;* or, *The Review of Reviews* for October, 1891, p. 309.

Pictures from Appledore.

Almost the only mention of the ocean in Lowell's poetry.

Last Poem.

My Brook. 1890. The poet received $1,000 for it.

Compare Lowell's two poems, "To the Past" and "The Sower," with
Bryant's poems of the same titles.

An Illustrated Lowell **Birthday Book** has been issued by his publishers.

PROSE.

Principal Writings.

My Study Window. Among My Books (First and Second Series).
Fireside Travels.

These include scholarly monographs on Chaucer, Keats, Spenser,
Dante, Carlyle, Abraham Lincoln, an interesting essay on Thoreau, and other critical work. A delightfully ironical essay is
the one entitled, "On a Certain Condescension in Foreigners."

Fireside Travels.

A series of letters addressed to William Story, the sculptor.
Called by Bryant the wittiest book ever written.

Posthumous Publications.

Letters of James Russell Lowell. Edited by Professor C. E. Norton.

Latest Essays and Addresses. (On Gray, Some Letters of Walter
Savage Landor, Walton, Milton's Areopagitica, Shakespeare's
Richard III., The Study of Modern Languages, and The Progress
of the World.)

The Old English Dramatists.

Last Poems of Lowell.

His Critical Writings.

Scholarly, sympathetic, individual, optimistic. Lowell admires the
writers he criticises. He is rich in material, and apt in figurative
illustration; while his views, taken from the high standpoint of
the sympathetic scholar, are comprehensive.

"They are at once subtle and masculine, independent and acute."

"He seems not so much to judge his author as to enjoy him. His perception is keen and discriminating; but he is expressing emotional effects rather than intellectual quality. Naturally, therefore, his essays are sometimes deficient in method. . . . Yet that man must be captious indeed who could object to writing so wise, witty, and gracious. . . . In genuine catholicity of taste, we venture to think no English critic of the past century has surpassed Mr. Lowell." — C. T. WINCHESTER.

A Characteristic Utterance. "It is one of the school-boy blunders in criticism to deny one kind of perfection because it is not another."

His Letters.

Delightful reading.

Models of epistolary writing.

It has been said that not one of the many communications sent by Lowell to the government during his years of diplomatic service was devoid of literary merit. "If there were many such despatch-writers, Blue Books would be as popular as three-volume novels."

When Lowell was in London, Lord Granville, then foreign secretary, invited him to dine, and apologized in his note for sending such short notice to "the most engaged man in London." Lowell replied, "'The most engaged man in London' is very glad to dine with the most engaging."

Extract from a personal letter: "I *will* have two or three quiet nooks into which I can retreat from the pursuit of my own title-pages. Let me be just the plain *man* to you, and forget that I ever took pen in hand except to write you a stupid letter. . . . If I did not think that I were better than my books, I should never dream of writing another. But I *do* dream of writing many, and such, too, as shall more fully express the real and whole me, and better justify the opinions of those who know me. You are a funny fellow, and I know you laugh at me sometimes; but you may laugh all day long if you will love me at the same time."

MISCELLANEOUS NOTES.

Tributes to Lowell.

"He has set a high example to his fellow-men of purity, manly dignity, faithful friendship, and honorable service."—CANON FARRAR.

"Never have I heard Lowell utter a word that would give another pain."—C. E. NORTON.

"His plentiful and original genius was so rich that he was never compelled, like many writers, to hoard his thoughts, or be miserly with his bright sayings."—E. C. STEDMAN.

"In British estimation Lowell was the man who most nearly united the literature and thought of the two great Anglo-Saxon nations."

"All the great gifts that lavish nature gave
By study, culture, art, were trained and formed—
As scholar, critic, poet—gay or grave—
The world to thee with heart responsive warmed."
                                        W. W. STORY.

"Great in his simple love of flower and bird,
   Great in the statesman's art,
He has been greatest in his lifting word
   To every human heart."
                                        SARAH K. BOLTON.

"O Lowell! I first gave to thee
My boyhood's love and loyalty.
My youth took fire at thy words,
And thou my manhood's spirit stirred
To lofty faith and noble trust."
                                        MINOT J. SAVAGE.

Whittier's verses on Lowell. 1891.

W. W. Story's poem. *Blackwood's Magazine*, November, 1891, and *The Critic*, Oct. 10, 1891.

O. W. Holmes's "At a Birthday Festival," Feb. 22, 1859, and "Memorial Poem." (The last appeared in *The Atlantic Monthly* for October, 1891.)

See *The Literary World*, June 27, 1885.

His Publishers for Thirty Years.

> One house; now Houghton, Mifflin, and Company.

His Voracious Reading.

> Lowell could read continuously for twelve hours, and retain what he read. In one of his letters, he calls himself "the last of the great readers."

> "He has profited by the literatures of all nations, but he has been the disciple of no one literary master."

> "Lowell read classical literature four hours a day, and paid little attention to the newspapers."

Lowell on Literary Style.

> "That exquisite something called style, which makes itself felt by the skill with which it effaces itself, and masters us at last with a sense of indefinable completeness."

His Introduction to Tennyson's Poems.

> Lowell first became acquainted with Tennyson's poems through a copy brought by Emerson from his first visit to Carlyle, in 1848, and circulated among his Harvard friends.

Lowell in Conversation.

> "His habitual manner had a mellow, autumnal glow. His serious conversation was suggestive and inspiring, and a sense of uplifting followed, as from seeing a play of Shakespeare, or hearing a symphony of Beethoven. But it was impossible for him to repress the bright fancies and droll conceits suggested by reading and conversation. Wit was as natural to him as breathing. . . . But epigrams and puns were the accompaniments, and not the end and aim, of his conversation: his perceptions were keen and just; his reading had been well-nigh universal; and, with his instant power of comparison, his judgments were like intuitions. His discourse often took on an airy and tantalizing form, and wreathed itself in irony, or flowered in simile, or exploded in artifices, until it ended in some merry absurdity. Such play of argument, fancy, humor, word-twisting, and sparkling nonsense was seldom witnessed, except in the talk of the Autocrat of the Breakfast Table." — F. H. UNDERWOOD.

A Lover of Nature and of Man.

> "Throughout his prose we find the same feeling for nature, and love for humanity, that distinguish his poetry. His whole literary career was but an outgrowth of his own broad, sympathetic, genial nature, interwoven with the acquirements of the scholar." — MRS. WRIGHT.

American Men of Letters who have known Diplomatic Service.

> John Lothrop Motley, George Bancroft, George P. Marsh, Nathaniel Hawthorne, Bayard Taylor, James Russell Lowell, Bret Harte, Francis H. Underwood, John Bigelow.

Lowell and His Literary Compeers.

> "He had more virility and mass than Longfellow, homelier philosophy and more musical utterance than Emerson, finer literary sense than Whittier, warmer human sympathies than Hawthorne, loftier and more serious imagination than Holmes." — C. T. WINCHESTER.

His Service to American Literature.

> "Of Lowell's service in strengthening and broadening our literature in the critical period of its development, too much cannot be said. As editor during an important epoch of *The Atlantic Monthly*, — the mouthpiece of the most remarkable group of authors that our nation has produced, — and later as editor of *The North American Review*, he had a chance which is presented to few literary men. His impress on the literary product of the period is everywhere visible. There are but few of the younger school of writers who did not receive their first impetus from a kind word of criticism or encouragement from this zealous builder of American literature." — F. L. PATTEE.

JOHN GREENLEAF WHITTIER.

JOHN GREENLEAF WHITTIER.

Lyrist, Reformer, Editor, Preacher.

EXTRACTS.

Then of what is to be, and of what is done,
　　Why queriest thou?
The past and the time to be are one,
　　And both are now.

My Soul and I.

Yet Love will dream, and Faith will trust,
(Since He who knows our need is just,)
That somehow, somewhere, meet we must.

Snowbound.

　　Life is ever lord of Death,
And Love can never lose its own.

Ibid.

For still in mutual sufferance lies
　　The secret of true living;
Love scarce is love that never knows
　　The sweetness of forgiving.

Among the Hills.

For of all sad words of tongue or pen,
The saddest are these : It might have been.

Maud Muller.

BLESSINGS on thee, little man,
Barefoot boy, with cheek of tan!
THE BAREFOOT BOY.

DEAR FRIEND! thy gift of love has brought
  More than thy early spring to me;
And words, to thank thee as I ought,
  Should all of bloom and fragrance be.
*(Written to a colored friend in the South upon the
receipt of some early spring flowers.)*

BE near me in my hours of need
  To soothe, or cheer, or warm;
And down the slopes of sunset lead
  As up the hills of morn!
MY BIRTHDAY.

WITH warning hand I mark Time's rapid flight,
  From life's glad morning to its solemn night,
Yet through the dear God's love I also show
  There's light above me by the shade below.
INSCRIPTION ON A SUN-DIAL.

AND thou, O Lord! by whom are seen
  Thy creatures as they be,
Forgive me if too close I lean
  My human heart on thee.
THE ETERNAL GOODNESS.

"SHOOT, if you must, this old gray head,
But spare your country's flag," she said.
BARBARA FRIETCHIE.

No longer forward nor behind
  I look in hope or fear;
But, grateful, take the good I find,
  The best of now and here.
MY PSALM.

PRAYERS of love like raindrops fall,
  Tears of pity are cooling dew;
And dear to the heart of our Lord are all
  Who suffer like him in the good they do.

THE ROBIN.

WHEN faith is lost, when honor dies,
  The man is dead.

ICHABOD.

AND Heaven's eternal years shall prove
That life and death and joy and pain
  Are ministers of love.

BETWEEN THE GATES.

OLD Floyd Ireson, for his hard heart,
Tarred and feathered and carried in a cart
  By the women of Marblehead!

SKIPPER IRESON'S RIDE.

THE pilgrims of the world went forth
  Obedient to the word,
And found, where'er they tilled the earth,
  A garden of the Lord!

A LAY OF OLD TIME.

I LOVED the work: it was its own reward.

  .   .   .   .

                It has come to be
In these long years so much a part of me,
I should not know myself if lacking it,
But with the work the worker too would die,
And in my place some other self would sit
Joyful or sad, — what matters. if not I?

THE BROTHER OF MERCY.

He lived to learn, in life's hard school,
   How few who pass above him
Lament their triumph and his loss,
   Like her, — because they love him.

IN SCHOOL-DAYS.

He prayeth best who leaves unguessed
The mystery of another's breast.
Why cheeks grow pale, why eyes o'erflow,
Or heads are white, thou need'st not know.
Enough to note by many a sign
That every heart hath needs like thine.

THE PRAYER-SEEKER.

What, ho! our countrymen in chains!
   The whip on woman's shrinking flesh!
Our soil yet reddening with the stains
   Caught from her scourging, warm and fresh!
What! mothers from their children riven!
What! God's own image bought and sold!
   Americans to market driven,
And bartered as the brute for gold!

Speak! Shall their agony of prayer
   Come thrilling to our hearts in vain?
To us whose fathers scorned to bear
   The paltry menace of a chain;
To us, whose boast is loud and long
   Of holy Liberty and Light;
Say, shall these writhing slaves of Wrong
   Plead vainly for their plundered Right?

FOLLEN.

We wait beneath the furnace-blast
　　The pangs of transformation;
Not painlessly doth God recast
　　And mould anew the nation.
　　　　Hot burns the fire
　　　　Where wrongs expire;
　　　　Nor spares the hand
　　　　That from the land
　　Uproots the ancient evil.

　　　　"Ein' feste Burg ist unser Gott."

THE TRAILING ARBUTUS.

I wandered lonely where the pine-trees made
Against the bitter East their barricade,
　　And, guided by its sweet
Perfume, I found, within a narrow dell,
The trailing spring flower tinted like a shell
　　Amid dry leaves and mosses at my feet.

From under dead boughs, for whose loss the pines
Moaned ceaseless overhead, the blossoming vines
　　Lifted their glad surprise,
While yet the bluebird smoothed in leafless trees
His feathers, ruffled by the chill sea-breeze,
　　And snow-drifts lingered under April skies.

As, pausing, o'er the lonely flower I bent,
I thought of lives thus lowly, clogged and pent,
　　Which yet find room,
Through care and cumber, coldness and decay,
To lend a sweetness to the ungenial day,
　　And make the sad earth happier for their bloom.

"YESTERDAY a strange thing happened in the meeting-house. The minister had gone on in his discourse, until the sand in the hour-glass on the rails before the deacons had well-nigh run out, and Deacon Dole was about turning it, when suddenly I saw the congregation about me give a great start and look back. A young woman, barefooted, and with a coarse canvas frock about her, and her long hair hanging loose like a periwig, and sprinkled with ashes, came walking up the south aisle. Just as she got near Uncle Rawson's seat she stopped, and, turning round towards the four corners of the house, cried out: "Woe to the persecutors! Woe to them who for a pretence make long prayers! Humble yourselves, for this is the day of the Lord's power, and I am sent as a sign among you!" As she looked toward me I knew her to be the Quaker maiden, Margaret Brewster. "Where is the constable?" asked Mr. Richardson. "Let the woman be taken out." Thereupon the whole congregation arose; and there was a great uproar, men and women climbing the seats, and many crying out, some one thing and some another. In the midst of the noise, Mr. Sewall, getting up on a bench, begged the people to be quiet, and let the constable lead out the poor deluded creature. Mr. Richardson spake to the same effect; and, the tumult a little subsiding, I saw them taking the young woman out of the door; and, as many followed her, I went out also, with my brother, to see what became of her.

A LEAF FROM MARGARET SMITH'S JOURNAL.

REFERENCES.

Samuel T. Pickard's *Life and Letters of John G. Whittier.*

W. J. Linton's *Life of Whittier.*

W. S. Kennedy's *Life of Whittier.*

F. H. Underwood's *Biography of Whittier.*

Margaret Sidney's *Whittier with the Children* (Illustrated).

Mrs. Claflin's *Personal Recollections of Whittier.*

Mrs. James T. Fields's *Whittier: Notes of his Life and Friendships* (Illustrated).

Shepard's *Pen Pictures of Modern Authors.*

Stedman-Hutchinson's *Library of American Literature.* Vol. VI.

Stedman's *Poets of America.*

Stoddard's *Poets' Homes.*

Theodore Wolfe's *Literary Shrines.*

Richardson's *American Literature.* Vol. II.

Haverhill's *Memorial of Whittier.* 1893.

Lowell's *Fable for Critics.*

Miss Mitford's *Recollections of a Literary Life.*

E. P. Whipple's *Essays and Reviews.*

M. W. Hazeltine's *Chats about Books.*

Allibone's *Dictionary of Authors.*

Appletons' Cyclopædia of American Biography.

Text-books of American Literature.

The Whittier Number of *The Literary World.* Dec. 17, 1887.

Scribner's Monthly. August, 1879 (Article by Stoddard).

The Atlantic Monthly. March, 1864. February, 1874. November, 1892. November, 1894.

Harper's Magazine. January, 1884 (Illustrated). February, 1883 (Illustrated).

The Boston Daily Advertiser. Dec. 17, 1877 (Autobiographic Sketch).

The Critic. Oct. 22, 1892. Jan. 28, 1893.

The New England Magazine. November, 1892 ("In Whittier's Land." Illustrated. "Whittier the Poet and the Man"). December, 1892 ("Whittier's First Printed Poems." Illustrated). June, 1893 ("Personal Recollections," by Charlotte Grimké).

The Cosmopolitan. January, 1894 ("Whittier Desultoria." Five portraits of Whittier).

NOTES. — Selections from Whittier's Prose are found in *American Prose*, Cleveland's *American Literature*, Stedman-Hutchinson's *Library of American Literature*, *Whittier Leaflets* (Riverside Literature Series).

For classifications of selected poems of Whittier, see Miss Hodgkins's *Guide to the Study of Nineteenth Century Authors*, and Alfred S. Roe's *American Authors and their Birthdays.*

OUTLINE OF HIS LIFE.

December 17, 1807.
September 7, 1892.

REMARK. — Whittier's life was notably uneventful.

Ancestry.

The Greenleafs are believed to have been a Huguenot family, who left France because of their religious convictions.

(See allusions to the name Greenleaf in the poem entitled, "A Name.")

"Generations of God-fearing ancestors were behind him [Whittier]."

Thomas "Whitier," the first of the family in America, was a contemporary of George Fox, and had much respect for his doctrines.

Rev. Stephen Bachiler, a maternal ancestor, founded the town of Hampton, N.H., and was the first minister settled there.

"It was the Bachiler eye, dark, deep-set, and lustrous, which marked the cousinship that existed between Daniel Webster and John Greenleaf Whittier."

Name.

Spelled in the old records in thirty-two different ways.

Original form probably Feuillevert.

Birthplace.

East Haverhill, Essex Co., Mass., the neighborhood of Hannah Dustin's heroic deed.

"Haverhill is the pleasantest village I ever passed through." — GEORGE WASHINGTON.

The Merrimack, Whittier's River of Song.

Homestead two hundred years old. Built by Thomas Whitier.

Described in *Snow-Bound* and in "The Fish I didn't Catch" (prose).

Home often visited by wanderers of varying characters. See sketch, "Yankee Gypsies," among Whittier's prose writings.

Now open to the public at all times.

It contains Whittier's historic desk and many other souvenirs of the poet.

For views, see Kennedy's *Whittier*, Underwood's *Whittier*, Pickard's *Whittier*, Vol. I., and *The New England Magazine* for November, 1892.

A mile from the home is Lake Kenoza (Indian word for "pickerel"), named by Whittier, and alluded to in his poetry.

See *The New England Magazine*, July, 1890 ("Old Haverhill." Illustrated); *Scribner's Magazine*, September, 1872.

Father.

"Quaker Whycher." A rough, decisive, sterling character.

Taciturn. "No breath our father wasted."

Mother.

Lovable, religious, kind-hearted.

Read the poet's characterizations of his parents and sisters in *Snow-Bound.*

She taught her children the Bible on "First-day" afternoons.

For woodcut of her face, see Underwood's *Whittier*, p. 48; also, Pickard's *Whittier*, Vol. II.

Education. (Non-collegiate.)

The Bible. Burns's Poems. (A copy was given to the boy by his schoolmaster.) The "Davideis," a poem by Ellwood, Milton's Quaker friend.

Read Whittier's poem on Burns.

"There were not a dozen books in my father's library."

"I had in my childhood a great thirst for knowledge, and little means to gratify it."

For an article on Whittier's boyhood, see *St. Nicholas*, October, 1887.

School in Haverhill, taught by Joshua Coffin, later the historian of Newbury.

See the poems, "In School Days," and "To My Old Schoolmaster."

The building is now standing; for a view of it as in the
poet's boyhood, consult Kennedy's *Whittier, Harper's
Magazine* for February, 1883, or Margaret Sidney's
Whittier with the Children.

Two Years at Haverhill Academy.

Tuition paid by money earned in making ladies' slippers at
twenty-five cents a pair. (Compare Whittier's poem,
"The Shoemakers," and the kindred production,
"Work," of his friend, Lucy Larcom.)

An omnivorous reader.

Dedicatory Ode, written for the new academy building in 1827.

Religion.

That of the Society of Friends.

The "Inner Light" glorified his whole life.

For view of the Friends' meeting-house in Amesbury, frequented by the poet in his youth, and again during the
years of his Amesbury life, see *The New England Magazine*
for November, 1892.

First Printed Poems.

In *The Newburyport Free Press*, June, 1826.

"The Exile's Departure." Sent by his sister without the
writer's knowledge.

"The Deity." Founded on 1 Kings xix. 11, 12.
("The turning-point in Whittier's career.")

For *fac-similes* of the two poems, look in *The New England
Magazine* for December, 1892.

Written at the age of eighteen.

The first poem signed with the author's full name was "The
Outlaw," printed in *The Haverhill Gazette*, Oct. 28, 1828.

NOTE. — Whittier wrote verses as soon as he could write at all,
and was often forced to use chalk and charcoal when pen
and ink failed him.

Friendship with William Lloyd Garrison.

Garrison's call to look up his new contributor to *The Press.*

The father discouraged the cultivation of the boy's talent, and
said to his caller, "Poetry will not give him bread." (Read

the statement relating to the poet's will, under Miscellaneous Notes.)

Joint newspaper work.

Through the reformer's influence, Whittier's verse became "the mallet of Thor."

Garrison was released from his imprisonment at Baltimore by Whittier's appeal to Henry Clay, which called forth Arthur Tappan's effectual response.

Consult Oliver Johnson's *Garrison and His Times* (Whittier wrote the introduction to this biography), and *The Life of Garrison by his Children*.

Read Whittier's poems, "To W. L. G." and "Garrison."

Teaches a District School.

Farm Life at Home in Haverhill.

Inspired his pathetic ballad, "Telling the Bees." (European tradition among the peasant people of inviting the bees to share in the family joys and sorrows.)

Advocacy of Abolition, involving the sacrifice of early political ambition.

Many and vigorous poems, "bugle-blasts in the van of freedom."

"The poetry was genuine, as the wrath was terrific."

A signer of the Anti-Slavery Declaration of 1833. (Massachusetts' youngest delegate to the Philadelphia Convention.)
He was prouder of this fact than of all his verse.

Secretary of the National Anti-Slavery Association. 1836.

Editor of anti-slavery journals.

Persecutions.

Mobbed in Concord, N.H., 1835, when in company with George Thompson, the English Abolitionist. (The same night his sister Elizabeth helped an Abolitionist, Samuel J. May, to escape from a mob in Haverhill.)

"I understand how St. Paul felt when he was thrice stoned."

Philadelphia office sacked and burned. 1839.

"He made himself the champion of the slave when to say aught against the national curse was to draw upon one's self the bitterest hatred, loathing, and contempt of the great majority of men throughout the land."

" For twenty years I was shut out from the favor of book-
sellers and magazine editors; but I was enabled by rigid
economy to live in spite of them, and to see the end of
the infernal institution that proscribed me. Thank God
for it."

His Counsel to a Young Friend. "My lad, if thou wouldst
win success, join thyself to some unpopular but noble
cause."

Consult Wilson's *Rise and Fall of Slave-Power* in America.

Representative to the Massachusetts State Legislature. 1835.

Journalistic Life in Haverhill, Boston, Hartford, Philadelphia,
Washington.

Editor of *The Pennsylvania Freeman.* 1838, 1839.

Editor of *The National Era*, Washington, which also championed
the principles of Abolition. Twelve years.

Contributors to his paper. Lucy Larcom, the Cary Sisters,
Mrs. Stowe, Grace Greenwood, Mrs. Southworth.

Uncle Tom's Cabin was first published as a serial in this
paper, 1850. The Novel of Abolition.

"Randolph of Roanoke," one of Whittier's best political
poems, appeared in the first issue of *The Era.*

Hawthorne's story, "The Great Stone Face," was first
printed in this paper, Jan. 24, 1850; and its author received twenty-five dollars for it.

Presidential Elector. 1848.

A Contributor to The Atlantic Monthly from its beginning.

Banquet tendered him by its publishers on his seventieth
birthday.

Member of the Atlantic Club (Saturday Club), Boston.

Life in Amesbury, Mass., with his sister Elizabeth. 1840–1864.

Their mutual devotion was a counterpart to that of Charles
Lamb and his sister Mary, of Wordsworth and his sister
Dorothy.

Elizabeth Whittier was "one of the rarest of women," and her
brother's complement in both temperament and intellect.

Semi-Invalidism.

Of many years' duration.

Whittier was a victim to severe headaches, and for many years was rarely able to write more than half an hour at a time. He attributed his delicate health to the method of "toughening" the constitution by exposure to cold, common when he was a boy.

Death of Sister.

The greatest sorrow in the poet's life.

See his poem, "To My Sister," the beautiful tribute in *Snow-Bound*, his "Last Eve of Summer," and "The Vanishers."

She had been his "most intimate and confidential literary friend." "He had for many years at his own fireside the concentrated wit and sympathy of all womankind in this sister."

Elizabeth Whittier also had poetical talent. Nine of her poems were published with some of her brother's in his collection, *Hazel Blossoms*.

His niece and adopted daughter, Elizabeth, presided over the Amesbury home after the death of her aunt, until her marriage.

Whittier lived twenty years deprived of all companionship of immediate family relatives.

Meets Dom Pedro, Emperor of Brazil, an enthusiastic admirer of his writings.

Closing Years at Oak Knoll, Danvers, Mass., with a cousin, Mrs. Johnson, and her family.

For a description of the spot, see Pickard's *Whittier*, Vol. II. pp. 614–616.

"I could not help a feeling of loneliness, thinking of having outlived so many of my life companions [after the birthday, 1888]; but I was still grateful to God that I had not outlived my love for them, and for those still living."

> "I sit alone and watch the warm, sweet day
> 　　Lapse tenderly away;
> 　And wistful, with a feeling of forecast,
> 　　I ask, ' Is this the last ? ' "

The Last Eve of Summer (1890).

Receives the Degree of Doctor of Laws from Harvard University. 1886.

Eightieth Birthday.

>Marked by the receipt of a thousand letters, messages, and gifts from loving and admiring friends, many of which came from colored schools in the South.

Death at Hampton Falls, N.H., at the home of Miss Gove, daughter of the "friend" in the poem, "A Friend's Burial."

>*Last Utterance.* "Love to all the world."

>For a view of the house, see Mrs. Fields's *Whittier*, and Pickard's *Life of Whittier*, Vol. II.

>In the vicinity had been laid the scenes of "The New Wife and The Old," "Hampton Beach," "The Wreck of Rivermouth," and others of his poems.

Buried in the Friends' Cemetery, Amesbury.

>The service was held in the garden behind his home, and, by the poet's request, in accordance with the simple forms of the Quakers. Lucy Larcom read "The Vanishers," the first poem written by Whittier after his sister's death.

>A song was chanted by the three surviving members of the Hutchinson family, the Singers of Abolition.

>For a description, see Pickard's *Whittier*, Vol. II., and *The New England Magazine* for January, 1893 ; for a view of the resting-place, consult the same magazine for November, 1892.

>The poet lies beside the loved ones immortalized in *Snow-Bound*.

Literary Executor.

>Samual T. Pickard, editor of *The Portland Transcript*, and Whittier's nephew by marriage.

A Nephew, a brother's son, is the only surviving relative bearing the poet's name.

Autobiographic Glimpses.

>Snow-Bound. "In School Days." "The Barefoot Boy." "Remembrance." "An Autograph." "My Namesake." "To My Old Schoolmaster." "At Eventide." "The Anti-

Slavery Convention of 1833" (*The Atlantic Monthly*, February, 1874). Introduction to Oliver Johnson's *Garrison and His Times.*

Prominent Traits in His Character.

Love of freedom and of country. Moral fervor. Faith in God. Self-effacement. Appreciation of his contemporaries. Keen enjoyment of his friends. Fondness for children and animals. Love of quiet and of silence. Tender sympathy for suffering. Indifference to fame. Sweetness of disposition. "His noble simplicity of character is the delight of all."

Read his description of himself in *The Tent on the Beach*, and in the Proem that prefaces his poetry.

Appearance.

That of a Hebrew prophet.

Tall, erect. Lofty, dome-like forehead ; "the upward and backward slope of the head was like that of Emerson and of Walter Scott." Olive complexion, black hair.

Dark, flashing eyes, firm and resolute mouth. Dignified carriage. Quaker costume.

Manner.

Kind and simple.

Voice.

Deep and sonorous. Fuller and stronger in reading poetry than at other times.

Habits.

" For forty years Whittier rarely failed to see the sun rise."

He never entered a " play-house." (A promise to his mother.)

His Friends.

William Lloyd Garrison. Charles Sumner. Bayard Taylor. James T. Fields and Mrs. Fields. Longfellow. Emerson. Holmes. Celia Thaxter. Lucy Larcom. Gail Hamilton. Lydia Maria Child. Sarah Orne Jewett. Colonel Higginson.

APPELLATIONS.

The Laureate of Abolition.

The Woodthrush of Essex. — *Holmes.*

The Quaker Poet.

The People's Poet.

Our Chief Bucolic Poet.

The Poet of New England History.

The Hermit of Amesbury. — *Longfellow.*

The Poet of the Moral Sentiment.

The Burns of America.

The Celibate and Prophetic Recluse.

The Hebrew Poet of the Nineteenth Century.

The High Priest of American Literature.

The Poet of Faith.

The Poet of Freedom.   (*Lowell his compeer.*)

The Champion of Right and the Enemy of Wrong.

The Galahad of our Table Round.

A Modern Bayard, "without Fear and without Reproach."

The Boanerges of American Poets.

Gentlest and Tenderest of all the Sons of Thunder.

A Poet Militant and Ministrant.

The Martial Quaker.

Our Merrimac Teniers.

The Poet of New England's Mayflowers.

The Boy Poet of Essex Farm.

The Poet of the Bright Side of Human Life.

The Bard of an Historic Time.

Our Foremost Balladist.

America's Shoemaker Poet.

The Patron Saint of Haverhill.

An Artist in Landscape.

Our Poet-Politician.

NOTES ON HIS WRITINGS.

His Poetry.

Vigorous, homely, unstudied, original.

Rhyme and Metre. Often incorrect. ("I should be hung for my bad rhymes anywhere south of Mason and Dixon's line.") The latter is but little varied; the prevailing measure is the iambic tetrameter used in rhyming couplets.

Evoked largely by contemporary events; "lacks the inherent element of perennial greatness."

Mainly lyric or descriptive.

Shows a "patriotic, democratic, and humane spirit."

"It has made freedom a duty and religion a joy."

"Whittier reaches the heart of the people as a poet of higher culture might fail to do."

Favorite Themes. Witchcraft, Quakerism, Slavery, Indian traditions, New England colonial history.

Local Associations of his Poems.

See illustrated articles in *Harper's Magazine* for February, 1883, and *The New England Magazine* for November, 1892 ("In Whittier's Land").

Voices of Freedom. 1833–1848.

The first poems that gave their writer reputation.

Some of the most stirring " Voices."

The Slave Ships. Follen. The Yankee Girl. The Christian Slave. Massachusetts to Virginia.

Snow-Bound. 1865.

The poet's masterpiece.

Inspired by Emerson's "Snow-Storm." (See prefatory lines.)

Written "to beguile the weariness of a sick chamber," the year after his sister's death.

The story covers three days and two nights.

A New England winter idyl.

Beautiful, picturesque, and artistic.

It suggests Burns's "Cotter's Saturday Night," Goldsmith's "Deserted Village," and Cowper's "Winter Evening" in "The Task."

Characters. (No one of the family survives.)

> The poet's parents, sisters Mary and Elizabeth, brother Matthew.
> Uncle, Moses Whittier. Aunt, Mercy Hussey.
> Schoolmaster. A student from Dartmouth College.
> The "half-welcome guest." Harriet Livermore.
> The "Queen of Lebanon." Lady Hester Stanhope.
> The "wise old doctor." Elias Weld, the family physician.

Annotated Version. In *American Poems, Masterpieces of American Literature*, and the Riverside Literature Series.

Whittier realized a profit of ten thousand dollars from the first issue of the poem.

The Tent on the Beach.

An idyl of life by the sea.

Scene. Salisbury Beach.

Campers. Whittier, Bayard Taylor, and James T. Fields.

Dedicated to Mrs. Fields.

Contains descriptions of the beaches of Hampton and Salisbury.

Idea. A group of tales read by Whittier to his two friends. Somewhat similar to Chaucer's *Canterbury Tales* and Longfellow's *Tales of a Wayside Inn.*

The Best Poems.

> The Wreck of Rivermouth. (Goody Cole, the witch who appears in this ballad, and also in "The Changeling," was Eunice Cole, who lived in a little hut in Hampton, avoided by all people.) The Brother of Mercy. The Changeling. Abraham Davenport.

Its Sale. Twenty thousand copies were quickly sold, being called for at the rate of a thousand a day.

"Whittier's art culminated in 'Home Ballads,' 'Snow-Bound,' and 'The Tent on the Beach.'"

Maud Muller.

Whittier did not like this poem because it was "too sad."

The author pronounced the "u" like "u" in cup.

Mabel Martin.

An amplification of "The Witch's Daughter."

Note the "Chaucerian freshness of the opening stanzas."

The house of Mabel's father, at Amesbury, stood until a few years ago. (For view of the scene, consult *Harper's Magazine*, February, 1883.)

Goody Martin was the only woman north of the Merrimack who suffered death for witchcraft.

When it was printed in book-form, the publishers sent Whittier a thousand dollars for the tale.

"The Witch of Wenham " is a companion tale.

Skipper Ireson's Ride.

Real name of rider, Benjamin Ireson.

Whittier unknowingly deviates from facts. (Consult John Chadwick's article in *Harper's Monthly* for July, 1874.)

The refrain was originally written without the use of the Marblehead dialect.

The story was told Whittier when he was at the Haverhill Academy by a schoolmate from Marblehead; the poem, begun at that time, was not finished until thirty years later.

The New Wife and the Old.

Founded on a legend connected with the family of General Moulton of Hampton, N.H., regarded by his neighbors as a Yankee Faust.

In School Days.

" *You* have written the most beautiful school-boy poem in the English language." — HOLMES, to Whittier.

Barbara Frietchie.

The best of Whittier's war lyrics.

The incident was given to the poet by Mrs. Southworth, the novelist.

For a discussion of the facts, see Kennedy's *Life of Whittier*, pp. 240, 241; and Pickard's *Whittier*, Vol. II., pp. 451-456.

"Inclosed is a check for fifty dollars, but Barbara's weight should be in gold." — His publishers.

The Countess.

One of the poet's most beautiful ballads.

Scene laid in Rocks Village, East Haverhill.

Heroine, Miss Mary Ingalls, a girl of remarkable beauty.

She married a French exile, Count de Vipart, and lived but a year after the marriage. The count, overwhelmed with grief, returned to his native land; but later he married again.

See three illustrations in *Harper's Magazine*, February, 1883 ; also, Wolfe's *Literary Shrines*, p. 123.

Cassandra Southwick.

A ballad of Quaker persecution.

Founded on historic fact.

Cassandra, a Quaker girl of Salem, Mass.

The poem is "full of heart-beats."

Mary Garvin.

"In Chase's *History of Haverhill*, there is preserved a letter from one Mary Wainwright, whose daughter had been carried away by the Indians and French, in which the mother asks that means be taken to get her child back before she should be perverted."

Miriam.

A sermon in poetry.

A Christian slave and favorite wife of an Oriental monarch inspires her lord to show Christian mercy toward one condemned.

The Pennsylvania Pilgrim.

Pastorius. A German jurist and scholar who came to Pennsylvania at William Penn's invitation, and founded Germantown; "the combined Bradford and Brewster of the colony." (Read prefatory note.)

Pastorius' memorial against slavery, drawn up in 1688 at a meeting of the Germantown Friends, was the first protest made by any religious body against negro slavery.

"A poem for Quakers."

"A truly erudite work for its limited sphere."

My Playmate.

"It is a perfect poem; in some of his descriptions of scenery and wild-flowers, Whittier would rank with Wordsworth." — TENNYSON.

"Ein' feste Burg ist unser Gott." ("The Furnace Blast.")

Set to the music of Luther's hymn.

Sung in the Cabinet of President Lincoln, in the Union camps, and by the Hutchinson family after the first battle of Bull Run to the soldiers encamped on the Virginia side of the Potomac.

The Vaudois Teacher.

The French translation of this became very popular among the Waldenses of Piedmont, who adopted it as a household poem.

Pæan.

Written after the formation of the first national anti-slavery party, at Buffalo, N. Y.

Laus Deo!

Called forth by the passing of the constitutional amendment abolishing slavery; suggested to the poet as he sat in the Friends' meeting-house in Amesbury, and listened to the bells proclaiming the fact.

"A Miriam's song of praise and thanksgiving."

The Last Walk in Autumn.

Contains appreciative stanzas on Emerson, Taylor, Sumner.

Follen.

" Our gifted brother Whittier has again seized the great trumpet of Liberty, and blown a blast that shall ring from Maine to the Rocky Mountains." — GARRISON.

Used with great effect by anti-slavery orators.

Lines on a Fly-leaf.

Portrait sketches of Gail Hamilton, Lydia Maria Child, Grace Greenwood, Anna Dickinson, and Mrs. Stowe.

Little Red Riding Hood

Phœbe Woodman, daughter to the writer's cousin at Oak Knoll.

The Singer.

A tribute to Alice and Phœbe Cary.

The Hero.

Dr. Samuel G. Howe.

Brown of Ossawatomie.

A tribute to the nobleness of John Brown's nature.

Poems on Daniel Webster.

Ichabod ! 1 Samuel iv. 19–22.

Written after Webster's famous speech of March 7, 1850, assenting to the Fugitive Slave Law.

This poem has been compared with Browning's " Lost Leader."

The Lost Occasion.

A superb eulogy, penned years later and in a tenderer mood.

Marguerite.

The story of an Acadian girl " bound out " in one of the families of Haverhill. (A thousand of the exiled Acadians were distributed among the towns of Massachusetts.)

The Cry of a Lost Soul.

Translated by Dom Pedro into Portuguese, who sent a copy of the translation to Whittier, accompanied by a well-mounted pair of the Amazonian birds whose peculiar cry and name suggested the poem.

Monadnock.

Compare with Emerson's poem on the same subject.

Indian Poems.

Inferior to Longfellow's *Hiawatha.*

The Bridal of Pennacook. (His best.) The Truce of Piscataqua. Mary Garvin. Pentucket. The Fountain. Funeral Tree of the Sokokis. The Grave by the Lake. Nauhaught, the Deacon.

Among the Hills.

(Whittier frequently summered in the White Mountains.)

"A pretty and melodious love-story, with a strongly realistic prelude."

Hazel Blossoms.

Sumner. The Prayer of Agassiz. John Underhill (the poet's favorite among his own works). In Quest, and others.

Religious Poems.

The Eternal Goodness. The Crucifixion. Palestine. My Soul and I. Andrew Rykman's Prayer. The Prayer of Agassiz. In Quest. A Christmas Carmen, and others.

Poems of Occasion.

Centennial Hymn. The Vow of Washington, 1889. The Two Hundred and Fiftieth Anniversary of the Founding of Haverhill (1890), and minor ones.

Hymns.

The Plymouth collection contains eleven by Whittier.

In a collection of sixty-six hymns prepared for the use of the General Congress of Religions at the Chicago Exposition, nine were taken from Whittier, a larger number than from any other writer.

"His hymns are so many acts of faith." — STEDMAN.

Lines from one of his last poems.

> "As the soul liveth, it shall live
>   Beyond the years of time.
>   Beside the mystic asphodels
>   Shall bloom the home-born flowers,
>   And new horizons flash and glow
>   With sunset hues of ours."
>
> *At Sundown* (January, 1891).

Songs of Three Centuries.

A collection of poems compiled by Whittier and Lucy Larcom.

Prose Writings.

Inferior to his poems.

Legends of New England. (Prose and verse.)

Justice and Expediency; or, **Slavery** Considered with a View to Abolition.

> Published in 1833, an issue of five hundred copies, at the writer's expense.   Arthur Tappan, the New York philanthropist and Abolitionist, at once caused ten times as many copies to be printed and circulated.

Supernaturalism in New England.

> Witch and ghost stories of his neighborhood.

Margaret Smith's Journal.

> Imaginary description of New England in early times.
>
> Sketch of Puritan intolerance.
>
> "A novel similar in nature to *The Household of Sir Thomas Moore.*"
>
> Originally contributed to *The National Era.*

Old Portraits and Modern Sketches.

Literary Recreations and Miscellanies.

> "Yankee Gypsies," "Evangeline," and other papers.

MISCELLANEOUS NOTES.

Tributes to Whittier.

"The world has lost one of its sweetest lyrists of its saddest wrongs." — *The London Chronicle*, Sept. 8, 1892.

"Emancipated millions will hold his memory sacred." — FREDERICK DOUGLASS.

"Whittier, like Hampden and Milton, is a character not produced in common times." — E. C. STEDMAN.

"He felt himself responsible to his heavenly Father, not for the actions of Joseph or Paul, but for those of John G. Whittier." — F. H. UNDERWOOD.

"With God's help he thought for himself, he said earnestly what he thought, — no more, no less, — and he did exactly what he said." — E. E. HALE.

"The love of liberty will not die out in the land while the youth of America learn and love the verse of the poet who combines the lofty inspiration of David with the sweet simplicity of Burns." — G. F. HOAR.

"His war poems were like the sound of the trumpet blown before the walls of Jerusalem."

"Whittier unites descriptive talent as related to natural scenery, the reformer's enthusiasm, and the patriot's sympathies."

"What Scott did for the scenery of Scotland, and the Grimm brothers for that of Germany, Whittier may almost be said to have done for New England."

"He is a sparrow that half sings, half chirps on a bush, not a lark that floods with orient hilarity the skies of the morning; but the bush burns, like that which Moses saw, and the sparrow herself is part of the divine flame." — DAVID WASSON.

"No poet ever lived nearer the great heart of humanity than he." — FRANCES SPARHAWK.

> "Gracious thine age; thy youth was strong,
>   For freedom touched thy tongue with fire;
> To sing the right and fight the wrong
>   Thine equal hand held bow or lyre."

W. H. WARD.

"All honor and praise to the right-hearted bard
Who was true to the Voice when such service was hard,
Who himself was so free he dared sing for the slave
When to look but a protest in silence was brave."

J. R. LOWELL.

"When our sad nation delved in deepest night,
To his pure spirit God was still in sight."

WILL CARLETON.

"A blameless memory shrined in deathless song." — O. W. HOLMES.
Holmes's poems. On Whittier's seventieth and his eightieth birthdays. Dr. Holmes wrote a third poem after Whittier's death.
Lowell's *Fable;* and his Sonnets, 1884, 1892.
Longfellow's Sonnet, "The Three Silences of Molinos."
For *fac-simile* of the original, see *The New England Magazine* for December, 1892.
Stedman's "Ad Vigilem."
John T. Chadwick's "A Thought on Whittier."
Allen E. Cross's "The Passing of Whittier."
Will Carleton's "Ode to Whittier." (Written for the Haverhill memorial services.)
See *The Literary World* for Dec. 1, 1877.

Position as Balladist.

Whittier ranks in this field first among American poets.

Homes.

East Haverhill. (See notes on the Birthplace.)
Amesbury. (Friend Street.)
His study, the "Garden Room." (Facing the garden.) Book-lined walls. Three pictures of interest, — The Haverhill Birthplace, The Barefoot Boy, and Barry's The Motherless, with lines by Mrs. Stowe written under it. (The last-named inspired one of his two poems called "The Sisters.")
Consult Stoddard's *Poets' Homes*, Kennedy's *Whittier*, Pickard's *Life of Whittier*, Vol. I., and Wolfe's *Literary Shrines.*
Newburyport. With his cousins, the Cartlands.
The house had been the early home of Harriet Livermore, the eccentric personage portrayed in *Snowbound.*
Oak Knoll, Danvers.
The estate where once lived George Burroughs, the athletic clergyman hanged for supposed witchcraft.
For view, see Mrs. Fields's *Whittier* and *The New England Magazine* for November, 1892.

His Pets.

In Amesbury a gifted parrot, Charlie, referred to in the poem, "The Common Question."

At Oak Knoll, a squirrel, two dogs, Jersey cows, and a mocking-bird.

"Whittier secured the love of every living thing that came under his care."

His Celibacy.

A house is shown in Marblehead, Mass., in which, according to tradition, lived the love of the poet's youth (Evelina Bray).

"Possibly there is reference to the same person in the poems, 'Telling the Bees' and 'In School Days.'"

Read the poems, "My Playmate" and "Memories."

"Circumstances — the care of an aged mother, and the duty owed to a sister in delicate health for many years -- must be my excuse for living the lonely life which has called out thy pity. . . . I have learned to look into happiness through the eyes of others, and to thank God for the happy unions and holy firesides I have known." — *Letter to a friend.*

Illustration of his Humor.

> "Ah, ladies, you love to levy a tax
>
>   On my poor little paper parcel of fame;
>
> Yet strange it seems, that among you all
>
>   Not one is willing to take my name —
>
> To write and rewrite, till angels pity her,
>
> The weariful words, Thine truly, Whittier."
>
> *Lines in a Young Lady's Album.*

Views on Marriage.

"Let me in all sincerity, bachelor as I am, congratulate thee on thy escape from single misery. It is the very wisest thing thee ever did. Were I autocrat I would see to it that every young man over twenty-five, and every young woman over twenty, was married without delay. Perhaps, on second thought, it might be well to keep one old maid and one old bachelor in each town, by way of warning, just as the Spartans did their drunken Helots." — *Letter to his publisher, Mr. Fields, at the time of the latter's marriage.*

Love of New England.

Whittier, like Thoreau, did not travel.

Note his verses: --

> "He who wanders widest, lifts
>
>   No more of beauty's jealous veil
>
>   Than he who from his doorway sees
>
>   The miracle of flowers and trees."

Benefactions.

> Generous.   In harmony with his verses: —
>
> > "O well-paid author, fat-fed scholar,
> > Whose pockets jingle with the dollar,
> > No sheriff's hand upon your collar,
> >   No duns to bother,
> > Think on't, a tithe of what ye swallow
> >   Would save your brother."
>
> In his will he made bequests to the amount of $66,000.

Ideal Message of Sympathy.

> To Mrs. Lothrop, "Margaret Sidney," upon the death of her hus-
> band, Daniel Lothrop, the publisher: "Let me sit in the circle
> of thy mourning; for I, too, have lost a friend."

His Self-Restraint.

> "He religiously curbed his tongue, and said of himself that he was
> born without an atom of patience in his composition; but that
> he had tried to manufacture it as needed."

His Optimism.

> "Of course the world is growing better; the Lord reigns; our old
> planet is wheeling slowly into light. I despair of nothing good.
> All will come in due time that is needed. All we have to do is
> to work — and wait."   (Written in 1881.)

Color-Blindness.

> Whittier could not recognize shades of red and green; but he appre-
> ciated yellow so keenly that he felt compensated for the defect.
> His face, in the opinion of an eminent authority on the subject,
> bore the characteristic look of the color-blind.

Modest Self-Estimate of His Verse.

> "I am not a builder in the sense of Milton's phrase of one who could
> 'build the lofty rhyme.' My vehicles have been of the humbler
> sort, — merely the farm-wagon and buckboard of verse, and not
> likely to run so long as Dr. Holmes's 'One Hoss Shay.' . . . I
> shall not dare to warrant any of my work for a long drive."

A Rule of His Life.

> Never to buy anything until he had the money in hand to pay for it.

Early Pseudonyms.

> Adrian. Donald. Timothy. Micajah. Ichabod.

Number of Poems composed between 1832 and 1865.

> Nearly three hundred, more than a third of which bore directly or
> indirectly upon the subject of slavery.

Literary and Anti-Slavery Labors.

"I cannot be sufficiently grateful to the divine Providence that so early called my attention to the great interests of humanity, saving me from the poor ambitions and miserable jealousies of a selfish pursuit of literary reputation. Up to a comparatively recent period my writings have been simply episodical, something apart from the real object and aim of my life; and whatever favor they have found with the public has come to me as a grateful surprise, rather than as an expected reward." (1867.)

Whittier and Calvinism.

"In no other of our poets do we find such traces of the conflict of old New England Calvinism as in the pages of Whittier, and it is in his help for freeing them from the thraldom of that nightmare that many owe him most. Whittier was born into a time and place in which the merciless old theology was supreme; and the more he came to know it, the more his Quaker soul recoiled [from?] and fought it. — EDWIN D. MEAD.

Read his poems, "The Eternal Goodness," "The Minister's Daughter," and "The Preacher" (George Whitefield, buried in Newburyport, not far from Whittier's home).

Concluding Paragraph of Justice and Expediency.

"And when the stain in our own escutcheon shall be seen no more; when the Declaration of Independence and the practice of our people shall agree; when Truth shall be exalted among us; when Love shall take the place of Wrong; when all the baneful pride and prejudice of caste and color shall fall forever; when under one common sun of political Liberty the slaveholding portions of our Republic shall no longer sit like Egyptians of old, themselves mantled in thick darkness, while all around them is glowing with the blessed light of freedom and equality, — then, and not till then, shall it go well for America."

Motto of "The Liberator," a paper edited at one time by Whittier.

"Unconditional emancipation is the immediate duty of the master, and the immediate right of the slave."

Our Journalist Poets.

Whittier. Bryant. Poe. Holmes. Lowell.

Illustrated Editions of Whittier's Poetry. (Houghton & Mifflin.)

Poems Complete. Three one-volumed editions.

Individual Poems.

Snow-Bound. At Sundown. Maud Muller. Mabel Martin. Ballads of New England. Poems of Nature.

Riverside Edition of His Works.

> Four volumes of poetry, three of prose.
>
> A number of the poems in this edition have notes written by the author.

A Characterization of Whittier.

> "His gallantry watched kindly on her way
> The humble maid that tossed the fragrant hay;
> His pity sought the fallen conquered brave,
> And left its tears upon an Indian grave;
> With flowers of justice and of love he strewed
> The Witch's child, by zealotry pursued;   .
> Even the soul in endless darkness thrown,
> Had pity from his muse; there was no moan
>   Escaped his eager ear!
> He pitied, with brave words that echo yet,
> Th' old soldier, prisoned for a paltry debt;
> He helped to give a new and honored place
> To an unjustly subjugated race;
> And though of peaceful lineage and creed,
> Yet he could fight when conflict was the need;
> And he could mould the silver of his song
> In solid shot, to hurl 'gainst shame and wrong;
> And tyrants fell, and fetters burst in twain,
> Before the fierce artillery of his brain."

WILL CARLETON.

A Group of Abolitionists.

> Whittier.   The Poet of Anti-Slavery.
> William Lloyd Garrison.   The Apostle.
> Henry Ward Beecher.   The Preacher.
> Charles Sumner.   The Statesman.
> Wendell Phillips.   The Orator.
> Harriet Beecher Stowe.   The Novelist.
> The Hutchinson Family, of Lynn, Mass.   The Singers.

OLIVER WENDELL HOLMES.

ESSAYIST, POET, NOVELIST, HUMORIST, SCIENTIST.

EXTRACTS.

BUILD thee more stately mansions, O my soul,
  As the swift seasons roll!
  Leave thy low-vaulted past!
Let each new temple, nobler than the last,
Shut thee from heaven with a dome more vast,
  Till thou at length art free,
Leaving thine outgrown shell by life's unresting sea!
                    THE CHAMBERED NAUTILUS.

      AY, tear her tattered ensign down!
        Long has it waved on high,
      And many an eye has danced to see
        That banner in the sky.
                        OLD IRONSIDES.

    AND, since, I never dare to write
      As funny as I can.
                THE HEIGHT OF THE RIDICULOUS.

      SILENCE like a poultice comes
    To heal the blows of sound.
                    THE MUSIC-GRINDERS.

You hear that boy laughing? — you think he's all fun,
But the angels laugh, too, at the good he has done;
The children laugh loud as they troop to his call,
And the poor man that knows him laughs loudest of all

THE BOYS.

THE mossy marbles rest
On the lips that he has prest
In their bloom.
And the names he loved to hear
Have been carved for many a year
On the tomb.

THE LAST LEAF.

My aunt! my poor, deluded aunt!
Her hair is almost gray;
Why will she train that winter curl
In such a spring-like way?

MY AUNT.

WHEN darkness gathers over all,
And the last tottering pillars fall,
Take the poor dust Thy mercy warms,
And mould it into heavenly forms.

THE LIVING TEMPLE.

GOD of all Nations! Sovereign Lord!
In Thy dread name we draw the sword,
We lift the starry flag on high
That fills with light our stormy sky.

ARMY HYMN.

When I talk of Whig and Tory, when I tell the Rebel story,
To you the words are ashes, but to me they're burning coals.

GRANDMOTHER'S STORY OF BUNKER HILL.

Lord of the Universe! shield us and guard us,
Trusting Thee always, through shadow and sun!
Thou hast united us, who shall divide us?
Keep us, O keep us the Many in One!
  Up with our banner bright,
  Sprinkled with starry light,
Spread its fair emblems from mountain to shore,
  While through the sounding sky
  Loud rings the nation's cry, —
Union and Liberty! One evermore!

      Union and Liberty.

While Valor's haughty champions wait
 Till all their scars are shown,
Love walks unchallenged through the gate
 To sit beside the Throne.

      The Two Armies.

Who would not, will not, if he can,
Bathe in the breezes of fair Cape Ann, —
Rest in the bowers her bays enfold,
Loved by the sachems and squaws of old?
Home where the white magnolias bloom,
Sweet with the bayberry's chaste perfume,
Hugged by the woods and kissed by the sea!
Where is an Eden like to thee?

      The Broomstick Train.

Little of all we value here
Wakes on the morn of its hundredth year
Without both feeling and looking queer.

      The Deacon's Masterpiece.

SENTENCES FROM THE AUTOCRAT.

Boston State House is the hub of the Solar System. You couldn't pry that out of a Boston man if you had the tire of all creation straightened out for a crowbar.

Put not your trust in money, but put your money in trust.

Passion never laughs. The wit knows that his place is at the tail of the procession.

Every person's feelings have a front door and a side door by which they may be entered. . . . Be very careful to whom you trust one of the keys of the side door.

The brain-women never interest us like the heart-women : white roses please less than red.

When a strong brain is weighed with a true heart, it seems to me like balancing a bubble against a wedge of pure gold.

The world has a million roosts for a man, but only one nest.

Facts always yield the place of honor in conversation to thoughts about facts.

I find the great thing in this world is not so much where we stand, as in what direction we are moving.

A man's opinions are of much more value than his arguments.

"This is the shortest way," she said, as we came to a corner. "Then we wont take it," said I.

I have known several genteel idiots whose whole vocabulary had deliquesced into some half-dozen expressions.

We never tell our secrets to people who pump for them.

Consciousness of unquestioned position makes people gracious in proper measure to all.

All men love all women. . . . The Court of Nature assumes the law to be that all men do so; and the individual man is bound to show cause why he does not love any particular woman.

Any new formula which suddenly emerges in our consciousness has its roots in long trains of thought.

Books are the negative pictures of thought; and the more sensitive the mind that receives their images, the more nicely the finest lines are reproduced.

HELEN DARLEY AND ELSIE VENNER.

She was a splendid scowling beauty, black-browed, with a flash of white teeth which was always like a surprise when her lips parted. She wore a checkered dress, of a curious pattern, and a camel's-hair scarf twisted a little fantastically about her. She went to her seat, which she had moved a short distance apart from the rest, and, sitting down, began playing listlessly with her gold chain, as was a common habit with her, coiling it and uncoiling it about her slender wrist, and braiding it in her long delicate fingers. Presently she looked up. Black, piercing eyes, not large; a low forehead, as low as that of Clytie in the Townley bust; black hair, twisted in heavy braids, — a face that one could not help looking at for its beauty, yet that one wanted to look away from for something in its expression, and could not for those diamond eyes. They were fixed on the lady teacher now. The latter turned her own away, and let them wander over the other scholars. But they could not help coming back again for a single glance at the wild beauty. The diamond eyes were on her still. She turned the leaves of several of her books, as if in search of some passage, and, when she thought she had waited long enough to be safe, once more stole a look at the dark girl. The diamond eyes were still upon her. She put her kerchief to her forehead, which had grown slightly moist; she sighed once, almost shivered, for she felt cold; then, following some ill-defined impulse, which she could not resist, she left her place and went to the young girl's desk.

"What do you want of me, Elsie Venner?" It was a strange question to put, for the girl had not signified that she wished the teacher to come to her.

"Nothing," she said. "I thought I could make you come." The girl spoke in a low tone, a kind of half-whisper. She did not lisp, yet her articulation of one or two consonants was not absolutely perfect.

"Where did you get that flower, Elsie?" said Miss Darley. It was a rare Alpine flower, which was found only in one spot among the rocks of The Mountain.

"Where it grew," said Elsie Venner. "Take it." The teacher could not refuse her. The girl's finger-tips touched hers as she took it. How cold they were for a girl of such an organization!

The teacher went back to her seat. She made an excuse for quitting the schoolroom soon afterwards. The first thing she did was to fling the flower into her fireplace and rake the ashes over it. The second was to wash the tips of her fingers, as if she had been another Lady Macbeth. A poor, overtasked, nervous creature, — we must not think too much of her fancies.

ELSIE VENNER.

REFERENCES.

Emma E. Brown's *Life of Holmes*. (Revised Edition, 1895.)

Stedman's *Poets of America*.

Arthur Gilman's *Poets' Homes*.

H. T. Griswold's *Home Life of Great Authors*.

G. W. Curtis's *Homes of American Authors;* his *Literary and Social Essays*.

R. H. Stoddard's *Poets' Homes*.

Shepard's *Pen Pictures of Modern Authors*.

Sarah K. Bolton's *Famous American Authors* (1887).

Lowell's *Fable for Critics*.

Stedman-Hutchinson's *Library of American Literature*. Vol. VII.

Haweis's *American Humorists*.

Richardson's *American Literature*. Vol. I., pp. 372–379 (Holmes as Essayist). Vol. II., pp. 204–218 (Holmes as Poet).

Charles Morris's *Half Hours with the Best American Authors*.

Allibone's *Dictionary of Authors*.

Appletons' Cyclopædia of American Biography.

Text-books and Cyclopædias of American Literature.

Scribner's Magazine. May, 1879 (Biographical Sketch by Underwood). January, 1895 ("Holmes as Professor of Anatomy").

The New England Magazine. October, 1889 ("Holmes at Fourscore." Illustrated. "Dr. Holmes's Pilgrim Poems").

McClure's Magazine. July, 1893 ("An Afternoon with Holmes." By E. E. Hale. Illustrated). August, 1893 ("Human Documents." Seven portraits of Holmes at different ages).

Harper's Magazine. January, 1876 ("Cambridge on the Charles." Illustrated). July, 1891 (Article by G. W. Curtis. Frontispiece, Holmes's portrait). July, 1894 (Howells's "Reminiscences of Holmes").

The Century Magazine. February, 1885 (Article by Stedman). February, 1895 (Mrs. Fields's "Reminiscences of Holmes").

The Harvard Graduates' Magazine. December, 1894 (Memorial Articles).

Littell's Living Age. Jan. 6, 1849. March 7, 1849 (Article on Holmes's poems. By Whittier). Oct. 8, 1853. Nov. 24, 1894.

The Holmes Number of *The Critic*. Aug. 29, 1884 (On his Seventy-fifth Birthday). *The Critic*. Oct. 13, 1894 (Illustrated Biographical Sketch).

The Atlantic Monthly. February, 1885 ("Reminiscences." By Holmes). December, 1894 ("Holmes." By the editor).

Poole's *Index of Periodical Literature* and its two Supplements.

Outlines for a Study of Holmes, Bryant, and Whittier (Leaflet).

NOTES. — Kennedy's *Life of Holmes*, published by Cassino, is now out of print.

    Dr. Holmes has written recollections of his past life to "serve as material to help some kind of memoir." These have been embodied in John T. Morse's *Life and Letters of Oliver Wendell Holmes*.

OUTLINE OF HIS LIFE.

August 29, 1809.
October 7, 1894.

Born the same year with Gladstone, Lincoln, Poe, Mrs. Browning,
Tennyson, Lord Houghton, Mendelssohn.

"I took my first draught of that fatal mixture called atmos-
pheric air on the 29th of August, 1809."

Paternal Ancestors.

Great-grandfather, John Holmes, settled in Woodstock, Conn.,
in 1686.

Grandfather. David Holmes, the "deacon" in "The One
Hoss Shay."

Captain of British troops in the French War, and later a sur-
geon in the Revolutionary Army.

Read Holmes's noble verses in memory of these two men in the
poem, "A Family Record."

Father.

Abiel Holmes. "A gentleman, a scholar, and a Christian."

A tutor and theological student at Yale ; married the daughter
of President Stiles. Minister for forty years over the First
Church, Cambridge (now the Shepard Memorial Church).

Charitable toward the Channing school of theologians.

Wrote *American Annals*, the first careful record of American
history after the Revolution.

"One of his last acts was to give a good book to every member
of his Sunday-school as they passed before the pulpit where
he stood."

Mother.

A Wendell, of Dutch descent.

The Wendells came to America about 1646. "I never meet a
Schuyler or a Cuyler or a Van Rensselaer without claiming
relationship with the owner of that name." — HOLMES, *in a
letter to the Holland Society, New York.*

An ancestor bought in 1735 a township (now Pittsfield) on the Housatonic River, of 24,000 acres, and married a descendant of Anne Bradstreet, America's earliest poetess.

The family arms may be seen on a window in a Dutch church at Albany, N.Y.

Granddaughter to Dorothy Quincy ("Dorothy Q."), who was aunt to Mrs. John Hancock, a second Dorothy Quincy.

Daughter of Hon. Oliver Wendell, an eminent lawyer.

See *Scribner's Magazine*, May, 1879.

Read Holmes's poem, "Dorothy Q."

Third of Five Children.

Cousin to Wendell Phillips.

Boyhood.

A happy one.

Spent in a home of culture, with three merry brothers, the youngest of whom, John (still living, 1896), is often referred to in James Russell Lowell's poetry, as "J. H."

"I cannot help thinking we carry our childhood's horizon with us all our days."

Early Schoolmates. Margaret Fuller and Richard Henry Dana, Jr.

"I was moderately studious, and very fond of reading stories, which I sometimes did in school hours."

Read Chapter VII., in his *Pages from an Old Volume of Life.* ("Cinders from the Ashes.")

Education.

His Father's Library.

Phillips Academy, Andover.

See poem, "The School-Boy," read at the centennial celebration of the academy, in 1878. (An annotated version of it is given in Houghton & Mifflin's *American Poems.* It has been illustrated also.)

Translated in heroic couplets the first book of *The Æneid.*

Harvard College. Famous class of 1829, including —

Professor Benjamin Pierce, mathematician.

Rev. James Freeman Clarke.

Rev. William H. Channing.

Hon. George T. Davis, a brilliant talker.

Judge Benjamin R. Curtis.

Samuel J. May, a zealous Abolitionist.

Judge George T. Bigelow.

Rev. Samuel F. Smith, author of "America." (See illustrated article, "Our National Songs," in *The New England Magazine*, July, 1890.)

Read the poem, "The Boys," written for the reunion of 1859. (In this the only classmate mentioned by name is the composer of our national hymn. The "speaker" was F. B. Crowninshield, and the "mayor," George T. Davis, of Greenfield, Mass.)

> "'The boys' we were, 'the boys' we'll be
> As long as three, as two, are creeping ;
> And here's to him — ah ! which is he ? —
> Who lives till all the rest are sleeping ;
> A life with tranquil comfort blest,
> The young man's health, the rich man's plenty,
> All earth can give that earth has best,
> And heaven at fourscore years and twenty."

Ad Amicos.

His scholarship admitted him to membership in the Phi Beta Kappa Society.

Gave the poem at Commencement.

Roomed in Stoughton Hall.

Charles Sumner, John Lothrop Motley, and Wendell Phillips were in Harvard at the same time.

Harvard Law School. One year.

Abandoned law for medicine.

Wrote for *The Collegian* the poems : " The Dorchester Giant," "Evening. By a Tailor," "Old Ironsides," " The Height of the Ridiculous."

Three Years in Europe, mostly passed in the hospitals of London and Paris.

A view of the Paris house in which he lived two years is seen in *McClure's Magazine,* July, 1893.

Read " A Prospective Visit," *The Atlantic,* July, 1886.

Degree of M.D. at Cambridge, 1836.
> Gained three Boylston prizes for medical dissertations.

Reads "Poetry; A Metrical Essay," before the Phi Beta Kappa
Society at Harvard.   1836.
> "The 'Metrical Essay' was the serious announcement that the
> poet was not lost in the man of science."
>
> "Its literary form is exquisite, and its general impression is
> that of bright, elastic, confident power." — G. W. CURTIS.
>
> "The delivery of this poem was a rich, nearly a dramatic, en-
> tertainment."
>
> One of the few successful Phi Beta Kappa poems.
>
> (Emerson delivered his oration, "The American Scholar,"
> before the same society, the following year.)

Publication of His First Volume of Poems.   1836.
> Three years before Longfellow's first volume, *Voices of the
> Night*, appeared.

Professor of Anatomy at Dartmouth College.   1838–1840.

Marriage with Amelia Lee Jackson, daughter to a Judge of the
Supreme Court of Massachusetts. Made his home in Boston,
and practised medicine. ("The smallest fevers gratefully
received."   Remark to a friend.)
> Lived for twenty years in the same house, Number 8, in Mont-
> gomery Place, and here all his children were born. (Notice
> verse alluding to it, in the poem, "Nux Postcoenatica.")
>
> Mrs. Holmes's habitually pleasant expression was attributed by
> one of her friends to her constant smiling at her husband's
> wit.

Parkman Professor of Anatomy and Physiology at Harvard.   1847–
1882.
> Relinquished medical practice.
>
> As lecturer, interesting, original, and stimulating.
>
> *Themes.*   Anatomy, physiology, histology, and microscopy.
> (He was wont to speak of occupying, not a "chair," but
> "settee," of medicine.)
>
> "I ought to tell you that, though he illustrates his medical
> lectures by quotations of the most appropriate and interest-

ing sort from a wonderful variety of authors, he has never been known to refer to his own writings in that way." — ARTHUR GILMAN.

Made Professor Emeritus. 1882. A rare distinction.

Invents the Stereoscope in its Present Form.

Obtained no patent. Might have made a fair fortune out of this ; "but," he said, "I did not care to be known as the patentee of a pill or of a peeping contrivance."

Becomes a Lyceum Lecturer. 1847.

Principal Subject. "English Poets of the Nineteenth Century."

Did not take kindly to the itinerant life involved ; he "preferred natural death to putting himself out of the world by such violent measures as lecterin'."

"I have somewhat felt as if I were a wandering spirit, and this great, unchanging multivertebrate which I have faced night after night, was one ever-listening animal, which writhed along after me wherever I fled, and coiled at my feet every evening, turning up to me the same sleepless eyes which I thought I closed with my last drowsy incantation."

"His lectures before the Lowell Institute were among the most noted of that distinguished platform."

Connection with The Atlantic Monthly.

One of its founders, perhaps the most brilliant of the galaxy.

Gave name to the magazine.

Lowell conditioned his editorship of the magazine upon Holmes's willingness to be a contributor. "You see the doctor is like a bright mountain stream that has been dammed up among the hills, and is waiting for an outlet into the Atlantic." — LOWELL.

Was identified with it more closely than any other one person, and for a longer time.

Breakfast Table Series of Papers.

The Autocrat. The Professor. The Poet.

A literary event.

A new revelation of Holmes. (At the age of fifty.)

Witty, satirical, sentimental.

"Took captive the English-reading public on both sides of the ocean."

Over the Teacups.   1890.

    ' Written in the white winter of the poet's eightieth year."

    "Full of the same shrewd sense and wise comment and ten-
        der thought."

Serial Novels.

    Elsie Venner.   The Guardian Angel.   A Mortal Antipathy.

Our Hundred Days in Europe.

Breakfast given by the editors in honor of Holmes's seventieth
    birthday. Dec. 3. 1879.

    (" Our brains are seventy-year clocks. The Angel of Life
        winds them up once for all, then closes the case and gives
        the key into the hands of the Angel of the Resurrection.")

See *Atlantic Monthly Supplement.*   June, 1880.

Delivers A Fourth of July Oration in Boston.   1863.

Second Visit to Europe, fifty years after the first.   1886.

    Everywhere warmly welcomed.

    Received the degrees D.C.L. from Oxford and LL.D. from
    Edinburgh.

    Read his description of the Oxford experience in *Our Hundred
    Days in Europe.*

Retired Life in Boston.

Death in the Beacon Street Home, and Interment at Mt. Auburn.

    " Last of the minstrel throng we held in honor,

        Ay, last and dearest, with hushed hearts we lay

      Our votive wreaths, where veiled, a pall upon her,

        She sits, his grieving city by the bay."

                            The Dead Poet.

Burial Service.

    Held in King's Chapel, his place of worship for many years.
    (Read his poem, " King's Chapel.")

    Conducted by Edward Everett Hale.

    Attended by many notable Americans, and by Mr. Arbuthnot,
    vicar of Trinity Church, Stratford, England.

    Two of his classmates, Rev. S. F. Smith and Rev. Samuel May,
    were present.

Religion.

An aggressive Unitarian.

Opposed to the Calvinism of his father.

Character.

Genial, humorous, sympathetic, fastidious, critical, hearty, happy, vivacious, optimistic. A lover of flowers. Fond of boating.

"He loves strongly his medical profession because he loves human nature." — HAWEIS.

"Unlike Tithonus, he secured from the gods, who gave him immortality, also eternal youth." — BOYESON.

He enjoyed socially the "Brahmin caste of New England."

A contra-type of Hawthorne in temperament and intellect.

"He has taken his troubles lightly, and his labors have sat easily upon him. He has laughed where many would have wept, and he has joked where some would have been serious, if not savage." — H. T. GRISWOLD.

He well illustrated his own words, "A true man's allegiance is given that which is highest in his own nature. He reverences truth, he loves kindness, he respects justice."

Appearance.

Small body; quick and nervous movements. A powerful jaw, and a thick underlip; winning expression. Of less than medium height. Called by Charles Kingsley, when seen in a frolicsome mood, "an inspired jackdaw."

Fastidious taste in dress.

"His words and his countenance were alive with power and feeling; the whole man, body and mind, seemed only a miraculous intellectual engine." — UNDERWOOD.

"I found him physically of the Napoleonic height, which spiritually overtops the Alps." — HOWELLS.

On the Lecture Platform. See Macrae's description in Shepard's *Pen Pictures of Modern Authors*, pp. 147, 148.

Children. Three.

Oliver Wendell. Justice in the Supreme Court of Massachusetts. Captain in the Civil War. Wounded at Ball's Bluff.

Note Holmes's stirring narrative, " My Hunt after the Captain," now printed in *Soundings from the Atlantic*, and
in *Pages from an Old Volume of Life*, chap. ii.

Author of *The Common Law*, and editor of *Kent's Commen-
taries*.

Edward. Lawyer.

Amelia Jackson. Mrs. John T. Sargent.

Autobiographic Pictures.

Prose. The Old Gambrel-Roofed House. My Hunt after the
Captain. Cinders from the Ashes. A Prospective Visit.
Our Hundred Days in Europe. Introduction to A Mortal
Antipathy.

Poetry. Dorothy Q. Parson Turell's Legacy. The School-
Boy. A Family Record. The Opening of the Piano (written upon the arrival in the home of an imported Clementi
piano). The Iron Gate. His poems in celebration of the
Class of '29, about forty in number.

All his writings are deliciously tinctured with the flavor of his
personality ; he is pre-eminently a self-revealing author.

" The Autocrat is his own Boswell."

APPELLATIONS.

The Autocrat of the Breakfast Table.
The Professor of the Breakfast Table.
The Poet of the Breakfast Table.
Everybody's Favorite.
Our Poet of Occasions.
The Blithe Toast-Master of the Nation.
Prince of the Table.
The American Montaigne.
Boston's Dr. Johnson.
A Boswell, Writing out Himself. — *Holmes.*
A Florist in Verse. (Also self-given.)
A Yankee Frenchman.
Our Typical University Poet.
The Laureate of Harvard College.
The Paragon among College Poets.
The Minstrel of the College that bred Him.
A Lyrist of Pathos, Humor, and Occasion.
The Liveliest of Monologists.
The Last of the Recitationists.
A Natural Songster and Balladist.
Our Laughing Philosopher.
A Merry Doctor.
Prince of Geniality and Generosity.
King of the Dinner-Table.
A Child of Nature.
A Proverb-Maker.
A Later Franklin in Riper Days.
A Writer of Society Verse.
Boston's Poet Laureate.
A Charming Egotist.
The Kindly Humorist, the Melting Poet, the Shrewd
    Essayist. — *G. W. Curtis.*

The American Hood.
Beloved Physician of Body and Mind.
A Wholesome Writer.
A Believer in the Reign of Law.
Our Merry Poet and Homilist.
The Wise and Witty Poet.
Our Welcome Guide, Philosopher, and Friend.
The Apostle of Local Contentment.
The Literary Embodiment of Cheerfulness.
A Clever and Versatile Writer.
Last Wearer of Great Laurels.

•

NOTES ON HIS WRITINGS.

General Comments.

His writings are light, graceful, easy, kindly, sometimes pathetic, sometimes humorous; clever, original, versatile; largely local, and of a decided medical flavor; unconventional in form and theme.

"His resources in the way of figure, illustration, allusion, and anecdote are wonderful."

"The spirit of his poetry is democratic."

"His prose is replete with poetic humor and analogy."

POETRY.

Classification

Characteristic among His Serious Poems.

The Chambered Nautilus. The Living Temple. Under the Violets. The Voiceless. Homesick in Heaven. Iris, her Book. Fantasia, the Young Girl's Poem.

Humorous Poems.

The One-Hoss Shay. How the Old Horse Won the Bet. The Height of the Ridiculous. The Ballad of the Oysterman. Aunt Tabitha. The Stethoscope Song. The September Gale. The Spectre Pig. The Hot Season. Contentment. Parson Turell's Legacy (Harvard's Presidential Arm-chair). The Broomstick Train, and others.

NOTE. — The first two and the last are published together in an illustrated form.

Humorous and Pathetic.

The Last Leaf. My Aunt. Bill and Joe.

"Smiles and tears come at the command of the master."

"Pathos has a curiously close connection with humor, both proceeding from a keenness of sensibility." — BARDEEN.

Patriotic.

> Old Ironsides. Ballad of the Boston Tea-party. Grandmother's
> Story of Bunker Hill. Our Yankee Girls. Brother Jonathan's
> Lament for Sister Caroline. Never or Now. One Country. A
> Voice of the Loyal North. Voyage of the Good Ship Union.
> God Save the Flag. Hymn on the Emancipation Proclamation.
> Union and Liberty. An Appeal for the Old South.

Compare Holmes's war poems with Lowell's.

> NOTE.— An annotated version of Grandmother's Story may be
> found in *American Poems*, in *Masterpieces of American Litera-*
> *ture*, and in the Riverside Literature Series.

Occasional Poems.

Numerous and varied.

These number in all more than one hundred.

"His verses have the courtesy and wit, without the pedagogy, of
the knee-buckle time." — STEDMAN.

Holmes is always felicitous in this department of literature.

Class Poems.

> Bill and Joe. Questions and Answers. The Old Man Dreams.
> The Iron Gate. Our Oldest Friend. The Boys, and many
> others.

>> " Pegasus draws well in harness the triumphant chariot of '29,
>> in which the lucky classmates of the poet move to a unique
>> and happy renown." — CURTIS.

>> " ' Why won't he stop writing ?' Humanity cries:
>> The answer is, briefly, 'He can't if he tries;
>> He has played with his foolish old feather so long,
>> That the goose-quill, in spite of him, cackles in song.' "
>>
>>   *The Smiling Listener.* — HOLMES.

Memorial Verses.

> In Memory of Lincoln. Edward Everett. The Shakespeare
> Tercentennial Celebration. The Burns Centennial Celebra-
> tion. At the Dedication of Halleck's Monument. · For the
> Laying of the Cornerstone at Harvard's Memorial Hall, and
> for the Dedication of the Hall. Funeral Services of Sumner.

Miscellaneous.

> For the Dinner given to Dickens in Boston. For the Meeting
> of the American Medical Association. At the Atlantic
> Dinner. A Farewell to Agassiz. Welcome to the Nations,
> July 4, 1876, *et alii.*

Birthday Poems.

On Washington, Daniel Webster, Lowell, Whittier, and Bryant.

Hymns.

"Lord of all being, throned afar." A Sunday hymn.

From *The Professor at the Breakfast Table.* (Long metre.)

"O Love Divine, that stooped to share." Hymn of trust.

From *The Professor at the Breakfast Table.* (Long metre.)

"Angel of Peace, thou hast wandered too long!"

Sung at the Boston Jubilee, June 15, 1869. (Ten syllables.)

Written to the music of Keller's "American Hymn."

"Father of Mercies, Heavenly Friend." Parting Hymn. (Common metre.)

"O Lord of Hosts! Almighty King!" Army hymn. (Long metre.)

"Thou Gracious Power, whose mercy lends."

Hymn for the class meeting. (Long metre.)

Vignettes of Wordsworth, Moore, Keats, Shelley.

Two Poems on the Pilgrim.

Robinson of Leyden. The Pilgrim's Vision.

Notes on Representative Poems.

The Chambered Nautilus.

"Elegy on a shell."

Originally printed in *The Autocrat.*

Whittier said of it, "That poem is booked for immortality."

The author's favorite among his poems.

Construction of Stanza. Interesting.

Dr. Holmes's book-plate is a nautilus, with the inscription, *Per ampliora ad altiora.*

Note the poetic legend in regard to this mollusk.

> "Long may he live to sing for us
> His sweetest songs at evening time,
> And, like his 'Chambered Nautilus,'
> To holier heights of beauty climb."
>
> WHITTIER.

Parson Turell's Legacy.

"As thoroughly Yankee as Tam O'Shanter is Scotch."

Agnes.

A story of colonial time in Massachusetts.

The scene is laid in Marblehead and Boston.

Compare with Edwin Lasseter Bynner's novel, *Agnes Surriage.*

Dorothy Q.

Dorothy Quincy was the poet's great-grandmother.

"That sprightly capture of a portrait's maiden soul."

The portrait hangs on the library wall of the Boston home.

See Houghton and Mifflin's illustrated edition of this poem, "The Boston Tea-party," and "Bunker Hill."

Views of the Portrait. — In the illustrated edition and in *Scribner's Magazine*, May, 1879.

A view of Dorothy's home, at Quincy, Mass., may be seen in *McClure's Magazine*, July, 1893; the same magazine article shows Dr. Holmes's library, with the picture on the wall.

The Last Leaf.

The allusion is to Major Melville, one of Boston's "tea-tippers," whom Holmes used to see daily pass his house.

Lincoln called this poem "inexpressibly touching."

"An artless piece of art." "The last leaf of his work to perish."

"One of those creations that are struck off at white heat, and remain unique in literature." —RICHARDSON.

An Illustrated Edition. ($10.00. Houghton and Mifflin.)

Printed in *fac-simile* of the author's handwriting, with history of the poem, and notes by the author. Designs by F. Hopkinson Smith and G. W. Edwards. (Also in less expensive form.)

Poe made an elaborate metrical analysis of the poem.

Observe its verse and stanza structure.

"It was with a smile on my lips that I wrote it; I cannot read it without a sigh of tender remembrance." (Written to his publishers a few months before his death.)

Old Ironsides.

(The war-ship Constitution.)

Written in an attic-room of the birth-home, when Holmes was but twenty.

Published in *The Boston Advertiser.* 1830.

It saved the ship from threatened destruction.

"A pet Boston ship, — built in that city; manned by Yankee crews; had often brought its trophies thither."

For an account of the ship, see Coggeshall's *History of American Privateers.* Note allusion to it in Longfellow's poem, "The Iron Pen" (read the prefatory note).

"There had been no American poetry with a truer lilt of song than these early verses [of Holmes], and there has been none since."

The Voiceless.

"A laurel-wreath laid upon the grave of mute, anonymous human suffering."

The School-Boy.

"Fresh in feeling, somewhat chastened by experience, but as beautiful as the memory of springtime."

The Song of Other Days.

A classic drinking-song.

Æstivation.

A Latin-English study.

Epilogue to the Breakfast-Table Series.

A humorous estimate of the posthumous value of his own works.

Compare with Swift's verses, "On the Death of Dr. Swift."

Holmes's Poetic Measure.

Varied. Dactyls and anapests used, as well as iambs.

In his longer poems the poet makes frequent use of the rhymed heroic couplet, Pope's favorite measure. "Holmes is the best American representative of the school of Pope."

"The movement is so perfect that one cannot conceive of the thought apart from its natural music. It is now as light and joyous as the flight of a bird; now as steady as the tramp of an army; now as gay and arch as the practised steps of a dancer, or as swift as an athlete in a race." — UNDERWOOD.

PROSE.

The Trilogy of the Breakfast Table.

The Autocrat. (1858.)

"A genuinely Yankee book, showing New Englandism at its best." (A later period than Hawthorne's New Englandism.)

Unique Form. "A cross between an essay and a drama." "A semi-dramatic, conversational, descriptive monologue."

A series of table-talks, mostly monologues, at a typical American boarding-house. Slight story.

"The tone of placid dogmatism and infallible finality with which the bulls of the domestic pope are delivered is delightfully familiar." — CURTIS.

"The most taking serial in prose that ever established the prestige of a new magazine."

Opening Sentence. "I was just going to say when I was inter-
rupted." (Holmes had written two papers of the kind more
than twenty years previous to this, which he characterized as
"the crude products of my uncombed literary boyhood.")

The Short Poems found here and there in the book are among its
most pleasing features; they are superior in this work to those
that occur in its successors.

Characters Sketched. "Mere pegs for wit and wisdom."

The Autocrat, "a Down-East philosopher."

The Landlady and the Landlady's Daughter.

"The young man named John."

"The old gentleman that sits opposite."

Our Benjamin Franklin.

The Divinity Student.

The Schoolmistress.

The Index. An interesting study, revealing "the whimsical discur-
siveness of the book."

Illustrated Edition. By Howard Pyle. ($5.00.)

The Professor. 1859.

Graver than its predecessor.

Contains more romance and theology, less discussion of social and
moral points, and a smaller amount of badinage and punning.

The story of "Iris," Holmes's loveliest creation.

Its best scene is the death of the Little Gentleman.

"The episode of the Little Gentleman is itself a poem."

The Poet. 1875. (Two novels intervened.)

More professional in its nature.

The first chapter is an excellent specimen of the writer's prose.

Novels.

"His themes are half Hawthornesque; but their treatment is that of an
analytical and tersely didactic Harvard professor."

His favorite subject is atavism, and the stories have been called "modi-
cated novels."

Elsie Venner; *A Romance of Destiny.*

First published in *The Atlantic,* as "The Professor's Story."

A study of inherited traits. Elsie is "a sort of human snake."

"The physiological theories and speculations in the book lie in the
debatable ground between science and superstition."

Consult *Macmillan's Magazine* for August, 1861, and *The National Review* for October, 1861.

Draw a parallel with Hawthorne's *Scarlet Letter* and with Whittier's story, "The Rattlesnake Hunter."

Suggested Class Readings.

The Apollinean Institute. Chapter IV.

The Event of the Season. Chapter VII.

NOTE. — "The site of Elsie's home, it is claimed, was suggested by the hills east of the Holmes mansion" [at Pittsfield].

The Guardian Angel.

A second study of heredity (through a vein of Indian blood), and consequent modified moral responsibility.

Hero and Heroine; Gifted Hopkins and Myrtle Hazard.

The "guardian angel," Master Byles Gridley.

"If any one would learn how to be his own Boswell, these five books are naïve examples of a successful American method."

A Mortal Antipathy.

"Holmes's essay, 'Crime and Automatism,' might well be taken as an introduction to the series [of novels]." — F. L. PATTEE.

Biography.

Memoir of John Lothrop Motley. 1879.

Read the introduction to *A Mortal Antipathy*, pp. 14–17.

Life of Ralph Waldo Emerson. (American Men of Letters Series.) 1884.

"As remarkable a study as one poet ever made of another."

"To share the inmost consciousness of a noble thinker, to scan one's self in the white light of a pure and radiant soul, — this is indeed the highest form of teaching and discipline." — HOLMES, upon the completion of the *Emerson Memoir*. (Read the introduction to *A Mortal Antipathy*, pp. 17–20.)

"These memoirs are model records of fact and character."

Miscellaneous.

Medical Essays. ("Fearless and original.")

Currents and Counter-Currents in Medical Science.

Homœopathy and its Kindred Diseases.

Mechanism in Thought and Morals. (A study of the functions of the brain.)

Pages from an Old Volume of Life.

Travel. Our Hundred Days in Europe.

MISCELLANEOUS NOTES.

Tributes to Holmes.

"A critic who punctured vice and folly with a lancet so smooth and keen it scarce inflicts any pain. . . . How we have forgot suffering in his and our own contagious smile!"—C. A. BARTOL.

"Holmes loves fact, yet often salutes with awe the superior angel of imagination. . . . Heaven send us on this side of the Atlantic a teacher so wise and generous, so witty, so tender, and so true!"—H. R. HAWEIS.

"I am confident that no writer since Walter Scott has given so much pleasure to so many English-speaking people as he."—JUDGE HOAR.

"If he should live to be the last leaf upon the tree of our noble band of New England authors, may no rude gust tear him away, but the gentlest of Indian summer dews loosen his hold."—JOHN BURROUGHS.

"A kindlier philosopher never made fun for himself or his fellows."—*The Westminster Gazette.*

"He has become a patriarch of our literature, and all his countrymen are his lovers."—GEORGE WILLIAM CURTIS.

"Perhaps more than any other American poet he has been loved for himself rather than for his poetry. . . . To him, as much as to Whittier, God is the Eternal Goodness; and he has not been able to think of God as wishing for anything else than the happiness of man. . . . He has been a preacher all his life of the most serious gospel of duty and fidelity."—GEORGE WILLIS COOKE.

"He is a Montaigne and Bacon under one hat. His varied qualities would suffice for the mental furnishing of half a dozen literary specialists."—JOHN G. WHITTIER.

"As a professional man, he has been thorough and successful; as a man of letters, versatile, brilliant, of the highest culture; as a citizen, patriotic; as a man, an exemplification of elegance of manner and kindliness of heart."—ARTHUR GILMAN.

"It may be said truly of Holmes, as Coleridge said of Goldsmith, 'He did everything happily.'"—F. H. HEDGE.

"By his life of spotless purity and transparent sincerity he has
crowned the literary life of New England with a diadem of
imperishable lustre." — Rev. WALTER CALLEY.

"There's Holmes, who is matchless among you for wit;
A Leyden-jar always full-charged from which flit
The electrical tinges of hit after hit;

. . . .

His are just the fine hands, too, to weave you a lyric,
Full of fancy, fun, feeling, or spiced with satyric,
In a measure so kindly, you doubt if the toes
That are trodden upon are your own or your foes'."

J. R. LOWELL.

"Beloved physician of age of ail!
When grave prescriptions fail,
Thy songs have cheer and healing for us all,
As David's had for Saul."

WHITTIER.

NOTE. — The verses above were the last written by Whittier, and
appeared in *The Boston Journal* a few days before his death.

Lowell's Fable for Critics.

Whittier's poem. *The Atlantic Monthly*, September, 1892.

C. L. Bett's poem. *The Critic*, Sept. 3, 1893.

Poems by Julia Dorr, Edith Thomas, Bret Harte, Edmund Gosse,
and others. (See *The Critic* for Aug. 30, 1884.)

A Whittier Wish for Holmes.

"Long may he live to make broader the face of our care-ridden
generation, and to realize for himself the truth of the wise
man's declaration, that 'a merry heart is a continual feast.'"

The Twofold Literary Man.

"Holmes's devotion to the Muses of science and letters was uniform and untiring, as it was also to the two literary forms of
verse and prose."

Holmes as Reader.

"Holmes's readings were like improvisations. The poems were
expressed and interpreted by the whole personality of the poet.
The most subtle touch of thought, the melody of fond regret,
the brilliant passage of description, the culmination of latent
fun exploding in a keen and resistless jest, — all these were vivi-
fied in the sensitive play of manner and modulation of tone of

the reader, so that a poem by Holmes at the Harvard Commencement dinner was one of the anticipated delights which never failed." — CURTIS.

"He always writes them [his college poems] with joy, and recites them — if that is the word — with a spirit not to be described. For he is a born orator, with what people call a sympathetic voice, wholly under his own command, and entirely free from any of the tricks of elocution. It seems to me that no one knows his poems to the very best who has not had the good fortune to hear him read some of them." — E. E. HALE.

Rank as Popular Writer.

In 1890 Holmes was voted by the readers of *The Critic* at the head of the list of American authors, receiving two votes more than Lowell and six more than Whittier.

Holmes and John Lothrop Motley.

Warm friends.

The historian once told Holmes that when he was worn out in his work in a foreign land, with few friends and amidst piles of manuscripts, two lines of the poet's writing braced him wonderfully, —

> "Stick to your aim: the mongrel's hold will slip,
> But only crowbars loose the bull-dog's grip."

Motley says of Holmes, "I hardly know an author in any language to be paralleled with him for profound and suggestive thought, glittering wit, vivid imagination, and individuality of humor."

Lowell and Holmes.

"Men who combine the culture of the Old World with the indefinable and incommunicable spirit of the New." — *An English writer.*

Our University Poets.

Holmes, Lowell, and Longfellow.

All alumni of New England colleges, and professors in their Alma Mater.

Their writings are imbued with the university culture and spirit.

Irving and Holmes.

"The rollicking laugh of Knickerbocker was a solitary sound in the American ear till the blithe carol of Holmes returned a kindred echo." — CURTIS.

American Writers of Metrical Essays.

Bryant, Emerson, Longfellow, Holmes, Lowell.

Long-Lived American Authors.

Bancroft nearly reached ninety years; Holmes saw his eighty-fifth birthday; Bryant lived to be eighty-four; Whittier, eighty-two; Emerson, seventy-nine; Longfellow, seventy-five; Motley, sixty-three; Cooper, sixty-two.

Poe is perhaps the only prominent American writer who died without manifesting to the full his literary ability.

Holmes on Biographers.

"There are but two biographers who can tell the story of a man's or woman's life. One is the person himself or herself ; the other is the Recording Angel. The autobiographer cannot be trusted to tell the whole truth, though he may tell nothing but the truth ; and the Recording Angel never lets his book go out of his own hands."

On Riches.

"Wealth is a steep hill, which the father climbs slowly and the son often tumbles down precipitately ; but there is a tableland continuous with it, which may be found by those who do not lose their head in looking down from its sharply cloven summit. . . . It cannot be repeated too often that the safety of great wealth with us lies in obedience to the new version of the Old World axiom, *Richesse oblige*."

On Woman.

"I would have a woman as true as death. At the first real lie which works from the heart outward, she should be tenderly chloroformed into a better world, where she can have an angel for a governess, and feed on strange fruits, which shall make her all over again, even to her bones and marrow."

"She who nips off the end of a brittle courtesy, as one breaks the tip of an icicle, to bestow upon those whom she ought cordially and kindly to recognize, proclaims the fact that she comes not merely of low blood, but of bad blood."

"God bless all good women ! To their soft hands and pitying hearts we must all come at last ! "

On Fame.

"Fame usually comes to those who are thinking about something else ; rarely to those who say to themselves, 'Go to, now! let us be a celebrated individual.' "

> " Ah, pensive scholar, what is fame?
> A fitful tongue of leaping flame;
> A giddy whirlwind's fickle gust,
> That lifts a pinch of mortal dust;
> A few swift years, and who can show
> Which dust was Bill and which was Joe ? "

" If your name is to live at all, it is so much more to have it live in people's hearts than only in their brains! I don't know that one's eyes fill with tears when he thinks of the famous inventor of logarithms; but a song of Burns's, or a hymn of Charles Wesley's, goes straight to your heart, and you can't help loving both of them, the sinner as well as the saint."

On Expressing Appreciation of Others.

" It is an ungenerous silence which leaves all the fair words of honestly-earned praise to the writer of obituary notices and the marble-maker."

On Wit.

" Its essence consists of a partial and incomplete view of whatever it touches. It throws a single ray, separated from the rest, — red, yellow, blue, or any intermediate shade, — upon an object; never white light; that is the province of wisdom. We get beautiful effects from wit, — all the prismatic colors, but never the object as it is in fair daylight."

" Keep your wit in the background until you have made a reputation by your more solid qualities: you'll do nothing great with Macbeth's dagger if you first come on flourishing Paul Pry's umbrella."

Holmes's Wit.

" If the Autocrat's wit is homely on one page, it is poetical on the next."

" Holmes has not only a command of witty phrases, but is a creator of wit in the concrete."

" As in the case of Hood, the fun in Holmes is always jostling the pathos."

" His sparkles of wit are like bubbles on a strong tide of feeling."

" His wingèd words always feathered an unerring arrow."

" His wit has been the solvent of bigotry. He has never, in all his fun, been a trifler with truth."

Wit and Humor.

References.

William Mathews's *Wit and Humor; Their Use and Abuse.* (S. C. Griggs, Chicago.)

Marshall Brown's *Wit and Humor.* (Silver, Burdett, & Co.)

Haweis's *American Humorists*, chap. i.

Whipple's *Literature and Life.*

Ben Jonson's Prologue to *Every Man in his Humor.*

John Weiss's *Wit, Humor, and Shakespeare.*

Appletons' Cyclopædia of Wit and Humor. 1859.

The North-British Review. August–November, 1860 ("American Humor").

The North American Review. January, 1849 ("Humorous and Satirical Poetry").

The Cosmopolitan. February, 1891 ("On Certain Latter-day Humorists." By Brander Matthews). January, 1894 ("Humor ; English and American." By Agnes Repplier).

Text-books on Rhetoric. Bardeen. Welsh. Kellogg. Waddy. Hart, and others.

The Two Distinguished.

Wit is unexpected.	Humor is anticipated.
Wit is intellectual.	Humor mingles heart with brain.
Wit is concentrated.	Humor is diffuse.
Wit laughs at things.	Humor laughs with them.
Wit needs words.	Humor may be shown in action.
Wit is the flash.	Humor is the electric atmosphere.
Wit is destructive.	Humor is creative.
Wit often lashes.	Humor is sympathetic.
Wit sparkles.	Humor glows.
Wit is based on imagination.	Humor is founded upon truth.

Interesting illustrations of the two may readily be found.

"Whoever has humor has wit, although it does not follow that whoever has wit has humor." — LANDOR.

"Humor is properly the exponent of low things; that which first renders them poetical to the mind. The man of humor sees common life, even mean life, under the new light of sportfulness and love; whatever has existence has a charm for him. Humor has justly been regarded as the finest perfection of poetic genius. He who wants it, be his other gifts what they may, has only half a mind; an eye for what is above him, not for what is about him or below him." — THOMAS CARLYLE.

Species of Wit.

> **Irony.** Sarcasm. Satire. Ridicule. Burlesque. Mock-Heroic. **Parody.** Pun. Repartee. Irish wit.

Some American Humorists.

> **O. W. Holmes. J. R. Lowell.** Mark Twain (Samuel Clemens). Artemus Ward (C. F. Brown). Bret Harte. Washington Irving. Mrs. Partington (Benjamin P. Shillaber). Josh Billings (Henry W. Shaw). James Whitcomb Riley. Charles Dudley Warner. G. W. Curtis. Frank R. Stockton.

The Atlantic Monthly.   (Named by Holmes.)   1857.

One of America's earliest and best magazines.

Established, through the enterprise of the firm of Phillips & Samson, Boston, to furnish literary support to the anti-slavery cause, and to encourage home authors.

Lowell was editor from its foundation until **1862, and** contributor for many years following.

Begun in a period of "storm and stress."

Made from the first an impression upon the public opinion **and taste.**

Coterie of Founders.   "The group is immortal."

> **O. W. Holmes. J. R. Lowell. H. W. Longfellow.** Louis **Agassiz. J. G. Whittier.** John **S.** Dwight. J. Eliot **Cabot. Charles E. Norton.** Judge E. R. Hoar. C. C. Felton. John Lothrop Motley. George T. Davis. Edmund Quincy. F. H. Underwood.
>
> Their periodic dinners (usually held at Parker's) were gatherings memorable for scintillations of wit and originality of thought.

Initial Rates of Remuneration.

> Editor's salary, three thousand dollars.
>
> Prose from the best writers, ten dollars a page.
>
> Average value of a poem, fifty dollars.
>
> "A paying American market for purely literary work began with the foundation of *The Atlantic.*"

Prominent Names associated later with the magazine.

> **T. W. Higginson. J. T. Trowbridge.** Rose Terry Cooke. James T. Fields. **W. D. Howells. T. B. Aldrich.** Horace E. Scudder.

Read Underwood's *Lowell: The Poet and the Man,* chap. v.

Holmes's Description of his own Method of Writing Poetry.

> "It cost him no trouble — a pen full of ink or two,
>
> And the poem is done in the time of a wink or two;

As for the thoughts — **never mind** — take the ones that lie upper-
　most,
And the rhymes used by Milton and Byron **and Tupper most;**
The lines come so easy! at one end he jingles 'em,
At the other with capital letters he shingles 'em, —
Why, the thing writes itself, and before he's half done with it
He hates to stop writing, he has such good fun with it !''

At the Atlantic Dinner. **1874.**

Last Poem.

Francis **Parkman. Published in** *The Atlantic Monthly,* February,
　1894.

Fondness for Trees.

Like Lowell and Bryant, Holmes had a passion **for trees, and de-**
lighted in monarchs among them. "I can generally **tell at a**
glance," he once **said,** "whether a tree is over fifteen feet
around; and when **I find one** that's larger than that, I measure
it and give **it a sort of mark of** approbation."

Vocation.

That of **a medical practitioner and lecturer;** his avocation, the writing of occasional poetry.

The Wyatt Eaton Portrait of Holmes.

See Selected Proofs of the Century Company. **Plate 47.**
Scribner's Magazine, May, 1879.

A Holmes Birthday Book (illustrated). Year Book, and Calendar have
been issued by his publishers.

Homes.

Birthplace. **An** historic house in Cambridge. (Now removed.)

Between the sites of Hemenway Gymnasium and Harvard's Law
　School.
Headquarters of the Committee of Safety just **before the Revo-**
lution.
On its steps Harvard's president stood and prayed for Prescott's
men as they marched **by** to Bunker Hill.
In it Benedict Arnold received his first commission.
Holmes describes it **in** the opening chapter of *The Poet at the*
Breakfast *Table* ("The Gambrel-Roofed House"). This de-
scription is found also in *American Prose.* See his allusion
to its destruction, in the introduction to *A Mortal Antipathy.*
For views and additional description, **see** *Harper's Magazine,*
January, 1876; *Scribner's Magazine,* **May, 1879;** *The Critic,*
Oct. 13, 1894.

The large old-fashioned key of the house is shown among the Cambridge relics in the city library.

296 Beacon Street, Boston. 1870–1894.

The library commands a sweeping view of the Charles, the river of Holmes's, Lowell's, and Longfellow's song; from one of its windows the poet could look over to the site in Cambridge of the home of his birth.

The home is filled with books, the collection numbering about six thousand.

For views, see *The New England Magazine* for October, 1889; *McClure's Magazine* for July, 1893; and Gilman's *Poets' Homes.*

Read Holmes's poem, "My Aviary."

Pittsfield, Mass. A summer home from 1849 to 1856.

House built on a portion of the large ancestral Wendell estate. Hawthorne, Catherine Sedgwick, and Fanny Kemble resided near, at Lenox. Longfellow frequently visited his wife's family home in the same town, the "Plunkett mansion," in the hall of which stood for years the clock that inspired his well-known poem.

"That home where seven blessed summers were passed, which stand in my memory like the seven golden candlesticks in the beautiful vision of the holy dreamer."

Read poem on "The Pittsfield Cemetery," and "The Ploughman."

Beverly Farms, Mass., with his daughter. A summer residence.

Two views of this home may be seen in *McClure's Magazine*, July, 1893.

NOTE. — "For twelve years Holmes lived at 154 Charles Street, Boston. At the foot of the garden were kept the boats that are familiar to the readers of *The Autocrat.*"

VERSIFICATION.

VERSIFICATION.

References.

James C. Parsons's *English Versification.*
Hiram Corson's *Primer of English Verse.*
Text-books on Rhetoric.

Elements of Versification. Rhythm. Cæsura. Rhyme.

I. *RHYTHM.*

Definition. — The division of a sentence by stress of voice into uniform portions.

Nature. — Accentual; not quantitative, as in Latin and Greek.

Elements.

1. FOOT. (Measure, number, metre.)

   Definition. — A unit of measure in rhythmical writing.

   Kinds. Determined by the relative position of the syllable receiving the periodic vocal stress.

      a. **Iamb.**   Devíce.   Longfellow's "Excelsior."
      b. **Trochee.**   Pállid.   Poe's "Raven."
      c. **Anapest.**   Intercéde.   Longfellow's "Sandalphon."
      d. **Dactyl.**   Beaútiful.   Scott's "Hail to the Chief who in triumph advances!"

   Substitute feet.

      e. **Spondee.**   Lóng dáys.
      f. **Pyrrhic.**   Into. (Both syllables unaccented.)

2. VERSE. (Line.)

   Definition. — A combination of two or more feet.

   Kinds.

      (1) As to length.

         a. Monometer.

   > "Here Skugg
   > Lies snug
   > As a bug
   > In a rug."
   >   BENJAMIN FRANKLIN.

b. **Dimeter.**

> "The unattained
> In life at last,
> When life is passed,
> Shall all be gained;
> And no more pained,
> No more distressed
> Shalt thou find rest."

Translation: LONGFELLOW.

c. **Trimeter.**

> "Just men no longer pine
> Behind their prison-bars;
> Through the rent dungeon shine
> The free sun and the stars."

WHITTIER's *Astræa.*

d. **Tetrameter.**

> "Oh, deem not they are blest alone
> Whose lives a peaceful tenor keep;
> The Power who pities man, has shown
> A blessing for the eyes that weep."

BRYANT's "Blessed are they that mourn."

e. **Pentameter.**

> "Unleash thy crouching thunders, now, O Jove!"

LOWELL's *Prometheus.*

f. **Hexameter.**

> "The bloom of young Desire, and purple light of love."

GRAY's *The Progress of Poesy.*

g. **Heptameter.**

> "Sir Patrick Spens is the best sailòr that ever sailed the sea."

Ballad of Sir Patrick Spens.

h. **Octameter.**

> "All at once, as we are gazing, lo, the roofs of Charlestown blazing."

HOLMES's *Grandmother's Story of Bunker Hill.*

(2) As to completeness.

a. **Acatalectic.** Complete.

> "Have you heard of the wonderful one-hoss shay?"

Anapestic tetrameter acatalectic.

b. **Catalectic.** Incomplete.

> "Dwindle, peak, and pine."

Trochaic trimeter catalectic.

c. **Hypercatalectic.** With an extra syllable.

"Our birth is but a sleep and a forgetting."

Iambic pentameter hypercatalectic.

3. STANZA.

Definition. — A combination of two or more verses.

Kinds.

a. **Distich.** (Couplet.)

"Dead he lay among his books!
The peace of God was in his looks."

LONGFELLOW's *Bayard Taylor.*

b. **Triplet.**

"The school-boys jeered her as they passed;
And when she sought the house of prayer
Her mother's curse pursued her there."

WHITTIER's *Mabel Martin.*

c. **Quatrain.**

"I know the way she went
Home with her maiden posy,
For her feet have touched the meadows
And left the daisies rosy."

TENNYSON's *Maud.*

Hymns. See Special Forms. (*g*)

Ballad Metre. See description of Common Metre,
under Hymns.

d. **Five-lined.**

"Not as all other women are
Is she that to my soul is dear,
Her glorious fancies come from far,
Beneath the silver evening star,
And yet her heart is ever near."

LOWELL's *My Love.*

e. **Six-lined.**

"But now his nose is thin,
And it rests upon his chin
Like a staff,
And a crook is in his back,
And a melancholy crack
In his laugh."

HOLMES's *The Last Leaf.*

f. Seven-lined.

> "O poor man's son! scorn not thy state;
>   There is worse weariness than thine,
> In merely being rich and great;
>   Toil only gives the soul to shine,
>   And makes rest fragrant and benign;
> A heritage, it seems to me,
>   Worth being poor to hold in fee."

LOWELL's The Heritage.

Short Chaucerian Stanza. See Special Forms.   (*c*)

g. Eight-lined.

> "Where are the swallows fled ?
>   Frozen and dead,
>   Perchance upon some bleak and stormy shore.
>   O doubting heart!
>   Far over purple seas
>   They wait in sunny ease
>   The balmy southern breeze,
> To bring them to their northern homes once more."

ADELAIDE PROCTER's A Doubting Heart.

Ottava Rima. See Special Forms.   (*d*)

h. Nine-lined.

> "When whispering strains with creeping wind
>   Distil soft passions through the heart;
> And when at every touch we find
> Our pulses beat and bear a part;
>   When threads can make
>   A heartstring ache,
>   Philosophy
>   Can scarce deny
>   Our souls are made of harmony.

WILLIAM STRODE's Music.

Spenserian Stanza. See Special Forms.   (*e*)

II. *CÆSURA.*

Definition. — A pause in poetry.   (Derivation, "a cutting.")

Kinds.

a. OF THE FOOT.   The ending of a word within a foot.

"The desert sun was sinking red."   (After "desert" and "sinking.")

b. OF THE VERSE.

    (1) At the end of every line. The poetic, or metric, cæsura. This is the slightest of all the cæsuras, and simply indicates the poetic form of the composition.

    (2) Within a verse, phrasing it. The grammatical cæsura.

"As it fell upon a day   (After "fell.")
In the merry month of May." (After "month.")

c. OF THE SENSE. The rhetorical cæsura.

"But, see, the Virgin blest   (After "see.")
Hath laid her Babe to rest."

Two of these pauses are often coincident.

When the metric and rhetorical pauses coincide, an *end-stopped* line is formed ; otherwise, a *run-on* line.

"Listen, young heroes! your country is calling." (End-stopped).
"She walks in beauty, like the night (Run-on.)
Of cloudless climes and starry skies."

The position of the cæsura in the verse is not fixed ; the ear demands changes of location, for variety.

The cæsura in the verse is sometimes followed by an extra syllable, sometimes preceded by one.

"I stand and calmly wait till the hinges turn for me."

"I hate the dreadful hollow, behind the little wood."

III. *RHYME.* (RHIME.)

Origin. — Obscure.

    Ascribed to the northern European nations, to the Arabians, and to the early Christians.

Orthography and Etymology. — Doubtful.

Nature. — Correspondence of sound between related syllables.

Use. — Constant in French poetry, rare in Greek and Latin, optional in English.

Kinds.

    a. SINGLE. (Strong, Masculine.) Decide, provide.

        (1) *Alliterative.* Similarity in initial sounds of words.

           Consonantal.

"Wild words wander here and there."
Common in Anglo-Saxon poetry.

Assonantal.

"Apt alliteration's artful aid."

Common among the Irish.

The two combined.

"Ye merry men all."

(2) *End.* (Terminal.) Correspondence of final sounds, usually at the end of the verse.

Consonantal. Distend, command.

Assonantal. Flee, lea.

Rich. Deplore, explore. Identity of sound throughout the rhyming syllables.

Perfect. Bells, tells. Betrays, displays. The common form in modern poetry. (See next topic.)

(3) *Middle.* (Leonine.) Correspondence between the middle and the close of a verse.

"When the deer sweeps by, and the hounds are in cry."·

(4) *Sectional.* (Line.) Correspondence within the line.

"Might trod down right; of king there was no fear."

b. DOUBLE. (Weak, Feminine.) Numbers, slumbers.

c. TRIPLE. Tenderly, slenderly. Annuity, gratuity.

Used effectively in humorous poetry.

Longer rhymes are found only among the Persians and the Arabians.

Requirements of Perfect Rhyme.

a. *Identity of vowel sound.* Moon, soon. Pleasures, treasures.

Violation. Love, move. "Allowable" rhyme when the vowel modification is but slight.

b. *Identity of subsequent sounds.* Fast, past.

Violation. Disease, increase.

c. *Dissimilarity of preceding sounds.* Soul, toll.

Violation. Confound, profound. (Rich rhyme.)

d. *The same accent on the rhyming syllables.* To know, below.

Violations. To ring, pleasing. The sea, truly.

Blank Verse. Unrhymed poetry.

This term is usually applied to rhymeless iambic pentameter.

a. Heroic Measure. (In English and in German verse.)

Iambic pentameter.

A characteristic form in English poetry.

Best adapted to lofty and dignified subjects.

Heroic blank verse was first used in English poetry the early half of the sixteenth century, by Henry Howard, Earl of Surrey.

Unrhymed.

> "But Winter has yet brighter scenes — he boasts
> Splendors beyond what gorgeous Summer knows;
> Or Autumn, with his many fruits, and woods
> All flushed with many hues."
>
> BRYANT's *A Winter Piece.*

This form is largely used in epic and in dramatic poetry.

First employed in dramatic poetry by Christopher Marlowe.

Rhymed. (The Popian couplet.)

> "It is too late! Ah! Nothing is too late
> Till the tired heart shall cease to palpitate."
>
> LONGFELLOW's *Morituri Salutamus.*

This form is often adopted for satiric and didactic poetry.

Used in the Drama of the Restoration.

Cæsura. This occurs in heroic measure most commonly after the fourth or the sixth syllable; variety of position, however, is essential to the artistic use of the metre.

b. Alexandrine Verse.

Iambic hexameter.

Named from a French poem on Alexander, in which this kind of verse was early employed.

The heroic measure of French poetry.

> "But silence spreads the couch of ever welcome rest."
>
> BYRON's *Childe Harold.*

c. Short Chaucerian Stanza. — (Rhyme Royal.)

Seven iambic pentameters.

Rhyme. — Verses one and three; two, four, and five; six and seven.

"And forests ranged like armies, round and round,
    At feet of mountains of eternal snow;
And valleys all alive with happy sound;
    The song of birds; swift brooks' delicious flow;
    The mystic hum of million things that grow;
    The stir of men; and, gladdening every way,
    Voices of little children at their play."
                            HELEN HUNT JACKSON'S *In The Pass.*

d. **Ottava Rima.**   (The Italian heroic measure.)

Eight iambic pentameters.

Rhyme. — Six lines of alternate rhyme, followed by a couplet.

"Deep in the forest was a little dell
    High overarchèd with the leafy sweep
Of a broad oak, through whose gnarled roots there fell
    A slender rill that sung itself asleep,
Where its continuous toil had scooped a well
    To please the fairy folk; breathlessly deep
The stillness was, save when the dreaming brook
From its small urn a drizzly murmur shook."
                            LOWELL'S *A Legend of Brittany.*

e. **Spenserian Stanza.**   (Long Chaucerian stanza.)

Eight iambic pentameters, followed by an Alexandrine.

Rhyme. — Verses one and three; two, four, five, and seven; six, eight, and nine.

"Look on this beautiful world, and read the truth
    In her fair page; see, every season brings
New change, to her, of everlasting youth;
    Still the green soil, with joyous living things,
    Swarms; the wide air is full of joyous wings;
And myriads, still, are happy in the sleep
    Of ocean's azure gulfs, and where he flings
The restless surge.   Eternal love doth keep
In his complacent arms, the earth, the air, the deep."
                            BRYANT'S *The Ages.*

f. **Sonnet.**

PURE CLASSIC FORM.   (Italian.)

Oldest extant.   1200 A.D.

Perfected by Petrarch.   (First half of the fourteenth century.)

Structure.

Number of lines.   Fourteen.

Their character.   Iambic pentameter.

Parts.

(1) **Octave.** Two quatrains.

(2) **Sestette.** Two tercets.

Rhyme.

Octave.

Verses one, four, five, and eight.

Verses two, three, six, and seven.

Sestette. Liberty allowed.

Two, or three, rhymes.

Never in couplets. (Not always observed.)

Illustration.

> "The holiest of all days are those
>> Kept by ourselves in silence and apart;
>> The secret anniversaries of the heart,
>> When the full river of feeling overflows; —
> The happy days unclouded to their close;
>> The sudden joys that out of darkness start
>> As flames from ashes; swift desires that dart
>> Like swallows singing down each wind that blows!
> White as the gleam of a receding sail,
>> White as a cloud that floats and fades in air,
>> White as the whitest lily on a stream,
> These tender memories are; — a Fairy tale
>> Of some enchanted land we know not where,
>> But lovely as a landscape in a dream."

LONGFELLOW'S Holidays.

Writers of the Italian Form of Sonnet.

Milton, Wordsworth, Keats, Mrs. Browning, Longfellow.

Other Sonnet Writers.

Sidney, Spenser, Shakespeare, Daniel, Drayton.

Sonnets were introduced into English by Wyatt and Surrey, in the reign of Henry VIII.

ENGLISH FORM BEFORE MILTON'S TIME.

Three quatrains and a final couplet.

Surrey used but two rhymes in his sonnets; Spenser, five; Shakespeare, seven.

NOTES. — A sonnet usually expresses but one sentiment.

It is often of a personal nature.

g. Familiar Hymn Forms.

a. IAMBIC MEASURE.

Long Metre. (L. M.)

Four tetrameters.

> " Eternal source of every joy !
> Well may thy praise our lips employ,
> While in thy temple we appear
> Whose goodness crowns the circling year."
>
> PHILIP DODDRIDGE.

Common Metre. (C. M.) Ballad Metre.

First and third verses, tetrameters ; second and fourth, trimeters.

> " I mourn no more my vanished years:
> Beneath a tender rain,
> An April rain of smiles and tears,
> My heart is young again."
>
> WHITTIER'S *My Psalm.*

Short Metre. (S. M.)

First, second, and fourth verses, trimeters ; third verse, tetrameter.

> "Come, ye who love the Lord !
> And let your joys be known,
> Join in a song of sweet accord,
> And thus surround the throne."
>
> ISAAC WATTS.

Hallelujah Metre. (H. M.)

Four trimeters followed by two tetrameters (or four dimeters).

> "If earthly parents hear
> Their children when they cry,
> If they, with love sincere,
> Their varied wants supply ;
> Much more wilt thou thy love display,
> And answer when thy children pray."

Six and Four Syllables. (6s & 4s.)

> "Come, thou Almighty King,
> Help us thy name to sing,
> Help us to praise !

Father all glorious,
O'er all victorious,
Come and reign over us,
　　Ancient of Days ! "
CHARLES WESLEY.

Seven and Six Syllables. (7s & 6s.)

" Jerusalem the golden,
　With milk and honey blest,
Beneath thy contemplation
　Sink heart and voice oppressed:
I know not, oh, I know not,
　What joys await me there ;
What radiancy of glory,
　What bliss beyond compare."
ST. BERNARD OF CLUNY.

Ten Syllables. (10s.)

" Abide with me: fast falls the eventide;
The darkness deepens; Lord, with me abide;
When other helpers fail, and comforts flee,
Help of the helpless, O abide with me!"
HENRY F. LYTE.

b. TROCHAIC MEASURE.

Seven Syllables. (7s.)

" Rock of Ages! cleft for me,
Let me hide myself in thee ;
Let the water and the blood
From thy wounded side that flowed,
Be of sin the perfect cure ;
Save me, Lord! and make me pure."
AUGUSTUS M. TOPLADY.

Eight and Seven Syllables. (8s & 7s.)

" Come, thou fount of every blessing!
Tune my heart to grateful lays;
Streams of mercy never ceasing
Call for songs of loudest praise."
ROBERT ROBINSON.

c. DACTYLIC MEASURE.

Eleven and Ten Syllables. (11s & 10s.)

" Come, ye disconsolate, where'er ye languish,
Come to the mercy-seat, fervently kneel;
Here bring your wounded hearts, here tell your anguish,
Earth has no sorrow that heaven cannot heal."
THOMAS MOORE.

Ten Syllables. (10s.)

> " Angel of Peace, thou hast wandered too long!
>   Spread thy white wings to the sunshine of love!
> Come while our voices are blended in song, —
>   Fly to our ark like the storm-beaten dove ! "
>
> HOLMES'S *A Hymn of Peace.*

d. ANAPESTIC MEASURE.

Eleven Syllables. (11s.)

> " How firm a foundation, ye saints of the Lord,
>   Is laid for your faith in his excellent word ;
> What more can he say than to you he hath said,
>   To you who for refuge to Jesus have fled ? "
>
> *Portuguese Hymn.*

Other Special **Forms.** (Less used.)

The Ode. Terza Rima. The Ballade. The Rondeau. The
Rondel. The Villanelle. The Triolet.
(See Parsons's *English Versification.*)

www.ingramcontent.com/pod-product-compliance
Lightning Source LLC
Chambersburg PA
CBHW021122270326
41929CB00009B/1001